It's a fine

for the hill

And once in a blue

sun and moon

Hills, folk and wildlife, 1935–62

Adam Watson

Dedicated to the many generous folk of the hill country who welcomed me in boyhood like a member of their own families

Publication of this book was aided by generous sponsorship from Bert McIntosh of Crathes near Banchory in Scotland and McIntosh Plant Hire (Aberdeen) Ltd, Birchmoss, Echt, Westhill, Aberdeenshire AB32 6XL ,
www.mphltd.co.uk

Published by Paragon Publishing, 4 North Street, Rothersthorpe, Northants, NN7 3JB, UK
First published 2011

* Clachnaben, Crathes, Banchory, Aberdeenshire AB31 5JE, Scotland, UK adamwatson@uwclub.net

ISBN 978-1-907611-58-2

Book design, layout and production management by Into Print
www.intoprint.net
01604 832149

Printed and bound in UK and USA by Lightning Source

Front photograph: Tom Patey, Mike Taylor, the author, Gordon Leslie at Bruachdryne tearoom, Braemar, 27 September 1954, ready for a fine day on the hill (Mac Smith)

Contents

Foreword by the late Tom Weir

When the author asked me to write a Foreword, I remembered the day when we met in December 1947. He was 17, in his last year at Turriff Senior Secondary School. Ours was an accidental meeting at Luibeg, occupied by deerstalker Bob Scott and his wife who sometimes gave accommodation to climbers. Allan McNicol (then 21) and I had booked for a week. Adam had come alone for his first winter week on the hills and already knew the Scotts so well that they treated him like a son.

Memorable days we enjoyed in that stormy week. By the time my 33rd birthday came on 29 December, enough snow had fallen for good ski-touring. Luckily we had a spare pair of skis, on which Adam practised with us, and now he could savour from the top of Sgor Dubh a mile of fast skiing on perfect snow. Our farewell was in a snowstorm at Braemar where Adam saw us off, and in his diary wrote *the end of the best holiday I ever had in my life*.

That first trip was only a beginning, for we were to have many good days ski-mountaineering and climbing in Scotland over the years. In 1950 Adam travelled alone to Lapland, before heading south to climb the highest rock peak in Lofoten. The finish was an epic journey on two fishing boats. In 1951, after hearing Adam's story of travelling on the cheap, and as Douglas Scott and I had talked often about visiting Lofoten, the plan was for Adam to find a trawler and we would head for Lofoten to spend the summer climbing. Adam's father then suggested coming with us to Bergen and motoring as far north as we wanted. It was a great trip, which I described in *Camps and Climbs in Arctic Norway*, published in 1953. We caught our own fish, between climbing rock peaks that leap from the sea and getting to know the friendly crofter-fishermen whose homes are on the shore of the Raftsund.

That line of Wordsworth's 'The Child is father of the Man' rings true in respect of Adam. At the age of nine, after reading Seton Gordon's *The Cairngorm Hills of Scotland*, he wrote to the author and got this reply: *It is a fine thing for you to have a love of the hills because on the hills you find yourself near grand and beautiful things, and as you grow older you will love them more and more*. Adam remembers the excitement of cycling to Crathie aged 13 to meet him.

It was appropriate that Adam should make the winter ecology of Scottish ptarmigan the subject of his university Honours thesis in 1952, where his enjoyment of lone ski-mountaineering made study possible even in the snowiest winter. This study was suggested by the Regius Professor of Natural History, V.C. Wynne Edwards, himself a keen cross-country skier and arctic biologist. In autumn 1952 Adam went to Montreal, where Pat Baird chose him as zoologist on the expedition by the Arctic Institute of North America to Baffin Island in 1953. Then Adam returned to Aberdeen to continue his ptarmigan study for a PhD.

Even Wynne-Edwards was impressed in 1962 when Adam took advantage of the Cairngorms carrying more snow than usual for April. At 5 am he set off from Invercauld carrying cross-country skis, which he had bought in Lapland for 50 shillings. With Ben Avon and Beinn a' Bhuird behind, he sped to Ben Macdui and Cairn Gorm, and then Braeriach and Cairn Toul. It was near 9 pm when he reached Luibeg after 38 miles, 34 of them on skis, with 8000 feet of climbing.

It was Adam who started his father climbing at the age of 48. He too became a keen mountaineer and ski-tourer. The three of us were always welcome at Bob Scott's house, and Luibeg was a home from home for Adam. Climbers liked Bob for his sharp wit and story-telling. His Obituary, written by Adam, appeared in the *Scottish Mountaineering Club Journal* in 1982.

Later I received a book by Adam. In the Foreword, Professor W.F.H. Nicolaisen wrote, *The Place Names of Upper Deeside is a sound book in every sense. In both scope and attention to detail, it surpasses everything published in Scotland so far*. An inscription in Adam's handwriting, in a copy sent to me, reads, *For Tom with deep gratitude for your early inspiration to me in 1947–49, and many good days then and since in some of the places named in this book*.

Acknowledgements

So many hill folk treated me like a family member that I felt one of them. I acknowledge the late Tom Weir for his Foreword and inspiration to me as a young mountaineer, and his wife Rhona for permitting me to publish photographs taken by him. Other photographers and other bodies named at the end of captions gave me permission. Captions without acknowledgement refer to photographs by me. My wife Jenny suggested the book's title. She says I always went outside first thing in the morning at Glen Esk and then Deeside to look at weather and sky, and coming in usually said optimistically "It's a fine day for the hill".

Introduction

This book is testimony to the idea that *Exploring for yourself by your own free will, without formal courses or training, is the best joy the hills can give* (my Preface, *The Cairngorms*, 1975). Now I would add 'without detailed planning', for my best days have been lone trips begun without such planning, indeed on the spur of moment and weather, almost chance events. Four chapters salute Scots to whom I owed much as a young naturalist and mountaineer, Seton Gordon, Bob Scott, Tom Patey and Tom Weir. They held to the above idea.

Reading Seton Gordon's *Cairngorm Hills of Scotland* in 1939 changed my life. I wanted to be in these hills at all seasons. Below, I write on that personal exploration of the Cairngorms, or the more expressive Am Monadh Ruadh the red hill-range, as some old folk called them. It was easier for me at lowland Turriff to reach the Dee side of the Cairngorms than the Spey side, by train or bus to Aberdeen and then bus up Deeside to Braemar, but I considered the Dee side better and the Derry finest of all. I got on so well with Derry deerstalker Bob Scott at Luibeg Cottage that he and wife Helen soon treated me as a member of the family. Luibeg became a home to me as well as a fine base. Sometimes I crossed the Cairngorms to Luibeg. In January 1949 I skied alone in deep snow from Coylumbridge, reaching Luibeg in the dark after the hardest day of my life thus far. Chapter 8 gives my diary account of it.

Although I always liked lone trips, I appreciated good company. My father gave up golf for the hills, after I persuaded him to take me there. We became good friends on the hill, far more than just father and son. When 17 at Luibeg I met Tom Weir, and soon we formed an unstoppable pair, sharing memorable days at all seasons. Later I knew Tom Patey well, early in the development that led to his becoming a mountaineer of world rank. Gordon, Scott, Weir and Patey were remarkable characters, apart from their interest in hills or their effect on me. Naming them may seem invidious, because I owed much to others, such as chronologically W.B. Alexander, George Waterston, Bernard Tucker, George Edwards, Eric Hosking, Desmond Nethersole-Thompson, Vero Wynne-Edwards, James Fisher, Robert Carrick, Mick Southern, Douglas Scott, Leslie Brown, Ben Battle, Pat Baird, Fritz Schwarzenbach, Housi Weber, Mac Smith, Reg Moreau, David Lack, and others. Another book!

Exploration by one's own free will is best pervaded by humility and wonder. Alien to this are avalanche alerts, 'challenge' walks, 'character-building', courses, Duke of Edinburgh Awards, guided walks, hill-runs, interpretive boards, marker cairns, outdoor centres, qualifications, rangers, route-cards, school outings, signposts, sponsored walks, tests of snowpack stability, text messages sent as avalanche alerts to mobile phones, transceivers, visitor centres, 'walk of the day', wardens, and 'wilderness walks'. Also alien are Munros, Corbetts and other anthropocentric designations, those who 'bag' them as if hills were shot birds, and assault, attack, battle, conquer, conquest, fight, vanquish and victory as if hills were enemies.

Many with flashing camera, global positioning, map, compass, mobile phone, and survival equipment are unsafe, as rescue accounts often reveal. Even climbers have been rescued after neglecting navigation on easy ground after completing rock climbs or ice climbs. Those who behave as if alone on an icecap when nobody else knows where they are and no help is possible, have greater inherent safety. They are also more likely to understand and appreciate the hill and its weather, snow, wildlife and indigenous folk.

The Cairngorms whetted my wish for the far north, where I went as soon as I could. Chapters 9 and 10 reproduce articles on a trip to Iceland with two fellow students in 1949. In 1950 I went north alone. Chapter 11 gives my diary extracts of a trip to climb solo in Swedish Lapland, and later I met Norwegian mountaineers who asked me to accompany them on an ascent of the highest rock peak on the Lofoten Islands. On my return, seeing the old hills of Dee or Spey was like meeting old friends again. Yet always I felt humility, for these old hills have abiding mystery, variety and wonder.

Chapter 1 A few early schooldays

My first memory in life was the morning I went to primary school at Turriff when five years old. The school had two large buildings, of soft red sandstone like most buildings in the town, from the quarry of Old Red Sandstone rock at Ardin near Delgaty. Our classroom on the left of the west building overlooked the playground, a sunny position facing south.

The pupils, like almost everybody else in the town and district, called the school *the skweel*, the Scots word *schuil* pronounced in Buchan as in the English word *squeal*. Turriff was *Turra*, with stress on *Turr*. Teachers forbade our using Scots to them, even though we overheard some of them using Scots to one another in a private room with the door open! They told us we must say Turriff School. As soon as they were out of hearing, back we went to *Turra Skweel*. The tarmac playground we called *the play-green*, so it may have been grass formerly. We were proud of Turriff. As a child I learned a common saying about the town. In response to the question: *Faar are ye gaan?* (Where are you going?), the answer was *Turra, faar sorra ither* (Turriff, where else for goodness sake?).

Our lady teacher ushered us to a series of desks attached to benches that each held two pupils. Girls sat on one side of the classroom, boys on the other. I happened to sit with dark-haired William Kelman, and behind us sat fair-haired Norman Sim. Bill, Norman and I instantly became friends. The friendship remained through our years at primary school.

On that first day our teacher gave each of us a hard slate and a slate pencil for writing. I still recall the unpleasant high-pitched scratching sound from writing on the slate. Pupils aged six were in the next classroom, and each age-group had a different room and teacher. A year later, we moved to the classroom for six-year-olds, again with slate and slate pencil. In the third class and thereafter, we advanced to the luxury of a paper jotter and a lead pencil each.

That first teacher was a kindly lady, who imposed firm and usually fair discipline in the class and outside. On one occasion, however, she took what I thought was unfair action on a pupil, unjustified because she did not give the recipient an opportunity to explain things. I cannot now recall exactly what the recipient had done, but that is not the main point. The incident happened shortly before the afternoon interval or what we called *aifterneen playtime*. During playtime, we all spoke about it and called it unfair.

Standing with two other boys, maybe Norman and Bill though I am uncertain of that now, I said "I'll stay outside at the end of the interval and not go to the classroom". Then I suggested we all do it, for three would count more than one. They agreed. We feared what might happen, but felt good to be rebelling.

Soon the end of the interval arrived, announced when the teacher came out into the playground to ring a loud hand-bell. The sheep flowed dutifully back into the classroom, while we hid behind a shelter shed out of sight. Eventually she realised our absence and came into the playground again, ringing her bell. This was to no avail, whereupon she summoned the janitor to search. Inevitably he soon found us and marched us to the classroom. There, an angry teacher confronted us, demanding to know why we had not returned. You could have heard a pin drop among the more than 30 pupils sitting in the class.

I had led the rebellion, so I spoke briefly: "I stayed out because I thought you'd been unfair". She managed to control her anger, and summarily punished each of us with a stroke of her leather strap (which we called *The Tag*) on one's outstretched right hand. As leader I was treated to be punished first. That was the end of it, and lessons resumed normally, but I recall seeing other pupils looking at us frequently and furtively. It had been a special occasion! When school ended for the afternoon and we came out, there was a buzz of excitement. We three were given respect as heroes, a respect that continued years later.

The boys often fought with fists, even in the youngest class, and bleeding noses and bruised eyes often resulted. I never saw the point of fighting and took no part in it, but was not ostracised or picked upon because of this. Perhaps this was because I got on well with all the boys, perhaps a result of my early rebellion, perhaps both. Bill was involved in many fist fights in that first year, Norman seldom. I did enjoy wrestling and became quite proficient, but it was friendly competition with no physical harm.

I saw no bullying among pupils in the primary or secondary school. Pupils who were obviously different did have nicknames, such as a boy from Little Turriff who always wore a kilt and whom we called Kiltie, but there was nothing derogatory about it. Two wartime evacuees, a boy Tinline from Glasgow (whom we nicknamed Tinny) and one Connon from London, were accepted totally into the fold, as much as if they had been in Turriff all their lives, despite their different accents and lack of familiarity with the Scots tongue of Buchan. Indeed, both became among the most popular of us. I see a difference in recent years when bullying has been rife and serious in schools across Britain. This includes the much-vaunted Banchory Academy near where I live. Education departments and teachers do not prevent it and often fail to take action. Despite all their detailed 'Bullying Strategies', often they cover it up.

Later in that first year I fell while racing with Bill and Norman round the tarmac playground. Slipping on wet leaves, I came crashing down on my right kneecap. This tore deeply into my knee and caused bleeding. My knee felt very sore and I saw bits of grit and dirt in the wound. Norman helped me to the classroom, while Bill ran to get the janitor and teacher. She picked out the grit, cleaned the wound, bandaged my knee carefully, and gave me a pat on the back. She bore no grudge about my infant rebellion!

So few vehicles came through Turriff that many boys noted each registration number in a competition to find who saw most in a week. Some resorted to invention to inflate their totals, but this was easily suspected and culprits would be asked to provide more evidence or drop out of the competition. There were no prizes.

A far rarer sight was to see a Chinaman or Negro, and when one appeared, always well dressed and very briefly in passing, we would stop to gawp at the strange visitor. A Chinaman to us was a *Chinkie*, a Negro being a *Darkie*. A common sight was an old tramp, well known across Buchan, who wore an enormous thick coat with many pockets and called at houses to ask for food. He had the nickname *Forty Pooches* because of his many pockets. The boys would call to him and shout "Forty Pooches", whereupon he would glower and point to his biggest pocket, saying he would put the catcaller into it. Local folk called a tinker or hawker a *cyaard*, not a term of distaste but simply factual, like the term *tinker*, referring to their trade of repairing holes in pots and pans. *Cyaard* comes from Gaelic *ceard*, a tinker or tradesman working with metal or a mechanic. Some old folk used the term *gaan-aboot bodie* or *gaan-aboot mannie*, literally going about, but meaning walking through and seldom staying long in one place.

My father told me that in the early 1900s he visited New Deer in Buchan, and overheard two old ladies talking to one another. Seeing a stranger, one said to the other "Ken ye fa that wid be?" This meant do you know who that would be? The other replied "The Deil a ken I, ken ee?" The reply meant The Devil do I know, do you know? This was like the Norwegian *kjenner de* or do you know, and points to the similarity of Norwegian and northern Scots.

Scots was already in decline when I attended Turriff School, a decline hastened by teachers and education authorities. If we schoolboys had said a *gaan-aboot bodie* (literally going-about body or person) for a tramp, this would have been considered as *aald farrant* or old fashioned. The term *ferlie*, meaning something unusual, I often heard from old rural folk. A few other words that I heard being spoken only by adults raised in rural parts, including my relatives, were *blaad* spoil, *deval* stop, *forfochen* tired, *looch* laughed, *sax*, *seeven*, *acht* and *twal* for six, seven, eight and twelve, *vrang* wrong, *vrannie* wren, and *vratch* wretch. The dialect was richest on high poor land with small farms and crofts, such as the Hill of Mountblairy, the Hill of Fishrie and the Waggle Hill. Nevertheless, it did beat strongly in Turriff too, and all pupils used it.

A very few children did not attend school because they were mentally retarded. Today they would be in an institution, with paid staff caring for them. In those years they stayed at home and were well-regarded in the community. Local folk called each of them a *feel*, a Scots noun similar to English *fool*. However, as in *cyaard*, a *feel* was not a term of distaste, but a factual description. A *feel*, usually male but occasionally female, would often stand or sit outside the house in the same prominent spot, where he would wave and smile to passers-by, who would return the compliment. The word *feel* for someone who is not mentally retarded has a quite different meaning implying dislike, just like the English word *fool*.

At Turriff School I led another revolt when about 14 years old. Norman and I were in the Boys Brigade, which met weekly at the school gymnasium in an evening. We respected the supervisor, who gave up his spare time to help. The BB in those days included a protestant religious element, which our supervisor had ignored. However, the Minister of the Church of Scotland, the Rev Peter Craik McQuoid, decided that too few of us had been attending his Sunday school and kirk, and he paid us a visit one evening at the gymnasium to say so.

Walking up and down our ranks like an army general inspecting a parade, he barked out demands that we must attend his Sunday school and kirk, and said he would keep a note of what happened and asked the supervisor to check weekly which of us had attended on the previous Sunday. The poor chap was no match for McQuoid's domineering attitude or his eloquence, and meekly agreed to the requests, though we could see the disapproval in his face. McQuoid then left and our normal activities resumed. In the dressing room at the end, we complained bitterly to one another but were reluctantly resigned to doing McQuoid's bidding.

Then I decided I would not comply. Although I realised that this might cause a showdown which I would be likely to lose, I was determined and prepared to use iron will to the limit, even if I were punished. When I told the others in the dressing room, they liked the idea, but were too frightened to rebel. Then I asked them to do the same as me and form a united front. If so, it would be harder for McQuoid to stamp out resistance and we might win. As we left, about a dozen had agreed to resist, and we walked up the street joyously. And resist we did!

We never told our parents, but simply avoided the Sunday events. At the next BB meeting, the supervisor remonstrated with us half-heartedly, but we refused to back down. That ended the matter, and McQuoid never again put his face inside the gymnasium at a BB meeting. We had humiliated him, but he got no more than he richly deserved for his overbearing arrogance. Later he became a County Councillor and rose to the exalted status of County Convener, neglecting his kirk job. I had never respected him and always found his sermons utterly boring.

Looking back at school, I think I was always a loner in the sense that I disliked organised group activities such as informal physical games and also formal physical training with gymnastics or football, dancing in groups, singing of hymns, music classes where the class sang, card-playing in groups, drill, marching, and even playing marbles with more than one friend. I was always poor at leaping over the 'horse' as part of a group in a gymnasium, and poor on the wooden bars and at drill, but fortunately allowance was made for my serious illness a year or two earlier. Anyway, I preferred to be on my own, out of doors walking or bird-watching or fishing or climbing, or in bad weather indoors reading or writing or drawing or looking at maps and photographs.

Nowadays, nanny-state government ministers decree that there must be compulsory physical education for much longer periods weekly at school, as well as more time on games and formal sport. They believe the ridiculous claim that such exercise will stop children becoming fat. Ironically, most of the ministers are fat and overweight from big lunches at taxpayers' expense. They promote the flag-waving that we must strive to make the country win at international competitive sports. I thank my lucky stars that I was at school in Aberdeenshire before the nanny-state jokers took over.

Chapter 2 Snow

View west from Old Bank House, Turriff in February 1937 (Adam Watson senior)

The first revelation I remember was the wonder of snow. When seven, I watched a heavy fall at Turriff in late 1937. I looked from a window as pale columns of snow crossed a dark sky and big flakes tumbled. For hours I watched flakes melt on a slate roof and then gradually persist until the snow hid all the slates. In the garden I waded in the deep snow, feeling it cold in my fingers until it turned grey and melted. A foot of white became an inch of grey as I stood on it. Each snowflake had variety, and each of the crystals comprising a flake. The airy mantle on branch, pavement and road absorbed sound. A strange hush pervaded the normally noisy town.

In 1938 I began to observe snow-patches in summer and have continued since. What began as an interest in snow for its own sake became of wider note in recent years because of climatic change. Seton Gordon's *The Cairngorm Hills of Scotland* added to my interest, for his descriptions and photographs of snow excited me as much as anything else in his book. After I first wrote to him in 1939 and he replied, in the early 1940s I sent him letters about patches I had seen, along with sketches and a photograph.

Walking three miles to my grandma's cottage over snow-blocked roads in 1940, I gazed at the intricate shapes of snowdrifts, the sparkling silver or pearly gold reflections of the sun on the snow, the brilliant light, the deep blue shadows, and the variety of snow underfoot and in my hands. It was magical. To the south gleamed the long snowy hill of Bennachie. Would I ever reach its silvery crest, I pondered? I wondered if anyone had been there in snow. Unlikely, I thought.

In 1941–42 I often saw Norwegian soldiers who had escaped to Scotland after fighting the German army's successful invasion of Norway. They felt at home because we spoke many words they knew, such as *bra* (fine) and *red*

AW at Morrone on 2 January 1947 (Adam Watson senior)

up (tidy). Part of the Commercial Hotel carried a Norwegian flag and a sign *Norges Hus* (Norway House). Daily I walked past it to school and often spoke with the Norsemen. Some sped on skis to Banff to collect Turriff's mail, after snow had blocked all the roads and railways, with the mail sent from Aberdeen by boat to Banff. I marvelled as they skimmed over fields where a man on foot sank to his knees or waist.

Up to the thighs in drifts on the road to my grandma's in 1942, I saw Willie Hutcheon skiing swiftly down a field to his Turriff office. Although later I realised that he was an inexperienced skier, his performance contrasted spectacularly with my laborious wading. A keen hill-walker and Cairngorm Club member, he had been to the Alps. It all seemed utterly unattainable.

To Banff's green links I cycled in 1942 and watched dumbfounded when showers cleared to reveal snowy peaks like arctic islands beyond a dark blue Moray Firth, the hills of Caithness and Sutherland. Winter or summer, I still find it thrilling to see this view, one of Scotland's finest.

In November 1942 my mother and I stayed a night at Lower Craggan near Grantown. In the morning I recall walking along the main road to climb a conical top to the west of it. Modern Ordnance Survey maps show it as at 295 m in Gaich Wood. In 1941 it had carried a pine-wood cut for the war effort, and now wavy hair-grass covered the ground. The graceful grass held raindrops, and no wind stirred to shake them off. Catching a sunray, they showed myriad spangles of brilliant shining colour. As I moved my head, each spangle changed colour across the spectrum. When an eddy moved the drops, they changed colour with a dancing motion. It was beautiful.

Walking through tall wet grass in shorts soaked me to the knees. Then the cloud to the south began to rise. As I reached the little top, Cairn Gorm appeared, thickly covered in fresh snow down to the top woods of Abernethy. The snow had a greyish hue in the gloomy light, dark clouds loomed, and veils of snow fell. Remote and mysterious, this far surpassed the summer views of hills whose outlines I now knew so well. Caught by the sudden wonder, I forgot about my cold wet legs and feet to gaze spellbound at the most striking prospect I had ever seen. One day, I decided, I must go to the hills in winter snow, not just look from below.

AW skis in thick ground drift in a gale high on Morven, 2 January 1968 (Tom Weir)

On 18 April 1946 when just 16, I first went in fresh snow to a high hill along with my father, Scottish mountaineer James Anton, and his brother in law Captain Bradbury, climbing to Ben Macdui, and on 30 December 1946 my father and I ascended to Derry Cairngorm on a bitterly cold day with a gale and heavy drifting. In my diary of 30 December I described my first glissade on hard snow as *Great fun*. I wrote: *A most enjoyable day, one of the best I've had in the hills.* Three days later my father and I climbed Morrone in fresh snow. Excited, I could not wait to return, and next day climbed it alone. Daily in the 1947 winter I walked miles down Deveron and learned much about walking on snow and ice. I watched ice spangles form on boulders at the river bottom and float to the surface, where they joined others to form the tinkling mushy ice that Scots call *grue*. When authors write about streams in frost and omit this fact, it reveals their poor observation. In late March there came a big thaw, which in Scots we called *a muckle fresh* or *a richt fresh*. The river then ran high with greyish water from snow-melting, a characteristic colour signifying what we called *snaa bree*, translated roughly as snow brew or snow water.

In December 1947 at Luibeg, skiers Tom Weir and Allan McNicol taught me my first lessons in skiing. Afterwards I could not get enough of this, to me amazing revolutionary way of travel into a wonderland of snow and ice. In snowy spells I never stayed in, whatever the weather. Even when crawling on hands and knees in storms, or sitting out squalls in snow-holes, I found snow so interesting that discomfort became secondary.

I learned to navigate when I could not see my ski-tips, occasionally my boots. The rhythm of skiing on flat ground or uphill was more enjoyable than walking, and the varied sounds of skis and sticks on snow added to the experience. Soon I found that different kinds of snow greatly affect one's ascent or descent on ski or on foot, and that a snow surface often changes greatly even within half an hour, sometimes within minutes. Unlike English with its few words for snow, the Inuit, Saami and boreal-forest Indians have many words for different kinds*. I once wrote notes on those that I knew and soon had 40 radically different types, excluding the special kinds that occur only on or under trees. Of course there are more than 40, because of intermediates and because in any case the number is limited only by the use put to the classification.

By small variations in feel and sound I learned to avoid starting an avalanche or falling through a snow-bridge. To ski or walk on snow at night relies greatly on feel and sound, for one cannot see small cornices or some changes in snow-type. To ski on moonlit fresh powder is wonderful, with the snow a delicate silky sheen, trees jet black, and hills soaring softly white against a velvety grey sky where only the brighter stars and planets shine. Silvery light floods the land, ice on pool and river glitters brilliantly, and clouds passing the moon turn to ethereal silky wisps, sending dark shadows moving across the snow. As the wind rises, cloud shadows race past and the light changes suddenly from second to second.

Rime cloaks the 10-m high granite tor on Beinn Mheadhoin summit, 9 January 1951

On 2 January 1968, AW skis towards Morven with the snowy breast of Mount Keen beyond (Tom Weir)

Blown snow has endless variety. Compared with blown water, soil, sand, or leaves, it is so light that wind whirls it high and packs it deep. Fresh white drifted snow makes a contrast on old grey snow or ice. I like to watch blowing powder pile up on my skis and change position by the second as the wind alters. It is interesting to see how hillocks or boulders or changes in slope gradient affect the drifting and the deposition of snow. Since 1985 I have used some of this knowledge to help Scottish ski-managers decide how to locate tows, pistes and snow-fences so as to minimise damage to soil and vegetation, and at the same time improve skiing.

During the late 1940s and since, I learned how ptarmigan, grouse and hares react to snowstorms and use snow for day-rests and night-roosts. It takes at least an hour for a skilled Inuit with the right tools to make an igloo or a skilled mountaineer to make a snow-cave, and yet only a few seconds for a ptarmigan to make a snow-hole. The bird chooses wisely. After thaws and frost on Lochnagar one day in November 1954, only small hard drifts remained. Scores of ptarmigan used steep hard snow at the cliff-top, above iced rocks plunging hundreds of feet to gloomy depths. They would have slept safe from fox or stoat. No human could have gone there without elaborate equipment, great expertise and iron will.

In snow on the Cairngorms I felt at home, but as a temporary visitor I knew I had to leave soon. To the ptarmigan, the snow and the hill are home to an extent that we cannot appreciate. The ptarmigan does not get lost, and teaches humility. In 1966 I wrote (*Scottish Birds*, p. 181): *Many climbers, fighting their way apprehensively in gathering darkness in a blizzard, have envied the ptarmigan preparing to spend a comfortable night on the exposed summits.*

AW skis in Glen Derry on 19 January 1952 (Tom Weir)

In the 1980s I replied to a letter from an ecologist who was interested in chionophilous vegetation. The typist asked what chionophilous meant. I said "It's an adjective for snow-loving, and chionophile is the noun". She said "You're a chionophile too". And yes, I am!

* The claim that the Inuit etc have many words for snow has been disputed, but Pruitt (1970) gave good evidence for many words and see also English (2008).

AW senior skis at Coilacriech near Ballater in January 1951

Chapter 3 With Seton Gordon

Seton Gordon had an extraordinary effect on my life. I do not understand why, and may never do so. There are spiritual issues of personality and stimulation that transcend rational analysis. His effect on me came from his book *The Cairngorm Hills of Scotland*. In 1939, our family was on holiday at Ballater, and on a wet July day we went to a summer-house with books and magazines. It is now a shop selling and hiring bicycles. That visit changed my life.

Picking up *The Cairngorm Hills of Scotland*, I turned its faded bluish-grey jacket to find a sketch map like no map I had seen, itself a work of art. On it I read place-names I had visited with my family, but now with a compulsive fresh enthusiasm.

The thick paper attracted me, old fashioned and yet of good feel. The photographs and simple captions took me to a new world, and I found the text riveting. The author portrayed a region of infinite wonder, where weather, wildlife, snow-patches, local folk and history added to the whole. It was as if an electric switch had been suddenly turned on in my head, so that now I saw the Cairngorms and the world in a new light. As soon as I could return to the summer-house I looked at the book endlessly, in a fever of excitement.

In my Foreword in 1979 for the re-publication of Seton Gordon's *The Immortal Isles*, I reflected on the effect that *The Cairngorm Hills of Scotland* had on me. *Books are one of the pinnacles of human culture and achievement. Few things can have a more revolutionary effect on the attitudes and beliefs of young minds in a receptive mood. That was so for me, with Seton Gordon's books. Only perhaps once or twice in a lifetime may a brief event, such as a casual glance at a book, or a sudden union of two like minds, become a clear turning point which transforms the rest of one's life. Suddenly, exciting new horizons and a whole new universe are uncovered, and one's previous existence seems dull and almost pointless by comparison. I was reading one of Seton Gordon's books in a library at Ballater, when such a turning point came to me. My parents had taken me to different parts of Scotland, but suddenly Deeside and the Highlands that I had thought I knew, became immediately relegated into distant memories of no importance. The fact was I had known them only in a superficial and trivial sense. The Highlands that Seton Gordon wrote about were utterly different, a place of endless beauty and variety with a wonderful wildlife and fine people, a place that could give infinite exploration, enjoyment and peace to human mind, soul and body. From then on I saw Scotland, its wild life, weather, skies, people and culture, with this different eye. Others whom I know had a spark lit in them by Seton Gordon's writings, and went on to become naturalists and writers themselves. And others unborn will have this magic in future.*

Back at home in Turriff, I avidly read Gordon's *Afoot in Wild Places* in the public library, and my mother promised to buy *The Cairngorm Hills of Scotland* for my birthday in April 1940. On 10 October 1939 I decided to send a letter to Seton Gordon.

Knowing he would be busy, I thought he would not reply. However, on an October Saturday when schoolmate Norman Sim and I played with toys at my home in Old Bank House, my father came with a big envelope, postmarked Isle of Skye and addressed to Master Adam Watson. It contained a hand-written letter on dark blue writing paper from Upper Duntuilm, dated October 22, and two enlarged photographs of the Cairngorms in summer and in snow.

Beside myself with excitement, I read his letter. He wrote, *Dear Adam, I was very glad to see your nicely written letter and the interesting pictures you drew. It was clever of you to draw Lairig Ghru so that I could recognise it at once. It is a fine thing for you to have a love of the hills because on the hills you find yourself near grand and beautiful things, and as you grow older you will love them more and more. I think you could manage to climb Lochnagar. Our daughter Catriona climbed Braeriach with me when she was 8. When we reached the Wells of Dee she was rather disappointed with them as she thought she would see a big river like the Dee is lower down. You must write to me again after you climb Lochnagar. I am sending you 2 photographs. Your friend Seton Gordon.*

So began a correspondence that lasted 38 years. On 11 February 1940 he wrote, *I was glad to get your last letter. You will be interested to hear that I have a very great friend who is now Governor General of South Australia. His home is at Dinnet, and he has often been with me on the Cairngorms, and as he is rather lonely so far away I sent him your first letter and he says in a reply I have just had "it is good to find one so young who is interested in Nature and the Hills". He sent back your letter – so it has been all the way to Australia and back. If you look on the map, you will see the great journey it* has made. *Thank you for the interesting picture of Rothiemurchus you sent, and the one of Carn Lochan and Cairngorm. I expect if we could see the Cairngorms now they would be* <u>*very*</u> *white. But we have no snow in Skye and Larks are in full song, and snowdrops have been out for three weeks, and last week one little yellow crocus came out. I have never known one so early. I am sending you one or two photographs as a New Year present and you must let me know, from time to time, how you get on.*

When I read his book in 1939, the place-names fired me to learn Gaelic. That autumn I tried with James Maclaren's *Gaelic Self-taught*, but reached only Lesson Five. I needed a teacher to help, but knew nobody who spoke Gaelic. Only in 1974 did I learn it at evening classes as a necessary basis for a study of Deeside place-names, and passed the O-Grade examination when aged 45, during 1975.

In November 1941 I received a copy of Dugald Macintyre's *Highland Gamekeeper*, with the inscription *For Adam. From your friend Seton Gordon, Upper Duntuilm, An t-Eilean Sgiathanach.* However I found Macintyre's writing and experiences less enthralling than Gordon's, and as a field naturalist he seemed dull by comparison.

Seton Gordon liked to know about birds I had seen, and I sent sketches of snow-patches, while he sent more photographs. On 21 March 1942 I wrote, *Dear Mr Seton Gordon, I am sorry I have not written you, but I thought while the storm was on a letter could easily be lost on the way* (snowdrifts had cut off Turriff for weeks). *The last of the storm was about a week ago, and there are still a few wreaths. Bennachie was sparkling with snow a few days ago when I saw it. I am writing a book about the Cairngorms, Rothiemurchus and Mar called My Mountains and hope to get it published* (I did not like this egotistical title, but my writer aunt Elsie S. Rae chose it). *I have put a few pictures in it and photographs. I have written 20 chapters and have to write 8 more. There are 25 pictures and photographs. Publishing is difficult just now so I will likely have to wait a good while if I get it done. I have printed 36,400 words in the 20 chapters. I think I will do about 20,000 more. Here is a list of the chapters I have done and will do. I send a photograph taken last summer below Tullochgrue, looking to Rothiemurchus. It is not very clear, but shows a few drifts, very conspicuous being Cuidhe Chrom in Coire Cas and a few others. I am standing in the heather. With good wishes From Your Friend, Adam'*

Sending two chapters, I asked for his comment. He replied that I had used too adult a vocabulary, and simple words would be better, such as hard rather than arduous. Arduous was a favourite word of his, and I had followed my mentor too much, though he was too diplomatic to say so. His comments made me see other flaws. Out of my 28 chapters, seven had identical titles to *The Cairngorm Hills of Scotland*, one was identical apart from a single word shifted, and two were identical but for an extra adjective. Though I had walked in the glens, I had not been there when snow lay, or on any high top or corrie in summer. My enthusiasm had leapt ahead of my experience. What I had written was worthless, so I threw it out and wrote to tell him. He replied that the work was not wasted and would be good practice for the future. How right he was!

About late 1943 he suggested I write to W.B. Alexander, Director of Oxford's Edward Grey Institute of Field Ornithology, because the EGI would be interested in having an observer in northeast Scotland. I wrote to Mr Alexander, who welcomed my offer. Often we corresponded and I helped in surveys run by the British Trust for Ornithology with his help.

On 20 February 1944 Seton Gordon sent a typical letter full of interesting varied comments. *Dear Adam Thank you for your letter. I see you wrote on Jan. 29th but it was not posted till Feb 6th, being a Sunday. That made me think what an outcry there would be in Skye if there was a Sunday post suggested here. It would be almost as bad as Sunday harvesting, which I cannot imagine in these parts, even now. It is curious but the Hebrideans feel very strongly about these things. I am glad you have heard from Mr Alexander and now you have got in touch with him you will be able to send him any interesting bird notes. I saw our local blackbird fly past yesterday with a bill full of straw and grass, and when I went to a raven's nest last night it seemed ready for eggs and well lined with wool. Last Thursday was the first really fine day this year and I went over to see if the Fulmars had arrived. They were on their cliff in force – courting or dozing in the bright sun. I hoped the weather would keep fine but yesterday it rained all day. Today Sunday is clear and I can see fresh snow on the Harris hills. The Edward Grey Institute are getting together a census of Woodpigeons in different areas. You should write to Mr Alexander and suggest that you are ready to be their correspondent for your area. Yesterday I saw redwings searching for worms about 10 feet from the kitchen window – very tame, and as you saw that white eye stripe and red flanks make them lovely birds. The young and the old of the wild swan are about the same size so I think you may*

have seen 2 Whooper and one Bewick's Swan. They are both wild species and sometimes go together. Bewick's is named after the great naturalist: it is the smaller of the two. They are lovely birds on the wing – I am glad you are going to be a good observer of birds – a splendid hobby –Your friend Seton Gordon.

At Rothiemurchus in July 1941, AW noted the big snow patch at Cuidhe Crom (curved wreath) on Cairn Gorm and sent the sole print to Seton Gordon. He saw the print again only recently when Pete Moore sent it, after finding it in the SG archive at the National Library of Scotland in Edinburgh (Adam Watson senior)

When George Waterston came to Huntly in 1944 to work on the BTO's Woodpigeon and Rook Investigations, I had already sent data on both species to the BTO, and Mr Alexander gave George my address. In my diary for 12 September I wrote: *My article about swallows mobbing a kestrel was published in The Banffshire Journal today. I received a letter from George Waterston, Secretary of the Scottish Ornithologists' Club, who is coming up to investigate rooks and woodpigeons.*

After George got lodgings in Huntly, he drove 20 miles to Turriff one afternoon. Seeing a solicitor's office at my address, with Stewart & Watson on the window, he entered. A typist ushered him to my father Adam Watson, then aged 48 and the sole solicitor. George said "Mr W.B. Alexander of the Edward Grey Institute at Oxford said I should see you". My father replied "It's not me you want, it's my son Adam. He's the bird watcher. Right now he is in the school, but he'll be home soon". Shortly I was delighted to meet George Waterston, a name I knew well from ornithological publications. He told me later of his surprise to see a schoolboy in shorts, but Mr Alexander had assumed from my detailed letters and survey reports that I was an adult!

George arranged to come next Saturday morning, 23 September, for a day in the field. Long ere the appointed time, I sat in feverish excitement at a window, gazing at the corner where his car would appear. When it did, I ran down to meet him in the street.

Many a good day George and I had over the next year. In July 1945 he, my father and I spent fine days at Ballochbuie and Lochnagar. He knew Oxford don Bernard W. Tucker, editor of *British Birds* and one of four authors of *The Handbook of British Birds*. I regarded Tucker as the crucial author because of his contributions on modern ecological aspects that greatly interested me. He and his wife had stayed at Braemar on holiday in 1943 and 1944, and George arranged for me to meet them there.

Later in 1945 and 1946 I spent many days with Bernard. A keen hill walker even if no bird appeared, he was interested in eagles, snow buntings, dotterel and alpine flowers. He and George showed me their diaries and discussed fieldcraft, observations and note-taking. They treated me as an adult. Only later did I realise my fortune in having such early discipline, although at the time aware simply of being on a wave of enthusiasm for the area and its wildlife. Had I not written to Seton Gordon or had he not replied, I would not have met George or Bernard, or been in early touch with Mr Alexander and the BTO.

On 11 April 1944 at Ballater I wrote in my diary: *I heard that Seton Gordon is staying at Crathie. My brother Stewart telephoned them, and I am going up to meet them at 4 pm tomorrow. Am I excited!* Next day I cycled to meet him. What surprised me most was his voice, high-pitched like that of lairds I had met near Turriff. In local terms he was 'a toff'. Because I knew he had spent his boyhood at Aboyne, I had expected an Aberdeenshire accent like mine. Later I learned the explanation, that he had been educated privately. Of far more import than his voice, however, was the content of what he said, about birds, people, weather and terrain. I was greatly stimulated.

Next day we walked far on trackless ground to eagle eyries, I wheeling my cycle for the first mile. When a curlew rose in song flight, he imitated its wailing whistle as it climbed high, and the crescendo of notes as it landed. When we saw a peewit, grouse, common gull or raven, he mimicked its call and occasionally got a response. He could not now hear birds, although their open beaks showed they must be calling. I thought of his ability at judging pibroch despite poor hearing. Deep musical ability may explain these skills continuing years after his hearing deteriorated. With the curlews' song, spring had come to the moor, and the pools felt warm. Water skaters crossed the surface and water beetles swam, each carrying its little air-bag. His collie Dara liked to tread a pool to dislodge from the underlying peat a gas bubble, which rose to be popped by the dog.

I remember his long loping stride. Later I learned he had his 58th birthday on 11 April, while my 14th fell on 14 April. Despite tall heather and my then short legs, I did not find it tiring to walk with him and did not delay him. He treated me like an adult and the conversation was adult. Also adult was to walk without need for map or compass, discuss terrain in detail, and share the appreciation of wildlife first seen or heard by one or the other. Unfortunately, the eyries that he showed me were unused, but he told me of many others and swore me to secrecy. I wrote in my diary: *Crossing the moor again, we found a dead fox. Then we parted where I left my bike, for I intended to cycle up another glen to check an eyrie he had described. I cycled along the track and sped down a steep brae. When I braked on gravel at a corner, I went head over heels past the handlebars and down a bank, skinning my knees and elbows. The bike was intact, though slightly bent, but now I felt sore and stiff, so I cycled by the main road to Ballater. It has been the best day of my life.*

On 15 April I saw my first occupied eyrie whose location he had described, and wrote to tell him. In his reply (below), he was surprised at the early hatch, but I have since seen even earlier ones in Deeside. The eagles and their homes excited me. This started me on the eagle observations I have continued since, later expanded by the North East Raptor Study Group and its eagle coordinator Robert Rae. Deeside eagles have now been monitored longer, 68 successive years, than anywhere else in the world.

On April 30 he replied, *Dear Adam Well done! I wish I had been with you. But you took a risk in putting the eagle off twice: she is very apt to desert, so I am glad you saw her go back. Keep the eyrie dark: do not tell any of your friends about it. You will, I am sure, realize your responsibility, for there are very few people I would have entrusted with the secret. The most remarkable thing is that you saw a young bird. Are you absolutely certain? Why I ask is that I have never known a young eagle hatched before April 29th, and as you saw the eaglet hatched on April 15 that is a record by two weeks. The eagle broods for 35 to 42 days, so you see how early that bird must have begun to sit. I am very glad that at least one eyrie is occupied. I have not seen a single used eyrie this spring. I went up to one here yesterday but saw no trace of the birds. I saw a golden plover's scrape – a fox quite near – I am afraid he was after lambs. Yes we had a good day for going back. We left Crathie 8.45 and got to Nethy Bridge before 11 and Inverness just after 12. It got finer as we went west and there were great heather fires burning in Skye when we got there about 6 o' clock. The weather here the day you found the eyrie was dull but fair: a little sun, then a sea fog at night. That was the last of the fine weather and we have had no really fine day since then and the wind blows day and night. By the way, you said nothing about whether you went across the hill road the afternoon you left me and whether you found the eyrie? I heard yesterday from Sir Malcolm Barclay Harvey from Australia written Jan 7, and he said he had a very nice letter from you – about the stamps. We saw no curlews on the Lecht but* of course we had not *much time. Dara sends her love. I would much like to see the photographs (of the eyrie) and will return them to you.*

Thereafter we corresponded and I bought more of his books. In 1944 and 1945, the school at Turriff closed for three weeks so that children could gather potatoes for the war effort. For this work, often wet and cold, we got eight shillings for an eight-hour day in 1944 and a princely ten shillings in 1945. I saved every penny to buy books, including Gordon's *The Charm of the Hills* and *A Highland Year*, and *The Handbook of British Birds* by Witherby, Jourdain, Ticehurst and Tucker (the Tucker I met at Braemar). The two by Gordon told much about the Cairngorms, especially *The Charm of the Hills*, unsurpassed for detail on snow-patches.

Bernard Tucker and AW at the Shelter Stone, 11 August 1946 (Adam Watson senior)

In September 1945 I wrote to tell him that Garbh Choire Mor held only two small patches on 2 September and all other snow had vanished on the Dee side of the Cairngorms. Although I thought it likely that the larger patch would survive, many warm days ensued in September and October.

I received a letter from him on 15 November, saying that climbers had found Ben Nevis free of snow, for both Observatory Gully and Gardyloo Gully were snow-less. At Garbh Choire Mor on 12 October he found quite a big wreath, though smaller than usual for the season. He thought it would last, but because of the warm snow-less autumn decided to visit again. He asked me to meet him on Friday 16 November for a visit next day, but I had school on the Friday. Just as I was to wire him about this, I got a wire from him: now he could not go on the Saturday. He suggested Tuesday 20th, but I had school examinations that day.

On 29 November came a postcard: on the Tuesday the drift was 17½ feet long and covered by more than an inch of fresh snow. My diary recorded heavy snow on the hills on the 25th, on Bennachie down to 1000 feet on the 26th, with strong winds, *so the solitary drift has lasted*.

In 1948 my father and I climbed in the west Highlands and I phoned Seton from Kyle of Lochalsh. He asked me to stay the night of 30 July at his house. In my diary I wrote *I have never seen such a hot day in Skye. While waiting in Portree I stayed out of the sun. The bus, scheduled to leave at 5 pm, did not arrive until 6 and then waited ¾ hour before setting off. Eventually I had a fine run to Duntuilm through interesting country.*

The bus reached Mr Gordon's house at 8 o'clock. He stood waiting at the roadside in bare feet, wearing a tattered shirt and kilt. After supper from Mrs Gordon, we walked to the bay below the house. Today was the hottest at Duntuilm since 1936, 81F in the shade, very high for a place with sea on three sides. Many terns fished the bay, coming from the Shiant Islands where thousands breed. We could see the Outer Hebrides clearly, with a magnificent sunset over Harris. As the sun sank, the sea turned to shimmering red, and greyish rays shot through the pink sky and vanished again. This is a lovely place, one of the most beautiful views out to sea that I have ever seen. In the low Corsican pines and Sitka spruces at the house are many song thrushes, starlings and house sparrows, but on open ground few small birds apart from numerous skylarks. I had an interesting talk with SG and went to bed at 11 o'clock. A strong light still lit the northern sky.

Mrs Gordon wakened me at 6 and he walked with me to the bus. On a sunny morning the journey to Portree was a delight, and also the boat to Kyle. Now hungry, I breakfasted in a Kyle café with Aberdeen climbers. Then I met my father and we drove north to climb Beinn Eighe.

I next saw Seton on 18 October 1948 when he lectured with slides to the Aberdeen Branch of An Comunn Gaidhealach on 'The Birds of the Hebrides'. Afterwards there came tea, followed by his playing the bagpipe, and Gaelic songs and clarsach-playing by local members. I recall his pibroch reverberating loudly in the cafe below the level of Union Street, and Cairngorm Club members Sandy Tewnion, V.C. Wynne-Edwards and Hugh Welsh attending.

After the meeting, Seton mentioned a talk I had given on 'The Birds of the Cairngorms' at the annual conference of the Scottish Ornithologists' Club in Aberdeen on 18 September. In the talk I mentioned the fairly large number and generally good breeding of golden eagles, and said there was a pair in almost every glen in the Cairngorms massif. A report in *The Press & Journal* exaggerated what I had said. Seton thought this had done harm, especially on Balmoral Estate, where eagles had ruined two grouse-drives, and the King, very annoyed, saw the press report and said "Well, this proves there are too many eagles". The Queen, Seton said, "wants to protect them, but I'm not so sure of the King".

However, I threshed it out with Seton, and I gained my point that my talk had been on the Cairngorms massif, excluding Balmoral and other parts of northeast Scotland where eagles are scarcer. Also the press had misreported, but my letter published in *The Press & Journal* had cleared up the errors. He thought Mar stalkers were still supposed to destroy eagles, but I said no, and he was glad to hear it. We parted most amicably after a fine conversation.

By now a student at Aberdeen University, I kept in touch by correspondence, but did not see him again until 1955. In February 1955, Jenny and I decided to marry, and arranged to wed on 19 March. Someone must have told Seton. I received a postcard dated 3 March, *Dear Adam, Is it true you are marrying a Golden Eagle -- or is it only a lying rumour, and you are really engaged to the Snowy Owl of B. M. D. (*Ben Macdui*)?. Anyhow, warm congrats to you both. SG.* In my Foreword to the re-publication of *The Immortal Isles* after his death, I wrote, *A romantic, Seton also had a puckish sense of humour. When I got married, I saw no reason for spreading the news. Shortly before my wedding day, I received a postcard*, as above. A classic SG card, it was the best I ever received from him.

In early May 1955 I put tents at 3000 feet to aid my ptarmigan study. Bob Scott told me that Seton was to stay on a Saturday night in Nell Macdonald's house at Greenfield near Braemar. I decided to call there with Jenny and my father on the way to my camp. My diary of 8 May records it. *Went up to Luibeg, and we climbed to the camp on Derry Cairngorm late in the evening. We had a talk with Seton Gordon on the way up.* Seton, now 69, gave us a great welcome. *It was a beautiful evening with soft purple light on the hills. Many deer grazed the Allanmore bog* as Nell gave us tea. Seton said we would hear ptarmigan cocks crowing at dawn. Despite rain, sleet and wind most of the night, at dawn we did hear a golden plover sing to the east and a ptarmigan crowing throatily near the tent.

On 18 May Seton wrote another postcard, *I should very much like to know (a P.C. would do) what the weather at and above 2500 ft is like. The storm may have just come before the ptarmigan have begun to lay: I hope so. The wireless says the Devil's Elbow was blocked! Here we have had much better weather than you with long hours of sun. I've been hoping to hear from you about your weekend on Derry Cairngorm. It was very good seeing you and kind of you to have called, and do tell your Father how glad I was to see him. I had never met him though I had the pleasure of meeting your Mother. Please tell the Snowy Owl that I think she is the perfect mate for a mountain and bird lover. Many congratulations to you both. Skye week is due to start Saturday. I fear hundreds of grouse must have lost their nests on Corndavon and Invercauld? We saw a pair of swifts at Tummel Bridge the morning after we saw you. SG.*

George Waterston told me that eagle expert Leslie Brown spoke at the Scottish Ornithologists' Club conference in 1946, proposing a national eagle survey by the SOC, but the Club turned it down when Seton Gordon and Fraser Darling opposed it. They wished to avoid giving estates an excuse to say eagles should be killed because the survey showed large numbers. However, grouse-moor estates persecuted eagles anyway, without a survey.

When Leslie came from Kenya in 1958 to work on a paper with me, and I told him some Scottish eagle news,

Garbh Choire snow bed, photographed by S. G. in early October 1910 — Just 50 years ago.

Christmas Greetings to Adam Watson and Adam Watson, younger, from Seton Gordon.

Snow patch at Garbh Choire Mor in 1910. Seton Gordon pasted his photograph on to a card and sent it as a Christmas greeting to AW, whom he called 'Adam Watson younger' (Seton Gordon)

he considered writing to the Duke of Edinburgh about eagle failures on Balmoral and threatening to tell *The Daily Express*. In retrospect I think this would have helped reduce such failures better than Seton's wish to keep information dark. At the SOC conference in 1948, James Fisher referred to the spirited discussion on eagle numbers after my talk as evidence of interest in the subject. He joked at the expense of the SOC about the eagle survey that Leslie Brown had proposed in 1946 and that the SOC, too easily swayed by Gordon and Darling, had rejected. James supported a survey and made his own estimate, based on less information than that held by Leslie, Pat Sandeman and others including me.

On this and other issues, George Waterston used to refer to Seton as Satan. Raymond Eagle's biography *Seton Gordon* tells how Seton irritated osprey wardens at Loch Garten and how *a misunderstanding grew between him and George Waterston.... For some time George Waterston was given to referring to Seton as 'Old Satan'!* I think Raymond overstated about Satan. Rural Aberdeenshire folk unfamiliar with the name Seton used Satan or 'Satty' Gordon as a way of pronouncing an unusual forename. In 1944–46, long before the osprey events, George and I knew this and

Seton Gordon on Carn an Tuirc, Cairngorms beyond, 7 August 1976

it amused George greatly. Thereafter, George always said Satan when referring to Seton in my presence, with that unforgettable George grin on his face.

Seton in his own book *A Highland Year* recounts (p. 51) how two men in a train compartment argued about an eagle's wingspan. Seton agreed with one man, and spotted him one eyeing up a label on Seton's luggage. This man trounced the other by asking 'Do you know who yon is?' 'No, indeed', came the answer. 'Well' said the first in triumph, 'yon is Setton Gordon'.

I next met Seton on 17 July 1966. I had gone to Ballochbuie with my father, and as usual called on Robert Brown, Balmoral stalker at Garbh Allt Shiel and internationally famed piper. Since 1945 I had known him well and spent many days with him on the hill and at his house. A sound observer, he protected eagles. On the way back I called at 5 pm to tell him what we had seen. Bob ushered us in, saying "Seton Gordon's here and hoping to see you".

With hand out to shake mine, Seton greeted me "How are you? I used to know your son". He said to me, with a wave of the hand towards my father "Your son there has been corresponding with me since he was a schoolboy." At first I thought he had mixed us up, because my beard had grown whiter and longer than the red one he had seen in 1955, whereas my clean-shaven father had a short back and sides. So, I replied to Seton "This is my father", introducing my Dad to him. Seton just grinned, without a word. I told this in the Foreword that I wrote for re-publication of *The Immortal Isles* (p. xiv): *A stranger might have thought Seton was just a confused old man, but the twinkle in his eye and the grin on his face told us this was another classic example of the mischievous Seton Gordon humour.*

Over tea, he said Bob Scott at Luibeg once told him "The only thing that'll bring Adam down off the hill is HUNGER". Then he asked Bob Brown to play. Bob Brown said the pipe would not do well with such short preparation, but Seton persisted and Pipe-Major Bob agreed. He asked us to come outside, because the notes would be distorted inside. He played a lament, the finest piping my father and I had ever heard. Bob walked slowly up and down, eyes closed as he concentrated on playing, a man transformed. The sounds came and went as soft eddies stirred among the old pines. We looked up to Lochnagar, entranced by the music and the setting. No one spoke. My eyes met Seton's, his face happy. It was a rare occasion that we would not forget. When Bob finished, Seton clapped his hands, and my father and I followed likewise.

The spell broke when my father said, "Well, I've a long way to go to Newburgh", and Seton said he must leave, as he was already late for dinner. After walking to the bridge we gave Seton a lift to Invercauld and spoke of Bob and his piping. A few years later, Bob retired at 65 in October 1970 to a cottage near Balmoral Castle. Sadly, he was not to live much longer. Seton wrote (Raymond Eagle's biography *Seton Gordon*), p. 283. *25 April. Very sad to hear from Follett, who rang before breakfast to say the Scottish News announced that Robert Brown had died suddenly. He had returned to Balmoral midday yesterday from a tour of Australia and at 4 p.m. he was away and we shall not hear his piping again. He will be a sad loss to piping and his many, many friends.*

Seton had known Balmoral stalkers back to his boyhood. In *A Highland Year*, he wrote (p. 53) *Charles Mackintosh, second stalker on the Balmoral Forest, I knew well, and often stayed with him. It was he, who, by supporting my weight on a ladder which he raised and held against his chest, enabled me to take my first photograph of a golden eagle's eyrie when I was a boy. His wife, I remember, was the baker of some of the finest scones I have tasted.* In his classic *Days with the Golden Eagle*, published in 1927, he generously dedicated his book: *To my friends the keepers and stalkers who have given me much valuable help in the writing of this book.*

In *A Highland Year* he wrote: *The deerstalkers on the royal forest of Balmoral were all fine men. There was a rather curious custom that, when on the hill, the royal rank of the 'gentlemen' was temporarily forgotten, and they were addressed with a familiarity that would never have been thought of elsewhere. This familiarity was sometimes a shock to the ambassadors of foreign nations who were present. I recall on one occasion an ambassador of Spain hearing one of the stalkers say to the late King George V: 'You will bide here (showing him a place of concealment for the deer drive) but there's the Laddie (the Prince of Wales), I dinna know what we will dae wi' HIM'. It must of course have been on the initiative of the Royal Family that this lack of ceremony was the custom 'on the hill', for the Balmoral stalkers were courtly mannered men with a fine Highland dignity and bearing.* Here, Seton showed a lack of identity with the stalkers. They spoke Aberdeenshire Scots but he did not. He erroneously construed their use of Scots as 'familiarity'. Hence, their 'lack of ceremony' did not result from the royal family's initiative.

Seton gave many lectures with slides, and came to Aberdeen to give one in August 1969. It shows his popularity among stalkers that Bob Scott of Luibeg told me "The wife and me gaed into Aiberdeen to see Seton's show. We saw a fair puckle (number) o Deeside staalkers there".

On Sunday 10 August 1975 I went to Beinn a' Bhuird to count dotterel and ptarmigan, with my father helping. After a long day we came to Alltan na Beinne. While we drank tea on the bank, a magnificent sunset flooded the Cairngorms. Then we heard a vehicle, and out came Invercauld laird Alwyne Farquharson and Seton. Alwyne had driven his land-rover up with the elderly Seton, and they had walked to the east corries.

He wrote on September 7 a typical memorable letter. *Dear Adam, Three weeks ago almost to an hour we met you and your Father in wild and barren surroundings, lit up by a glowing aircraft 6 miles to the SW* (Loch Etchachan). *I wrote an article, and the Editor of The Field (London) said it would be in the issue of Sept. 4, which I have not seen, but you may like to keep an eye open for it. I drove back to the West next morning; the heat was almost overpowering -- But the heat wave had gone by the Saturday of that week when Angus Macpherson (of Invershin and aged 98) and I judged the piping (and mist was on the tops) at Glen Finnan. I must congratulate you, quite seriously, on your beard. It is indeed one of the most distinguished beards I have seen for a long time, and reminded me of the Highlander of 70 years ago. Very few Solans passing this year – indeed it was only yesterday that I saw my first. The local fishermen say the Herring hereabout have been fished out, and, 'No Herring no Solans'. I hope most of the eagles in your area have been successful this year and that there have been no Eagle Rustlers! Best wishes to you all. Seton Gordon.*

It was astounding for an 89-year-old. I would have missed him had my father and I not stayed to see the sunset, and I wanted a day with Seton if we could arrange it. Knowing that he stayed a few days annually at Invercauld, I phoned Alwyne, who said he would be delighted to arrange a day with Seton and me, and would phone me on Seton's next visit in 1976.

On 5 August, Alwyne phoned and asked me to come next day in the afternoon. On 6 August, he and his wife had tea with Seton and me. To join us came the Keeper of the Privy Purse from Buckingham Palace, who knew Seton well. Alwyne suggested I return next morning for a whole day out. When I arrived, I found Seton outside the back door. He and I spoke with head-keeper Donald McDonald while the laird took lunches to a vehicle. Seton had just seen a buzzard above Craig Leek.

Alwyne drove up Glen Callater and then to Carn an Tuirc. Completely ignoring scenery and wildlife, Seton on the front passenger's seat told Alwyne a stream of humorous anecdotes about Violet Barclay-Harvey and other Deeside gentry, while I sat in the back, amazed at this side of Seton that was foreign to me. It seemed out of place from his writings and past talk with me, but showed his complexity. His gossip ended when we dismounted on the plateau.

Now, fine views and wildlife absorbed his attention totally. In an obituary by me in *Scottish Birds*, the journal of the Scottish Ornithologists' Club, I wrote about our trip. *Though slower, he still had a steady step on the plateau. Remarkably, his blue eyes sparkled as keenly as ever, and his conversation was full of excited comments on snow-patches, birds, place names and the Cairngorms range itself, which I believe was the most beloved part of Scotland to him.*

I spotted a few birds far away and said they might be dotterel, but Seton thought golden plover. He rested a telescope on the vehicle while Alwyne and I used binoculars. Simultaneously Seton and I said "Definitely golden plover", a good eye for a 90-year-old.

At Christmas 1976 he sent a card about recent photographs purporting to show Nessie of Loch Ness. It was typical SG. *Dear Adam, What is your verdict on the recent pictures of Nessie? Before it is too late, I do wish you could obtain, in writing, from some of the old people on Loch Ness-side, their Gaelic name for the 'Beast of Loch Ness'. I am sure some of the old people have it. I am rather out of touch with that area. Best wishes to yourself and the Family.*

Also when 90 he lectured at Braemar for the Scottish Wildlife Trust. In my obituary I wrote: *The slides were ancient and blurred, but his word pictures were as good as anything he ever wrote. Describing the dawn sun rays catching the gold hackles on a brooding eagle's neck, he had us there with him, over 50 years ago......Only days before his death, The Field published a letter of his about Whooper Swans, simple and evocative as usual. It was a good farewell from the grand old man.....The grand old man has gone, on 19th March 1977 at Brackley in Northamptonshire, only a fortnight short of 91.* The date brought memories to Jenny and me. On that very date in 1955 at our wedding party, my father had read Seton's plain postcard, but it contained a far more memorable message than the many greetings telegrams that he announced.

In his Foreword to the re-publication in 1980 of Seton's book *The Golden Eagle*, ornithologist Desmond Nethersole-Thompson wrote about him. *Many regarded Seton Gordon as a Highland character and almost as an eccentric. In any part and in any company he was certainly easily and instantly recognised in his kilt, bonnet and jacket. But eccentric he was not. He was a courteous, kindly, cultured man of great ability and sensitivity.*

After my obituary on him appeared in *Scottish Birds* during summer 1977, I received a letter from daughter Caitriona, written on August 22. *Dear Adam I thought I would write and say what a good and stimulating obituary you wrote about my father in Scottish Birds, quite the best I have seen, and a really excellent description of him. I still remember him getting your letters and showing them to me, when you were 8 or so, and he was always very impressed.* She asked if I could send her prints of my photograph that accompanied the obituary, *for myself and my stepmother, and brother in Vancouver, and sister in Australia, she also was very impressed by your writing. I hope this is not a great bother, but it is a very typical stance of him, and the famous kilt! Yours very sincerely, Caitriona Macdonald Lockhart.*

After re-publication of *The Immortal Isles* with my Foreword, John Harrower of St James's Deeside Gallery at Dinnet wrote on 25 January 1980. *Dear Adam, This morning I received my copy of The Immortal Isles, which I had ordered the very day I read the review in the P & J, and I have lost no time in delving into it. I have also read your Foreword with the greatest possible pleasure. I too knew him in different ways most of my life though not so closely as you. As a boy I admired him from afar, in later years I corresponded with him, and finally got to know him here on Deeside. He was a great poet. He understood the 'Magic of Things' and could translate it into words – a great gift. Thanks for a good job well done! Sincerely, John H.*

In that Foreword I gave a few quotations as examples of Seton's value as an author. I wrote: *Seton Gordon's first books were mainly on natural history and wildlife photography, but even his most specialist books on these subjects showed his sensitivity and perception of the beauty of nature, his extraordinary variety of interests, and his deep appreciation of Scotland's history and Gaelic heritage. Nothing could exemplify these points better than The Immortal Isles, his beautiful book about the Outer Hebrides. Take any few pages at random and you will find a fascinating mixture of sensitive, romantic descriptions of the islands and their beautiful skies, seas, and light, local place names and their meanings, legends and local customs, fine accounts on the flowers, birds, and seals, enthusiastic stories about his camping trips to photograph uncommon nesting birds from hides, and a reverence for the local people......Seton Gordon was a masterly describer of an incident or event, and often did this so well that for a moment the reader was there with him.......Here is an example from The Immortal Isles: Before we set sail on the return journey to Uist we sat down to a wonderful tea: drop scones, newly made and light as a feather, freshly churned butter with the scent of the flowers of the machair in it, and the richest of sweet cream. Or the last paragraph of the book, one heard often the wild elusive call of a wandering greenshank. Sometimes he fluted beside some hill tarn; sometimes one disturbed him at his feeding on the ooze beside a sea-pool at low tide. There are few bird-calls more wonderful than the cry of the greenshank. In his voice the spirit of the wild places lives: his love-song, heard at an immense height above some lonely Highland pine forest in spring, is deathless music that remains in the mind of him who hears it so long as memory lasts.*

Seton's books emphasised Gaelic place-names and meanings. Too many authors invented derivations that flew in the face of Gaelic usage or local pronunciation. Seton consulted Professor W. J. Watson, a native Gael and outstanding pioneer of place-name study. Seton's books refer to him, and the *Highways and Byways* books include Watson's sections.

In my obituary I wrote of him. *With his passing ends the period of wholly exploratory naturalists in Scotland and their extraordinary breadth of interests. He was long the last practitioner, overlapping for decades with the modern period when scientific method dominated ornithology. Astride two centuries, Seton had a timeless attitude, exemplified by the patched, decades-old kilt he wore on every occasion, sun or snow, mansion or bothy. Plate 28 might have been in Harvie-Brown's time, showing nothing to indicate the real date – August 1976.* (J.A. Harvie-Brown was an outstanding Scottish naturalist in 1880–1907.)

I wrote in my obituary of him: *Gordon began writing articles to newspapers and magazines in his late teens, and published his first book Birds of the Loch and Mountain in 1907 when he was just 19. Others soon followed. A pioneer in bird photography, he took photographs of Golden Eagle and Greenshank that are still classics. He was also a pioneer of camping on the high tops. These early books brimmed with enthusiasm and already showed his wide interest in birds, rare plants, snow-patches, the old Caledonian forest, piping, weather, folk lore, history, place names, the survival of Gaelic, and a deep appreciation and knowledge of the Highlands. He also described vividly some winter climbs and storms. A natural hillman, he never over-wrote the difficulties or dangers and was at home in the Cairngorms winter or summer, alone or in company......His most detailed study was of Golden Eagles; he and his wife Audrey spent 167 hours watching a Speyside eyrie in 1924.....Leslie Brown noted that Gordon had not condensed his observations into tables from which others could benefit by doing their own statistical analyses. The fact is Gordon was a pre-tables man. As with many fine naturalists, most details within his exceptional experience will have died with him. He was a masterly describer of things in breadth, of incident, of anecdote. Detailed analytical research was not his way, and this is as true of his contribution on place names and history as on ornithology. Nor could one expect it, as his training had been different; the change did not start in field ornithology until David Lack's papers in the mid 1930s. However, analytical researchers and men interested in problems often fail to interest the layman, and seldom excite him as Gordon did for many. Future Scotsmen will read him when many of the analysts have been forgotten.*

In my Foreword to the re-publication of *Days with the Golden Eagle* in 2003, I wrote: *A pioneer naturalist and bird-photographer, Gordon was also ahead of his time as a hill-walker and nature conservationist. Unlike many authors on hills or wildlife, he did not stress or overstate difficulties, and eschewed egotism and anthropocentrism. He wrote simply, describing scenes so vividly that many readers imagined they saw them, or felt they were standing on the hill beside this timeless outstanding naturalist and writer.*

Chapter 4 Hills and wildlife, 1935–43

I first saw the Cairngorms when too young to remember the occasion. My first clear memory, still vivid, was the first morning I went to school at Turriff in August 1935. Turriff is a small town by the river Deveron at the western end of the lowlands of Buchan in northern Aberdeenshire and south of Banff on the Moray Firth. However, in the early 1930s my parents liked to holiday at Ballater and Grantown, and my father took photographs that included me, in years that I do not now remember. A few early events at school I recount in Chapter 1. They point to my later liking of lone days on the hill or observing wildlife, and my determination while doing so, irrespective of weather.

The town centre of Turriff lies on a south-facing slope beside the Burn of Turriff, a tributary of the nearby Deveron. From upper parts of Turriff one can see hills towards the upper Deveron and to the south the striking outline of Bennachie with other nearer hills, Tillymorgan and Foudland. In 1935–37 I knew their shapes but the hills did not yet excite me.

When seven I recall going to Bennachie on a warm summer day with my father and elder brother Stewart, while my mother and my father's mother stayed by the car at a croft. Among beeches nearby, the path contained a yard-deep dry gully, above a fan of washed-out gravel. It amazed me. I could not think how rain could do this and nobody whom I asked could explain it. Thereby began a lifelong interest in soil erosion. The hill seemed immense and we found it stiff going. When we reached two thirds of the way up, we turned, the Mither Tap towering far above.

Also when seven, I remember the Linn of Dee's rocks, pools, gnarled old pine-trees, and gravestone to one who had drowned. Well I recall my mother's dire warnings to stay well back from the edge.

At Grantown I was curious to see a big fish-shaped pink object on Cairn Gorm, shining in reflected sunlight, but vanishing in shade. Wondering what it could be, I kept asking people, but nobody knew. It surprised me that my parents and others had not noticed it and were not interested when I pointed it out. I wanted to go there, see what it was, and stand beside it. Years later I found at close range that water flowing down the Great Slab of Coire an Lochain gleamed in the sun, and avalanches that tore lichens off the rock maintained the granite's pink colour.

In summer 1938 I knew the shapes and locations of snow-patches visible from the roads in Speyside or Deeside, and saw that most of them had melted by autumn. I liked their distinctive shapes, but had not yet thought of setting foot on the patches.

Reading Seton Gordon's *The Cairngorm Hills of Scotland* in early July 1939 changed all that (Chapter 3). Thereafter I wanted to be on the hills, the higher the better, and asked my father to help. Over the next few days he took my brother and me on walks far longer than before. The first was to the Sgor Mor in Glen Dee.

In 2009, Dave Hewitt asked me to write a short note on the first hill I ever climbed, and he published it in *The Angry Corrie* (No 75, p.8). I wrote of seeing Seton Gordon's book and then persuading my father to take me to the Cairngorms. *His most energetic sport had been golf, but now he drove past the Linn of Dee to the White Bridge, and he, my 12 year-old brother and I climbed north. When we reached the horizon, another appeared beyond, then another, and another. The boggy slope seemed endless. We became tired, and I wished I had longer legs, but my father and brother also took rests. Finally there came the summit tors, where a dense haze augmented the impression of a vast wild landscape. As we walked back, I recall picking out stretches of short grass and running down them, until we reached the car and looked back at the great Sgor Mor. I wanted more and more.*

On a second trip we went to Morrone above Braemar. My parents knew the McGregors of Tomintoul croft very well, having stayed on their honeymoon around 1922 when Mrs McGregor's father James Downie still lived there after years as a part-time paid mountain guide. When my father drove to Tomintoul in July 1939, we visited the McGregors. Mrs McGregor gave me a glass of frothy warm milk straight from her cows, which grazed knee-deep in a flowery meadow. Then we walked up the path, again slow and tiring, and turned at the tall cairns below the summit, but the cairns are a good viewpoint to see the Cairngorms. I looked through my father's telescope at snow-patches on Beinn a' Bhuird, Ben Macdui and other high hills. Below us, miles of old pinewoods stretched unbroken, from east of Allanaquoich westwards to Glen Dee, and from the Linn of Dee eastwards to well past Corriemulzie.

Later in that week, my father drove his car near the Colonel's Bed in Glen Ey, and on other days to Loch Builg, the

Linn of Quoich and the Falls of Garbh Allt, and each day we walked to a place of interest. No locked gates barred the private roads. We met a Ballater man who spoke of climbing Lochnagar by what he called The Ladder, but I thought he was too keen to impress us and exaggerate the difficulty.

On a windy day in October 1939 we returned to the White Bridge and the Chest of Dee with its swirling dark pools. I recall a feeling of great space for miles to Beinn Bhrotain, An Sgarsoch and other remote hills. I still feel it every time I go there.

In 1939 I began to explore the Turriff area at all seasons by cycling and walking to wood, bog, river and loch within five miles in lowland Aberdeenshire and Banffshire. By 1942 I expanded this to river-gorge, moor, coastal cliff, beach, and low hill within 15 miles, and by 1946 within 25 miles. Then an area of great variety, its farmland soon became far less attractive as taxpayer's money flowed to intensify agriculture. A wonderful variety of naturally regenerating boreal woodland of birch and Scots pine excited me beyond measure. Again with taxpayers' money, the Forestry Commission encouraged and authorised its clear-felling and replacement by monotonous conifer blocks.

From 1939, school pals and I walked miles to find birds' eggs. We used the Scots names, such as *blackie* a blackbird, *mavis* a song thrush, *stormcock* a mistle thrush, *yalla yite* or the diminutive *yalla yitie* a yellowhammer, *peesie* or *peesie-weep* or *teuchat* a lapwing, *whaup* a curlew, *skirly wheeter* an oystercatcher, *craa* a rook, *heedie craa* a hooded crow, *craggit heron* or *craggie* a heron, *cushie doo* a woodpigeon, and many more. A few of the names resembled the calls of the birds. *Peesie* and *peesie-weep* brought to mind the bird's plaintive alarm call, *whaup* the slow wailing notes at the start of the curlew's song, *skirly wheeter* the excited shouting of oystercatchers as they arrived in spring on their home shingle. English names such as oystercatcher and rook we never used, though we knew what they meant.

We climbed many trees to nests. At first we climbed easy short trees with many side branches, but when aged 13 and over we advanced to taller trees with few side branches. The most climbing took place at the huge rookery near Hatton Castle. We gained the added advantage of selling the eggs to an egg-packing station at Turriff, for transport to the south.

Gnarled old Scots pines carried the biggest and often the most nests per given tree, but usually you had to swarm up by putting your legs round a side bole and then pull with your hands, so you had to rely on friction from your clothes holding you temporarily. A monkey is far better at this. Often you could get an easier start by getting a shoulder from a pal. I found I could easily climb short conifers with few side branches, such as planted Scots pines, because with my long arms and legs I could reach branches high above.

My best friend Norman Sim was small in height, though quite strong, and too short to reach high branches. Instead, he swarmed up by putting his legs round the tree and moving them in unison, slower than me but effective. For old Scots pines and old beeches, Norman's method was the only one that worked.

Norman excelled at climbing very difficult trees, just natural ability plus determination. He came into his own with old beech trees. These had a widely-spreading canopy of strong boughs, and many rooks nested near the outer ends, a spot where a few side-branches often formed a good receptacle for a stick nest. A given bough might have several nests at its far end. Climbing the main bole or a side bole was hard enough, given the smooth bark of the beech. Once you were high up, however, the only way to reach nests at the far end of an upper bough was to crawl horizontally along the bough, with the bough supporting you. Norman was a master at this, crawling along, putting the eggs in a bag, next moving to other nests nearby, and then reversing to crawl back and lastly climb down the main bole. Had he slipped, there was little to hang on to, and a fall could have been fatal. I never even tried it on the biggest beeches. I did notice that boys short in height could do this more easily than taller ones.

In 1939 I scaled a few rocks near Turriff, on my own, for my friends were not interested in trying it. On a south-facing, steep 15-foot outcrop of slate rock near my grandma's cottage I drew a sketch of half a dozen routes, with notes on the difficulty. When a taller and stronger 18, I returned to find all the moves no harder than easy or moderate, but to a wholly inexperienced 9-year-old with a short reach, the rock posed a big challenge.

To reach the outcrop I walked a narrow tree-clad ridge with small rocks on both sides, past a 20-foot vertical outcrop on the north side. Easy vegetated ledges led to the mid-point, but slightly loose holds on the top vertical wall faced down, so I never climbed it despite several attempts. Returning at 18, I found the moves difficult and dubious because of loose slate rock.

A vertical outcrop on the south side, rising for 30 feet in shade above steep slopes covered in wood rush, seemed

At Gleann Einich in July 1940, honeymoon lady, AW, mother, AW senior, brother Stewart (honeymoon man with A. Watson senior's camera)

far too intimidating when I was 9, and I never attempted it. Other rocks lay at an easy angle and I walked up them in gym shoes in dry weather. I told nobody about my rock climbing, for fear of being forbidden. My parents never discouraged my going alone then or later on, and never showed anxiety to me about this. Grateful was I for this freedom.

In April 1940 we drove to the White Bridge and walked to the suspension bridge that then spanned the Geldie Burn. Deep fresh snow lay on Beinn Bhrotain and falling snow obscured the summit. Through my father's telescope I searched this complex hill of many shoulders and tops. I wanted to cross its high snowy slopes and wondered if some day I would.

During July 1940 we stayed near Grantown on Spey with the McDougalls who worked the croft at the Craggan. Mrs McDougall's father Robert Grant lived with his wife at the Lower Craggan, after retiring as head gamekeeper at Muckrach near Dulnain Bridge. Often I walked with him to the end of his garden to admire the Cairngorms, especially the dark blue cone of Cairn Gorm, which looks so impressive and mysterious from the north. He delighted me by singing *Allt an Lochain Uaine*, that lovely Gaelic song once popular on both the Dee and Spey sides of the Cairngorms. I learned to sing it and never forgot it. He told me the Gaelic name for the Cairngorms was Am Monadh Ruadh the red mounth. While a keeper, he had often been a guide taking Muckrach guests to Cairn Gorm, where they drank at the cold spring of Fuaran a' Mharcuis, visited perennial snow at Ciste Mhearad, and got 'refreshments' at Glenmore Lodge. It seemed a far-away world.

One day my father drove to Glenmore Lodge and we walked to An Lochan Uaine, which Mr Grant said means the green lochan. I marvelled at the strange grey-green water, the fallen trees below the surface, and the mystery of the place. Mr Grant said old folk believed that fairies washed their clothes in the lochan and so caused the colour.

On another day in July 1940 I recall the panorama outside the then Aviemore Hotel, with the snow wreath of the Cuidhe Crom prominent at the top of Coire Cas. Later that day, my father, mother, brother, mother's sister Elsie and I walked from Coylumbridge through Rothiemurchus by the Lairig Ghru path. My father in the lead took a wrong turn, so we found ourselves facing Gleann Einich, and spent some time before regaining the right path to the Cairngorm Club footbridge. Near the outer trees we stopped on a conical hillock that gives the finest view of the Lairig. I was sorry we had to go back, now that we had come so near to that mysterious pass.

Next day we visited Barrie's Cairn near Whitewell. Through my father's telescope I looked closely at the hills, admiring the three high corries of Braeriach and the gulf of the Lairig Ghru.

My aunt left next morning by rail, but the rest of us drove to Whitewell and walked up Gleann Einich to the Lower Bothy. Past the defile of Caigeann Beanaidh we met a well-equipped couple walking north. He worked in a Keith bank and they had spent their honeymoon at the Lower Bothy. In a week they had climbed Braeriach, Sron na Lairige and Sgoran Dubh, and had descended from Braeriach to the Pools of Dee and down the Lairig Ghru. I regarded them as heroes and listened with amazement to what they said. They assured me that I would be able to do the same when some years older, but I did not believe it. On return to Keith they sent a letter to my father, saying how they enjoyed meeting us. Then I lost touch with them.

Fifty years later, in summer 1990, their daughter phoned out of the blue to say her parents had bought my books on the Cairngorms and had seen me on TV. She asked if I could visit their home at Friockheim to celebrate their 50th wedding anniversary. I did, and spent a pleasant hour reminiscing with them. In 1940 they seemed tall to me, but in 1990 I found them shorter than average. It was like revisiting 50 years later a walk that you did when 10 years old. The walk that seemed so long has shrunk astonishingly.

After parting from them in 1940 we walked to the Lower Bothy, quite a big wooden building in good condition. In the visitors' book I read of the hill walks by my two heroes. Outside I sat on a wooden bench, looking through a telescope at striking views of Braeriach and Sgoran Dubh. Next we crossed Am Beanaidh by a footbridge and climbed hillocks over to Loch Mhic Ghille-chaoile. As we stood on its beach, endless waves broke to leave frothy foam in lines on the coarse pink sand, a sight and sound I still remember as if yesterday. Beyond, the black cliffs of Sgoran Dubh soared into thin mist. Then we walked four miles down the gravel road to Whitewell. It had been my most exciting day yet on the hill.

In November 1940 I noticed a slight pain in my left chest, which became constant in December, but I ignored it because I felt fine. While the family stayed at Ballater in late December, deep snow fell and hard frost set in, conditions that normally delighted me. However, one morning when we walked the road to Pannanich among snow-encrusted spruces out of the sun, I felt the cold in my very bones. More than anything I wanted to stand before a hot fire. Shivery and unwell, I told my parents for the first time that I had a pain in my side, and had felt it for weeks. The Ballater general practitioner said I probably had pleurisy and should stay in bed. Next day, my father drove us by Aberdeen to Turriff, because snow blocked the direct road by Strath Don. Buchan's farmland lay snowbound, a cold grey-blue colour as I looked from Whiterashes, where tall clouds tinged red and blue threatened more snow. I sat wrapped in blankets, feet on a metal hot-water bottle. I felt cosy, and enjoyed looking at the snow and the snow-clouds.

At Turriff, Dr James Hunter treated me for pleurisy, but after days without recovery, now into January, he suspected worse problems. Inserting a syringe needle into my back, he withdrew nasty-looking and smelly brown liquid for analysis. I had empyema. Infection had gone beyond my lung, into the pleural cavity.

During mid January, again in blankets, I accompanied my father by train to Aberdeen and then by ambulance to hospital. From the looks of Dr Hunter the day before and now the looks of the surgeon, I judged I must be very ill, though I felt fine, provided I kept warm. The surgeon operated next morning. They kept my wound open for six weeks, with a tube into a container to remove any remaining foul matter. Those weeks taught me to endure searing pain twice daily when a nurse or doctor adjusted the tube, and occasionally at other times if I turned in sleep or moved while sitting in bed.

Long after my body temperature had fallen to normal and the staff proclaimed easy sailing, I had a strange experience. Waking in the middle of the night, I felt an odd chillness about my body and the air. I seemed to be partly disengaged from my body, as if floating in air, looking on as an outsider. Though not a happy feeling, it did not alarm me enough to call for help, and I was more concerned in trying to understand events. After what seemed a long time in limbo, I fell asleep. Next morning, my temperature was above normal, when after a night's rest it should have been below. The nurses wondered why, and I just told them I had been awake in the night. Afterwards I thought I might have been near death, but then reasoned that I must have had a hallucination, induced by the poisonous matter still in my pleural cavity.

The nurses told me to stay in bed except when going to the toilet, but often when no nurse was about I tiptoed barefoot to a window, holding tube and container in both hands, to take a brief look at snow lying or snowflakes falling. Lucky was I that a nurse or matron never saw me.

In bed I had much time to read and write. I filled a small notebook with pencil writings on the Cairngorms, laid out in chapters with crayon drawings. The book has drawings of a kilted Seton Gordon-like man using a telescope, and emphasises hills with snow-patches as well as winter snow. A series shows the Upper Bothy in Gleann Einich with no snow, then 'snow is coming', and finally in December 1940 deep snow everywhere including the bothy roof. I did not know then that snow blows off the roof of an exposed bothy. The notebook has incorrect drawings of a golden eagle with a tiny eyrie and a ptarmigan nest like a blackbird's, but I had not yet seen either in reality. I included drawings of other wildlife that I had seen. I still have the wee black notebook.

Nurse Michie in hospital heard of my interest in Deeside and often saw me. A relative of the Rev J.G. Michie who wrote *Deeside Tales*, she had walked as a girl to the great Monaltrie Moss to dig peats, and said the old folk had whisky stills there. This excited me. I wanted to go there with her and see that great peat-moss.

After six weeks the surgeon decided that I had recovered more quickly than expected, and in March 1941 my father came to take me home by train, without blankets. At Turriff, Dr Hunter forbade school, church, and Sunday school, and allowed only short walks, gradually increasing after some weeks to two miles, while I recuperated. I wanted more, but he kept telling me I'd had a narrow squeak and must take care. While in my father's car on his way to see clients, I looked at Bennachie and distant Corryhabbie from the Brunt Smiddy on the Banff turnpike, and at Ben Avon from the high crofts of Fishrie. Often I wondered if I would ever walk the hills again, but it made me happy just to see them.

While in hospital and afterwards I had much time to think, and this included wondering about philosophy. I was pleased about the doctor's order to omit church and Sunday school. Tedious and uninspiring they had been for years, but now I questioned organised religion seriously. I could not reason why I should obey a minister standing in quaint robes within a pulpit, telling many including me how to behave. I found sermons, songs and bibles too man-centred, and it seemed absurd to believe the earth and its life were put there for man's use and dominion.

I thought of the Cairngorms and the beauty of nature, which spiritually meant so much more to me. When the time for restarting school approached, my father said I would of course attend church and Sunday school. I told him my thoughts and begged him not to compel me. Although a kirk elder, he let me be. I regarded this as a lucky escape, but many years later he told me he had been having his own doubts, and in a few years he gave up his eldership. Indirectly, my non-attendance freed Sundays for reading and exploration, and his resignation as elder later freed Sundays for hill trips.

In summer 1941 my mother and I stayed with Robert Grant and his wife at Lower Craggan near Grantown on Spey for a few days. One day we took a bus to Aviemore, and at Nethy Bridge I noticed some corries that I had not seen before, especially the steep red screes of Coire Dearg on A' Choinneach, and the northern hollows of Beinn Mheadhoin. A double snow-patch in Coire Dearg lay on a crag beside a waterfall, and I could not understand how snow could lie at such a steep angle. Only later did I realise that a slope which seems vertical when viewed face on, can be at quite a low gradient.

Mr Grant showed me how to grow vegetables and told me about Speyside's countryside, folk, gamebirds and other wildlife, Gaelic, and place-names. The old crofters on the Dava and towards Duthil still spoke fluent Strathspey Gaelic. I asked him to pronounce the names that so fascinated me on maps and books, and he obliged for a willing pupil. We fished for trout in nearby burns and the mill-lade. Intently I listened to this gentle man who must have been 60 years older.

After I returned to school in late September 1941, on doctor's orders I had to omit gymnastic classes, dancing, football and other team games for two years. This suited me, for I disliked all these activities. Despite losing almost a year's school, I found myself no worse off. During my time away, I had done much reading, writing and thinking, and now the teacher in my last year of primary school instructed English grammar and writing brilliantly. I liked both, and thrived with her iron discipline in the subject and her well-behaved class. The only thing I pined for was the Cairngorms. I hoped fervently I would be fit enough to return one day.

In 1942 I began to explore further around Turriff, going on cycle runs and then walking to woods, lower hills and moors. One sunny Saturday in June I cycled to Mountblairy and walked to the top. Old Scots pines used to cover the hill and capercaillie thrived, but the trees had been felled for the war effort. Now I walked through grass, blaeberry and heather where curlews called. Vividly do I remember approaching the top, at each step seeing more of the scores of hazy hills rising in far away Caithness, Sutherland and Ross out of the blue Moray Firth.

Then I noticed further east in the firth an extraordinary sight, a naval fleet at anchor in sheltered waters east of Portsoy. The ships must have been eight miles away, but seemed big, with battleships, aircraft carrier, cruisers, destroyers and anti-aircraft balloons attached high above the bigger ships. Through a telescope the ships appeared enormous, and I watched people standing on deck. Afterwards I thought it was maybe an escort for a Murmansk convoy. I skimmed quickly back to Turriff on the bike to tell my parents, who listened briefly. How could they be so uninterested? I had not yet learned that what excites one person may bore others!

During early July 1942 I stayed a few days with Mrs Farquharson at Piedmont beside the Roman Catholic Chapel of Braemar. A Gaelic speaker who cleaned the chapel, she treated me like a son. I recall her telling me: "Laddie, your reid hair, white skin and freckles will mak lassies' herts sair" (hearts sore), though I did not understand then what she meant. She said "If you ging (go) to Morrone, tak care to watch oot for that wild witch the Cailleach Bheathrach. Her rocky hoose is there. They say she likes the reid-heided lads". About 40 years later, Braemar shopkeeper Johnnie Stammers told me about the Cailleach, with similar words. By then my red hair had started to fade, but Johnnie spoke as if the Cailleach were real. He said "Watch yersel for the callach, rufus, she wis a gey lass wi the ginger-heided men". In the late 1970s I found that "the rocky hoose" was Tigh na Cailliche Beathraiche, the house of the wild old woman. In my book on place-names, published in 1984, I described it as: *An unusual serrated rocky ridge west of Braemar with vertical blocks of rock almost like gigantic masonry.* It stands prominently on the western skyline of Morrone as seen from Braemar.

In 1942 at Piedmont I met Mrs Farquharson's adult daughter Mary. For years she had gone in summer to hills on the Dee side of the Cairngorms and the Mounth, and showed me scores of small black and white photographs. I admired her enthusiasm and knowledge, which increased my desire for the hill. Seeing her prints made me want to be on the hills that she had photographed.

A local businessman, Turriff's sole climber Willie Hutcheon appointed my father as solicitor. In July 1942, Willie asked him to go to the Lake District, where they climbed the main hills. They enjoyed it, mainly for the good company of other walkers on the hills and in a boarding house.

For a week in August 1942, our family stayed on holiday at Cattie farm near Alford, where we feasted on cherries and climbed hills south of Bennachie. On public roads we cycled or took a bus. One day my father, brother and I cycled far to Lumsden and the Dufftown road, stopping at the then occupied Silverford farm. There followed another long slow ascent up boggy ground, but eventually we stood at the top of the Buck of the Cabrach, and enjoyed a hazy view of miles of rolling high moors and peat-hags descending to the great bowl of the Hich (High) Cabrach.

Empyema had not yet finished with me, for a boil two inches wide rose within two days on my back, close to the operation mark and obviously containing the last of the poisonous matter from my pleural cavity. On arrival in late evening in Turriff, my father phoned the doctor, who said he would lance it next morning. In the night I woke, feeling chilly and partly disengaged from my body, exactly the experience that I had had in hospital. At first I wondered if I might be near death again, but then remembered the two associations of events, and rationalised that it must be hallucination due to poisonous matter. Next morning the doctor lanced the boil. Later I had no ill effects of the empyema, other than my left chest growing more slowly than my right, and remaining smaller. It still is.

In November 1942 I recall going with my parents to visit a Dufftown family where the father was a business colleague of my Dad, and seeing a cock pheasant that the father had shot. It lay in a porch. The brilliant iridescent colours of a few loose feathers fascinated me. Ignoring the social games and musical records being played by the two sons and their friends, all a few years older than me, I went to the cold porch on my own and collected every loose feather carefully, much to the surprise of everyone later. Equally it surprised me that everyone could be so unaware of the feathers' beautiful colours and delicate structure. When the Dufftown father saw my deep interest, he told me to help myself by pulling out any feathers I wished. I took a few dozen treasures home and often appreciated looking at them.

Suddenly in April 1943 I became interested in birds when I saw paintings of British birds in an encyclopaedia. As soon as I saw the coloured plates, I could not lay the book down. Turriff had no electricity till 1947, but when I went to bed I looked at the plates by torchlight until I remembered every species, with the captions hidden by a piece of paper. I began to identify species in our garden and elsewhere, and borrowed books from the Turriff public library. Abel Chapman's *The Borders and Beyond* absorbed me with his knowledgeable descriptions of moors and estuaries. His writings on gamebirds opened a light to me on fieldcraft, especially his accounts about roost-holes of red grouse in snow and other aspects of grouse behaviour. I thought how can one author like him know so much and travel so much in wild places? I wondered if I might ever see a roost-hole in snow. I thought I would try one day, and it would be a wonderful achievement to find one.

In July 1943, Willie Hutcheon asked my father if he and I would join him and his son Willie to climb Ben Macdui. My Dad could not go because of business. Knowing my interest in the Cairngorms, Mr Hutcheon asked if I could come. Dad said yes, if I wanted to. I could not wait. Coming off a train at Ballater, we cycled to Luibeg, where we stayed the night with gamekeeper James Beattie and niece Miss George. Next day we walked up Glen Derry to Loch Etchachan. Above the loch, a cold rainy wind blew and mist crept to 3100 feet, so Mr Hutcheon decided to turn, for young Willie was only 10 years old. Nonetheless, this was great adventure to me. I liked being with one who did not exaggerate the difficulty.

After we cycled to Braemar, they carried on to Ballater while I stopped with Mary Farquharson's mother and walked to Tomintoul croft. Mrs McGregor welcomed me, and I recall smelling the dark pine panelling in the old house and sitting in the sheltered garden with a fine view of Braemar. Then I climbed to the row of cairns far up Morrone, where I sketched snow-patches on the White Mounth, Carn an t-Sagairt and the Cairngorms. In the heather I saw an egg of a red grouse, its upper side bleached by sun, its lower side showing dark markings. Years later I found that this often signifies a snowfall, when a hen lays an egg on the snow because she cannot find her nest. At the time it was a strange mystery.

One evening Mary said: "Tomorrow I'm going to walk with botanist Grant Roger and an Aberdeen medical student up Glen Quoich and down Gleann an t-Slugain. Would you like to come?" I had never tackled anything remotely as long, but looked forward to it excitedly. We crossed Dee by a commandos' suspension bridge and walked up Quoich. Wading Allt an Dubh-ghlinne, we continued east below the great snowdrifts high on Beinn a' Bhuird, and crossed Quoich Water by crawling along a fallen pine. We looked at anthills where the acrid smell of formic acid rose as we put our faces near the teeming reddish-brown insects.

Now we climbed through tall heather to a wide moor with spacious views of Ben Avon, and down to a bothy at the top of the Slugain. In good condition, it held deep springy bedding of dry heather, and unused food tins and candles. This unselfish behaviour impressed me. We walked down beautiful green lawns in a rocky defile among birches, and then on a path down the glen. Thousands of green tiger beetles basked on the hot path and ran off as we approached, in numbers far greater than I have ever seen since. Lastly we waded across Dee and walked to Braemar, where Mary's mother gave us tea and cake. My companions praised my stamina, and though sunburned I did not feel tired. It had been the best day of my life.

Next day I cycled to Luibeg. The Canadian lumber camp at the foot of Glen Lui held many buildings, a cinema, a bridge made of logs over Dee, and a railway on the bridge for taking timber to lorry transport on the south bank. The bridge offered a short cut. At the Black Bridge further up Glen Lui, the Royal Engineers had removed nearly all the planks, in readiness for renovations. They helped me over, one carrying my bicycle, and wished me good luck. Outside Derry Lodge, other army men on training wished me well. When they heard I would call on Mr Beattie, they said they respected the tough man they nicknamed Buffalo Bill.

At Luibeg, Miss George gave me tea, and then I headed for Carn Crom, by far the biggest hill I had yet climbed on my own. It lacked a path and I had not been there before, so it was high adventure. I climbed to the cairn on the west top. A cloud layer gave a dark shade to the hills, although Derry Cairngorm and Ben Macdui were brighter. On Carn Crom I walked slowly among grey boulders when my eye caught the bright dark eyes of the first ptarmigan I had ever seen. I described them in *The Cairngorms* (by D. Nethersole-Thompson and A. Watson), *Watson saw his first pair at the age of 13....he vividly remembers the two quiet birds sitting like stones, the cock's bright red combs and beautiful black, grey and white pattern and the very yellow hen, the same as the crusty lichen on the granite rock she was sitting on.* Now, after decades studying the ptarmigan, I admire it deeply, and like seeing and hearing it more than any other bird.

Slowly I crept away from the pair on Carn Crom, and shortly came upon a second pair. Then I walked to the east top, which had no cairn until the 1950s, and looked at a superb view. Scanning cliffs, corries, hills and glens with a telescope, I was happy. A pair of eagles soared, accompanied by a young bird. I rose to walk towards the Little Cairngorm, but then turned, for mist fell on Derry Cairngorm. Although very interested in maps, ground and terrain, and although having a compass and knowing how to use it, I had not navigated in mist, and knew I should try it first on lower hills. It astonished me how easily I had climbed this steeper hill than the Buck a year earlier, without a rest, and how quickly I descended. Then I speeded on my bicycle down Glen Lui to Braemar, to tell Mary Farquharson and her mother about the most exciting day of my life.

Chapter 5 With Bob Scott o the Derry

The first time I saw the Derry I thought it was the finest part of the Cairngorms, and still do. In July 1943, Willie Hutcheon of Turriff took his son and me to Ben Macdui, staying at Luibeg with James Beattie and his niece Miss George from Glen Livet, two grand speakers of northeast Scots. Often I returned. Beattie and I climbed the Beinn Bhreac, walked the glens, fished, and shot his rifle at targets. They treated me as one of the family. We ate boiled salmon, fried trout that I caught, eggs from the hens, potatoes from the garden, and sometimes venison or stag liver from Mar Lodge. My father became Mr Beattie's solicitor, and we visited him and Miss George after he retired to Glen Livet.

Braemar folk called him Aal Beattie. In my obituary on Bob Scott in the *Scottish Mountaineering Club Journal*, I wrote of Beattie. *I got on well with him, but he took a hard line with most people entering his domain. Even the Commandos were wary of him, calling him 'Buffalo Bill'. To one unfortunate camper whom he ejected, he announced "Haud up the glen, and if ye dinna like that haud doon the glen".* In a letter to me in August 1945, Miss George wrote: *very few folk are going through just now, although one morning Mr Beattie found two young fellows up to the eyes in Donald's* (the horse) *hay. They got a rude awakening and had to quit the district immediately, hurried on by Mr Beattie's forcible sayings, not printable!*

Outside the bothy, I once saw a hiker give a bottle of beer to him and one to my elder brother Stewart. Drinking it at a single draught, Beattie wiped his moustache with his hand, smiled, and exclaimed triumphantly "A peety it wisna fusky, billies" (whisky, chaps).

Most who stayed at Luibeg bothy remember it as 'Bob Scott's bothy', but Beattie used it for the same purpose, charging a shilling a night, which Bob later copied. To a stalker on the minimum agricultural wage, this was a useful perk. Hikers got free firewood, but Beattie expected a hand with sawing and chopping wood. A big man, he always spoke loud northeast Scots, which imposed authority. His hard line prevented widespread poaching by servicemen who were training at Derry Lodge and further into the Cairngorms, and by Canadian lumbermen at their sawmill below Glen Lui. Also he had instant wit. When my father asked his cure for a cold, he said, "Twa gills o fusky an awa to yer bed".

I met Bob at the Linn of Dee Cottage in 1946 when I called briefly to discuss eagles, but my first long chat with him was on 4 May 1947 when I came with my father and Eric Hosking. I, just three weeks from reaching 17, preposterously described him in my diary as *a nice young chap*! Then we went to the Knock to see Bob's older brother Frank, *a huge, imposing chap well over 6 ft and with a freezing look.* Later that summer I met other brothers, gamekeeper Ronald from Arndilly by Craigellachie, and Walter (Wattie), a year younger than Bob, who died at Ballater in August 2000.

My father and I next met Bob on 10 May 1947 when we called at Luibeg. Miss George gave us tea with Beattie and Bob. My diary runs: *Met Scott (Linn of Dee) who is taking Beattie's place in a short time. He has been catching many young foxes up Glen Connie and Glen Ey. JB was showing him around and showing off very much to Scott all the time, boasting and telling tall stories.* On 17 May my father and I went to Ben Macdui. I wrote on this. *Beattie alas now away but saw R. Scott at work* outside the cottage. In late afternoon we *saw two estate road-men at work on the Derry road -- marvels! Scott isn't going to take on the job unless the road is repaired.*

Passing in late May and June, I found Luibeg empty. Mr Beattie and Miss George had gone to Glen Livet and Bob had not moved in yet. On 2 July, when I walked to Luibeg through the Lairig Ghru from Coylumbridge, I saw Bob again and met Mrs Scott, who gave me a fine cup of tea. I enjoyed their company and they asked me to come back.

On 11 July 1947 I did, excited about staying at Luibeg again. Cycling from Braemar, I sheltered under the Bridge of Ey from torrential rain, but another downpour caught me in the open in Glen Lui and soaked me. Drying at the fire in the Luibeg kitchen and drinking tea, I chatted with Mrs Scott and her mother. I learned that Mrs Scott was Margaret Helen Dickie, an Aberdonian born in March 1906, whereas Bob started life at Linn of Dee Cottage on 19 August 1903, one of a family of 11. In 1983, the *Transactions of the Gaelic Society of Inverness* contained a paper on *Aberdeenshire Gaelic* by me with David Clement, after many interviews with Jean Bain, the last fairly fluent speaker

Milking at Luibeg, Bob Scott's father on left, about 1890 (courtesy of Margaret Wiseman nee Scott)

of Deeside Gaelic. We wrote: *Mrs Bain told us she had wheeled the baby Bob in his pram for a walk along the road. Bob's father died in 1916 and had Gaelic as his first language, but his mother had no Gaelic so the children spoke none either. Their main speech was Aberdeenshire Scots.* Bob did show Gaelic traces, though, pronouncing the *t* in *castle*, and Stewart with a long *oo*. His father was an indigenous Mar stalker, and his mother hailed from lowland Aberdeenshire.

Bob often spoke of his father and the many other deerstalkers on Mar in the years of the Duke of Fife. Head stalker Ronald McDonald gave orders for the day in Gaelic each morning to the deer staff. An obsessive stag-shooter, the Duke easily became angry when he lost a stalk. Once in the early 1900s, a different McDonald from the Bynack, nicknamed The Brogach (Gaelic meaning The Lad) because he had been the youngest in the family, accompanied a second stalker on a deer drive at Cairn Toul. The head stalker had sent them to the Slichit gully on Coire an t-Saighdeir of Cairn Toul, in case the driven stags broke away to escape down the gully. The two men drank whisky and conversed instead of paying attention to the driven stags, which did break away and escape. Infuriated, the Duke told Ronald McDonald to ensure that they see him at Mar Lodge when they came off the hill. He told them "You walk like fools, you talk like fools, and you <u>are</u> damned fools". They expected to be sacked when they reported to his office next morning, but he apologised for what he had said. John Duff in 2003 told the story in more detail, as given to him by the Brogach's son Donald.

After his father died, Bob left school at 12 years old to be a pony-man gillie, and later for 12 seasons on Glen Ey as rifleman gillie. In his spare time he cleaned chimneys as a favour for folk on Mar. As he stood on the roof doing this for old Ceitidh Chaluim (Calum's Kate), through the open chimney he heard her talk to herself in Gaelic.

In the 1930s he had a winter job with Aberdeen County Council, operating a tarmac-mixing machine at the Lion's

Face below Braemar, and repairing bridges and roads. He showed me a small black and white photographic print of many roadmen with shovels when they cleared the snow-blocked Cairnwell road in spring. Another interesting photograph of his showed the train on the railway that carried deerstalkers from Dalmunzie near the Spittal of Glenshee up to Glen Lochsie Lodge. On the Council staff he worked with Bill Brown, who later ran the Council's road depot east of Aboyne, and they became firm friends until death. During summer in the 1930s, Bob worked as a Mar fishing gillie, developing his excellence as an outstanding salmon fisher. He and Helen lived at Woodside, a white cottage with a red corrugated iron roof, in Little Inverey.

While I stayed at Luibeg in July 1947, Bill and son Andy in his 20th year arrived late one evening, laden with food and beer, and at midnight went with Bob for *an all-night fishing trip to Clais Fhearnaig loch, but had only one bite.* Next forenoon we all fished the Derry Burn with worms and *got many trout, about a dozen each, some 8 or 9 inches but mostly small.*

In 1947 I spent much time studying eagles. Ex-stalker Fred Maclaren at Corriemulzie disliked them because they killed deer calves, "I once saw four and twenty hinds' calves lying at the side of a nest" in a Mar tree. When I told Bob he laughed loudly, for Fred had a reputation for exaggerating. Bob said "Adam, I doot if he was ivver even at the fit o the tree".

As well as liking eagles, Bob and I often discussed red deer. In 1947 I began a long-term study of them, published in the *Journal of Applied Ecology* in 1971. Most observations came from the Derry beat. Isabel Duncan, who later worked as a deer gillie with Bob, wrote an article about him in 1972 when he retired from Luibeg, and quoted what I said when she interviewed me: *Bob knew all the stags in the group of twenty or so that lived around Luibeg; individually, by differences in their faces as well as antler differences. He could tell them apart even if they had cast their antlers.* He showed me how to do it. Shepherds use it for knowing sheep, as do people recognising one another.

I told Isabel that *I first met Bob when I was a schoolboy of sixteen and was mad keen on the Cairngorms and their wild life. Instead of being patronising like most adults in such a situation, Bob gave great friendship and enthusiasm, introduced me to many things I knew nothing of and accepted me almost as a member of his own family. I think some of my keenness also rubbed off on him and we spent many great days on the Derry hills, enjoying that marvellous hill country and its equally marvellous wild life. In some ways this was the best time of my life. No one took Bob's peremptory remarks as a personal attack; it was all just part of the free and easy relationship between keeper and climber that was Luibeg in those days. Those who went there a lot found themselves spending less time climbing and more time sawing wood, mending bridges, feeding deer, going round fox traps, measuring rain gauges and ski-ing halfway down the Derry road to meet 'Morgan the post'. There was no compulsion in any of this; it just came naturally, given Bob's enthusiasm and his outgoing attitude to people.*

Isabel wrote of Bob and Patey. *One of Bob's favourite climbers was the late Dr Tom Patey. He first came to Luibeg as a young boy, bearing a letter from his father, asking Bob to keep an eye on him. Over the years their friendship developed, and when Tom did a spell as locum in Braemar in 1961, he spent much of his spare time at Luibeg.* Bob had overstated to Isabel, for Tom first met Bob at the bothy when 16, not a young boy, and did not spend much spare time at Luibeg in 1961.

Bob kept a necessary discipline over campers to remove litter and dig latrines. My wife Jenny walked with him in 1948, years before I first met her, to check English scouts after twice telling the leader to dig latrines. When he saw that they had continued to foul the grass, he exploded. Jenny recalls him shouting, "Get doon that bloody glen an tak yer bloody shite wi ye".

He told stories brilliantly, and in 1947 I wrote *he was very amusing, especially when talking of experiences with the 'Arabs' and the 'Eyeties' in the war,* the word *vino* (wine) recurring frequently in his Italian stories. He told how a German submarine torpedoed his troopship on its way to Africa, and how a destroyer picked up the troops. The army used his expertise in the Royal Engineers, where he erected bridges and made roads.

In the bothy he often stood in front of the large open fireplace, where he dominated the room. Often he put an arm to hang on a wire draped across the fireplace for hikers to dry wet clothes. On one occasion Kenny Grassick lay in a sleeping bag on a bench high up, under the roof, his teeth in a broad smile as Bob told a story. "Grassick", Bob said, "fit are ye daein sittin up there grinnin like a crocodile?" and he stressed his northeast speech-rattle when

AW enjoys a fine day on Cairn Toul, 9 July 1946 (Adam Watson senior)

pronouncing *r*. His loud laugh "Ha, ha, ha" gave punch after a story.

On 20 July 1947 he asked me to accompany him round his fox traps, and I wrote *each trap is hidden under a moss causeway leading to a dead deer as bait in a pool of water*. He showed how he prepared the pool, causeway, bait, and trap. By summer 1947 the Royal Society for the Protection of Birds gave £10 for each successful eagle nest on a beat, and asked me to verify those in Deeside, Speyside and Angus. On 20 July I *told Scott about the eagle-protection scheme and got him keen*. Willie Grant, stalker at Linn of Dee, became enthusiastic, and I authorised rewards for them up to the late 1950s.

Previously, Frank and Bob had liked eagles. Though not going out of his way to persecute them, Willie said if an eagle passed within shooting range it would take a risk. After I told him of the scheme, he showed interest in it. Then he accompanied me to eyries on his beat, climbing crags and trees, and handling eaglets. He became a keen observer and gave me notes on the prey items. The prey included water vole, stoat, mole, adder and blackcock besides the usual grouse, ptarmigan, rabbit and mountain hare. When rewards later fell to £15 for two successful nests, Willie and Bob lost no enthusiasm, having been 'bitten by the bug'.

Bob protected other birds. When the oystercatchers returned to Luibeg, it was a welcome sign that spring had come. Bob liked watching the parents drop earthworms for the young, saying they were "teaching the chicks to eat worms". Once he saw a stranger walk to the oystercatcher's nest. About to pick up an egg, the man jumped when Bob bawled with oaths. To the cringing English egg-collector who quickly put the egg back, Bob shouted. "Haud doon that glen, ye bugger. Ye'd better nae come back or I'll string ye on a tree for the heedie craas (hooded crows) to pick. Tell yer bloody freens (friends) nae to hairry (harry) oor birds or they'll get waar (worse)". The man never returned!

Apart from crows, the only birds that Bob disliked were goosanders, because they ate young salmon. He and other Deeside keepers burned their nests and shot the ducks swimming with their poor downy ducklings, often point blank from bridges as the mothers hurried downstream with their downy chicks. Because of this I omitted goosanders when telling Bob the birds I had seen. In June 1955, Jenny and I spotted a goosander with six ducklings swimming down the Luibeg Burn just outside the cottage. Hoping he had not seen them, we drove to the Black Bridge and then further down to the Lui Bridge to delight in watching them swim to the river Dee.

On snowy days, Bob threw bread to a robin and a dunnock that frequented the heap of dung from the horse and poultry, and they came into the shed or barn or henhouse at our feet. We often watched crossbills feeding on seeds from cones in the trees. They too were tame, accustomed to seeing folk. They came to the gutters to drink, and landed on a skylight window only two feet from us. before using their strong beaks to extract pieces of cracked putty and swallow them. It contains linseed oil, so maybe they regarded it as food.

I often heard Bob tell of old Charlie Robertson the 'watcher' at Corrour Bothy. Bob once told Charlie he had seen an old man of over 90 going to Braemar on a push bike, and Charlie said, his head shaking and voice shooting up and down the scale, "Oh man, he never had a shower of rain in his life! He was gardener at Mar Lodge and took shelter in a shed whenever a drop fell. And me half soaked on the top of Beinn a' Bhuird." Charlie walked from Corrour Bothy to Braemar chapel every Sunday. Fond of whisky, on the return he would be drunk by the time he reached Inverey, but continued resolutely to Corrour. Bob told of Charlie once becoming stuck in a barrel with his head in first, while searching for a "drop o whisky", and having to be helped out. When Bob asked about a long day that Charlie spent on the hill, old Charlie responded "After we got to the Geldie it was just one continuation of the wheel all day".

In December 1947 I went to Luibeg for my first week of lone winter walking. Alone I was not to be, for on the first evening I met Tom Weir (who then called himself Tommy) and Allan McNicol. Tommy's confidence and mountaineering experience impressed me. I accompanied them on several hill walks and my first days on ski. After that, I could not get enough ski-touring, much of it based at Luibeg.

Tom and I often returned to Luibeg, and Bob affectionately called him "Little Tommy Weir". To the bothy in 1948 came kilted Bruce Cockie with Major his golden Labrador. Inclined to overstate, Bruce went up the Lairig on 22 December. "My neck was sunburned and my moustache frozen in the shade, and after scaling huge black crags above Pools of Dee, I traversed the Carn a' Mhaim ridge, one leg on one side and one on the other", he told us, gravely. He did not see the joke in Tom's quick response, "Well hung, sir!" Bob could imitate Bruce's nasal voice perfectly when saying "Major".

Helen gave board to visitors at Linn of Dee Cottage in 1946 and continued this at Luibeg. Her visitors' book for a year at the Linn ran to four pages, but in her first year at Luibeg 11 pages, nine each in her third and fourth years, next a long run of about four per year, and lastly two or three pages per annum. She had many folk from abroad as well as Scotland and England. I noted Canada, Newfoundland, USA, France, Switzerland, Netherlands, Denmark, Norway, Sweden, Hungary, Egypt, Kenya, Uganda, South Africa, Iran, Pakistan and New Zealand. Many comments showed appreciation of superb hospitality and friendliness. Professor V.C. Wynne-Edwards wrote on 4 January 1948: *Our best thanks to the Scotts for a grand holiday. Their motto must be: 'Nothing but the best is good enough, and nothing is too much trouble.' This is the recipe of perfection.*

Bob liked a three-course dinner every evening. His sole dislike was steamed pudding, which he called "fog", the Scots word for moss. When I was with him and his pony on high ground, he would say "Adam, there's naething good for a horse to eat here, jist dry heather and fog".

In June 1948, Bob, my father and I found a young eagle in a nest outside Bob's beat. My diary records: *I photographed it, and with the aid of Bob who held its head with my sweater I ringed it.* This pair liked fox cubs as food for eaglets. In 1947 I saw two big cubs on the nest.

Then Bob and I found a third fox cub at that pair's eyrie in 1948. Bob cut off its tail and later presented it with tails of foxes killed on his beat. A Department of Agriculture inspector checked tails, paying ten shillings each. Once Bob shot a wild cat and skinned its tail so that only the bones showed. Handing it in with fox tails, he received ten shillings extra. During November 1952 at McGill University in Montreal, seal biologist Dean Fisher told me of a

Bob and Helen Scott with visitors at Luibeg Bothy, 14 July 1947

bounty scheme for seal noses, run by British Columbia's Department of Fisheries. The Indians became adept at making artificial noses to raise their income. This reminded me of Bob, and Dean laughed at the story.

To the bothy in September 1948 came Willie Campbell Dyer, a Kent farmer of Scots extraction who wore a tweed suit with knickerbockers, topped by a deerstalker hat. Callater stalker Jock Wright said to Willie at Braemar games "Faar the hell are ye a keeper? I've nivver seen that tartan (tweed pattern) on knickers (Scots for knickerbockers) afore." Willie had a loud voice and hearty laugh. My father and I came to know him well on his trips, and Jenny and I stayed with him on our way to Lapland in 1955.

On 6 September I wrote: *Dyer discovered a wounded stag lying unable to move below Sron Riach, and after he slit its throat and gralloched it he came to Luibeg. He and Bob set off walking, and I rode Punchie to ease my sore foot* (I had a sprained ankle). *Ben Macdui was a grand sight, cliffs beautifully etched and shadowed in the sunlight and white billowy clouds racing over the plateau. The stag lay on the path and had been shot a week ago. A fox had eaten his hindquarters almost completely, a ghastly sight. He must have suffered terribly. Luckily Dyer had a knife to put him out of pain. We loaded him on Punchie and walked to Luibeg, past a dead weasel on the path.*

A notable visitor in the late 1940s and 1950s, Malcolm Smith of Aberdeen had unsurpassed knowledge of the cliffs and possible routes on them. Out of respect, young climbers vacated the bothy armchair for Mac if he arrived after them. An all-round mountaineer, he had also long been a keen naturalist with particular interest in beetles. Mac was an articulate speaker and writer, interested in an unusually wide range of topics. He enjoyed a good intellectual argument.

Sandy Tewnion, a visitor in the late 1940s, had climbed on the coastal cliffs of Longhaven pre-war. While on army leave in October 1943 he climbed Ben Macdui, and on the way to Loch Etchachan heard a sound like a footstep, and then two more. Knowing the legend of Am Fear Liath Mor (the big grey man) that was said to haunt Ben Macdui, he thought this must be the spectre. A strange shape approached in the mist, and in fright he fired thrice with his revolver, but the shape came again and he turned and ran to Glen Derry. When he wrote about it (Bibliography), he decided that there must be a rational explanation, such as wind among rocks and whirling mist.

Blown up in Normandy during summer 1944, Sandy had his wounded foot treated in hospital. The specialists said he would never walk the hills and should pursue other interests. They had not reckoned on his determination. After getting a lift to the uninhabited Bynack Lodge where he stayed a week, he set himself the task of walking further each day. Painfully he did, and gradually developed his walking, using a stick and often stretching his foot to avoid cramp. Eventually he walked and camped on the high corries, and walked the hill in winter snow. We shared enthusiasm for the Cairngorms and wildlife. My diary for 16 July 1948 records: *Met Alex Tewnion who likes going to the Cairngorms although he has a partly paralysed leg,* and at midday on 27 August 1949 *Sandy Tewnion appeared not long after and we settled in the bothy to have a conversation that went on into the smaa oors, interrupted only by meals and brews of tea. We bedded down about midnight but talked until 3 am before falling asleep.*

An unusual visitor to the bothy was a stocky walker whom Bob called The Birmingham Highlander and who despite his Brummy accent claimed Scots ancestry. Always in a kilt, he announced proudly to all that he wore no underpants. One day he told Bob he would go to the Shelter Stone. On his return journey, he climbed beside a steep long tongue of snow and then took a short cut by crossing it. Bob said "His feet gaed oot anaith (went out beneath) him, his kilt flew up abeen (above) his heid, and the snaa tore a piece o skin the size o my hand aff his airse. When he come (came) to Luibeg he showed me the wound. He hid to ging to hospital in Aiberdeen to get a skin graft. I said 'Fit aboot nae underpants noo'? Next spring he came in his kilt again withoot underpants as if naething hid happened".

The Birmingham Highlander showed us how he would slow a glissade, using a board with shoulder straps and two meat-hooks that went into the snow when he leaned back. Again the snow pushed up his kilt, and his bottom rivalled his kilt in redness. In *Cairngorm Commentary*, Tom Patey wrote of him as a megalomaniac, but this was incorrect and overstated. Bob used to say "crissadin", which added amusement to his stories of this eccentric.

Another kenspeckle bothy-visitor was Davy Glen, a leading light in the Carn Dearg Club, a climbing club of Angus. The champion 'diddler' (a form of mouth music) of Angus, he soon had listeners' feet tapping to his rhythm. An old-style storyteller, he held an audience by word, gesture, and expressive face. He used a dash of licence, or as Bob

Bob and AW release a tawny owl that flew into Derry Lodge, 3 October 1948 (Adam Watson senior)

said "bloody lees" (lies). Once he came into Luibeg kitchen while Bob, Helen, my parents and I sat there, and told us tales. In one, he slid down a rainbow from Lochnagar to shake hands with the King on Balmoral lawn. In another, he invented a machine for Angus road department, which carried road-metal uphill at the touch of a finger. Some thought him crazy, but Davy knew the northeast Highlands well at all seasons, especially Glen Clova. A small shelter high above Glen Doll still carries the name Davy Glen's Bourach.

In early April 1949 I spent many days at Luibeg checking eyries with Bob and skiing alone on the corries and high tops. I recall the Turners, an English honeymoon couple, both keen walkers. One day I went to Cairn Toul with them and then skied on the Buidheanach. On the way up, *At Corrour the Dee was high and we had to wade through cold water but it was refreshing once the circulation returned. Mr Turner crossed with his pack, back for his wife, and crossed with her on his back.*

Out for an evening walk up Glen Derry, Mr Turner took a shortcut by leaping a peaty backwater. He landed short of the far side, and sank in water and peat to his shoulders. Cold, wet and fear sapped his strength, and he thought his end had come. Holding heather tips on the far bank with a few fingers, slowly he pulled nearer, hoping the tips would not break. After five minutes he staggered out on the bank for a rest, before walking to Luibeg. He arrived late and in darkness, covered in wet black peat from head to toe, and badly shaken.

Bob's favourite fellow-stalker Willie Grant and I got on very well. A fast man on the hill and a crack shot, he and I shared a deep interest in Mar's Gaelic place-names and culture, as well as its country and wildlife. On 30 September 1948, a wonderful day of sun, blue sky, fleecy cloud and sharp visibility, he asked me to take photographs of him stalking in Glen Derry. During another day we crawled towards stags, but could get no nearer than 300 yards. Despite this, he killed one with a shot through the neck. Unsure of our position, the rest milled and this gave him time to shoot two more. The stags then saw our position and began to walk away. Willie stood up and shouted, whereupon they halted to look at him for a second. In that very second he shot another stag, felling it with a bullet in its neck. This made a remarkable total of four. At Dublin in the summer of 1949 he won the international clay-pigeon shooting prize for Scotland, England, Wales and Ireland.

In 1949 I spent several weeks helping Willie and Bob with the stalking. In October 1949 we saw remarkable healing on a wounded stag. Two weeks before, it had been wounded and escaped with a broken foreleg. Willie spotted it again while spying for stags on the evening of 5 October. Frank, Bob, Willie and I climbed the Sgor Dubh next morning, taking two ponies. Then Frank, Bob and I walked to the Sgor Mor. Meanwhile Willie crawled towards where he had seen the stag. It still lay there and he killed it with a shot in the neck. It had lain with its leg in a spring of cold clear water with green moss. Willie said he had seen this several times, and had known such a stag eventually recover to walk and feed.

My diary records this. *This stag still retained most of its velvet which had hardened on to the antlers – this could be explained by the retardation of growth due to the broken leg (and the little feeding possible). However, when we examined it later in the larder, its kidney fat was still intact, although it had begun to draw on the fat reserves on the hindquarters. In late November, Willie once shot a stag in perfect condition and amazingly fat. Wounded in the leg before the rutting-season, it had not gone to the rut, so its fat increased instead of being exhausted in the rut.*

On 25 June 1950 I walked from Braemar, met Willie in his red MG sports car, and we raced up Glen Ey almost to Altanour Lodge and later to the Linn of Dee, *Willie a speed ace, shaving off the grass at every corner down the steep hills on the Glen Ey road. Willie's father Charles was home now, a great old man, heart set on stalking and the hill, and head full of the old Gaelic place names. We had a grand evening together. Then I went to bed and fell asleep with the sound of the Linn in my ears.* Willie asked me to buy a Gaelic dictionary in Aberdeen for him, so that we could investigate Charles' names, and I did. Although Bob knew many Mar names, he distorted some Gaelic pronunciations, whereas Willie, Charles and relative Ian Grant excelled in the number of names and their correct pronunciations in the Braemar dialect of Gaelic.

After the 1949 season, Bob and Helen spent a few days in Aberdeen, staying with Helen's relatives. My diary for 25 October runs: *On Thursday, Tommy* (Weir) *arrived from Glasgow by train and I took him up the Mitchell Tower, a great view of Aberdeen, dead clear. Afterwards we met Bob and Mrs Scott for tea at a cafe, Bob in great form, showing photos of stags. They are on holiday just now, going home on Saturday, but told us not to use the bothy when we go up tomorrow, but to warm up the house for their arrival.*

Bob got on well with hikers. In the stalking season he asked them to avoid land east of Glen Derry and Glen Lui, but go anywhere to the west, which walkers liked better anyway. Some offended innocently without knowing. Rarely, a few knew the rules but ignored them, such as in October 1965 when Bob's party had a blank day on Beinn a' Bhuird as hundreds of stags streamed out of Mar into Glen Avon after seeing hikers.

When Bob returned to Derry Lodge and saw the hikers, he was told they were from the Cairngorm Club, and he asked the senior member for a private word. Later he told me, "Yon Sheriff mannie Smith, fit div ye caa (what do you call) him", and I replied "Aikman Smith", at which Bob continued "I tellt <u>him</u> aff ahin the lodge. I said how the hell can ye expect me to get bloody stags on Beinn a' Bhuird when you and a crowd o Cairngormers come on the same hill. Fit the hell made ye go there? Aabody kens nae to go there in the staalkin season. Christ min, ye pit aa (Christ man, you put all) the bloody stags on Beinn a' Bhuird into Inchrory". The man identified himself as Sheriff Aikman Smith and assured Bob he would tell the club to avoid Beinn a' Bhuird in the season.

Bob said to me, "I got an apology letter fae the Smith mannie". Years later, when John Duff and I visited Bob, John

Bob with a young golden eagle on 13 June 1948

said "Yes, I think Aikman Smith was your finest hour", to which Bob replied briefly, "I gied (gave) him a line o my mind, I tell ye". Smith had a fearsome reputation in court, but Bob minced no words and treated all visitors equally, irrespective of status.

I often helped Bob to cut trees. He showed how to avoid sticking a saw or axe, how to split trunks with wedges, and then cut the trunks by circular saw. He instructed how to cut, stack and dry peat, grow potatoes and other vegetables, look after ferrets, ponies and poultry, and rear poultry and turkeys. In his workshop with many tools, he showed me how to sharpen axe, saw, knife and scissors, care for tools, clean a chimney, maintain roofs, mend punctures and boots, and repair furniture. He often said "I'm a jack of all trades and a master of none".

Once he showed me how to make a pine candle. I had often seen him do it but now he wanted to instruct me.

Choosing a pine log that was red with resin and about 15 inches long, he chopped it with a sharp axe into pieces an inch wide. With a knife he shaved a thin sliver of wood towards him from the top of a piece, without cutting the sliver. He repeated this until the top of the piece was a mass of slivers curling into the air. Then he left the pieces to dry. He could kindle a fire of coal, logs or peat with one match on a pine candle. To use paper was beneath contempt.

Bob had a good knowledge of his ground and of likely weather to come, though not exceptionally good like Alick Sutherland of Gaick or John Robertson of the Spittal of Glenmuick. He always led a stalking party on his beat, but outside the season would follow me if dense mist came down. He believed old sayings about weather, such as "The aald moon is in the new moon's airms, so we'll get a storm". I never argued, because I liked to hear the sayings.

For his dogs he had great affection. Terriers had to be bold to drive a vixen from her cubs, and he played with them to raise their fighting spirit. Lying in an armchair with Jiffy on his knee, he brought a hand down like eagle claws, "Here's an eagless to catch ye", whereupon Jiffy snarled, trying to catch his hand. Then he would play affectionately with Jiffy.

He tamed a white hen that jumped on his lap to get a piece of bread when he sat outside. Drapimg his big ferret round his neck, he stroked it while it sank claws into his jacket and sniffed his face. He tamed the Luibeg stags with potato peelings and other food, and announced the food-time by rattling a pail with a stick. The tamest stag also ran to the scullery window when Helen opened it to offer a pancake. Bob named the first tame stag Beattie, after his predecessor. Then one year the shooting tenant killed Beattie during the rut, when it left the safe vicinity of the cottage, though he and Bob had agreed beforehand that a different stag be shot. Bob told me he thought the tenant's breaking of word was disgraceful.

He showed me how a spring of water turns vegetation bright green, producing a good bite for deer, and how stalkers bled a spring diagonally, using a spade to spread the water over a bigger area. Bob and Willie wanted to extend this on the Derry's heather slopes. Later I learned from books that a spring carries nutrient-rich groundwater that encourages the smooth grass favoured by deer and sheep.

Daughters Margaret and Eileen were away most of the time, Margaret in the Women's Auxiliary Air Force and Eileen at a job. In these years I spent far more time with Bob and Helen than their own daughters, and they treated me like a grown-up son. In 1969 at the public bar of Mar Lodge many years later, Bob spoke to an Englishman with a tape recorder about the days when I was with him, "Adam wis a great lad, a great freen o oors." I could not have had a greater compliment.

I knew the relatives well, especially Helen's elder sister Mary (nicknamed Dolly) who had been barmaid at the Royal Athenaeum Restaurant in Aberdeen, her brother Jimmy a sailor in the merchant navy, and her mother and father, and I stayed at their house in Aberdeen when I went with Bob and Helen there on weddings and funerals. I even began to look like a Mar employee, for Bob gave me his old jacket. The Mar tartan had a nice pink hue with blue and red streaks, fitting a Mar hill with heather in gay bloom. Wearing the jacket, I often accompanied Bob round fox traps, at target practice with his .22 rifle, and down to Braemar, where local indigenous folk treated me as if I were a close relative of Bob and a Mar loon (boy).

At first he used a bicycle or his pony and trap for going to Inverey or Braemar, but by 1948 a motorbike, taking a shortcut from the Black Bridge to Claybokie and then by the Victoria Bridge to Braemar. Often I went with him. I recall beautiful evening light on pine and birch as we sped along the old track, with magnificent views up Glen Ey, Glen Dee and Glen Lui. After a beer at Invercauld bar, Bob would stop on the way home at friends' houses in Braemar and as far up as the Linn of Dee, for he was one of the most sociable persons I have ever known. All were indigenous folk, before the days of holiday homes and 'white settlers'. It was a real community then. Now, that has long gone.

Later he bought an old second-hand car, which needed many repairs. As he turned the corner north of the Linn of Dee one evening, he said "God Almichty wife, the haill (whole) steerin wheel's come aff in my haans". Stepping on the brake and clutch, he came to a shuddering stop in the dark. I ran to the Linn of Dee Cottage to tell Willie Grant, who brought a torch and tools, and in a few minutes we had the car safe. On 14 September 1949 at the same spot we smelled burning, and blue smoke appeared through cracks in the dashboard. Bob shouted "Christ, the bloody car is on fire". Bob told Helen to get out, while he and I opened the bonnet. The smoke streamed from the fuse-box. One

Luibeg Cottage in September 1951 with bothy and barn to the left, Glen Derry and Beinn Bhreac beyond

fuse did not work, and Bob used my penknife to fix it temporarily. Helen *was scared stiff all the way home that the car would burst into flames.* On the way, Bob joked as if he were old Charlie Robertson in his quavering Highland accent, "Good heavens, we smelled burning. I thought my time had come and I would never see my nice house in Inverey again".

In August 1948, Bill and Andy Brown appeared at Luibeg, keen on fishing. We walked miles to Poll Sgeir Dhearg where the river Dee foams in a fast torrent between rocks. Bob took out thick gut with a triple hook, tied a lead weight, and proceeded to jerk the 'snigger' hook through the water. Masterly at predicting where fish would lie, in two minutes he foul-hooked a salmon. Far from 'playing' it half an hour till it tires as in fly-fishing, he pulled it out immediately and killed it swiftly with a blow to the head. The rest of us fished vainly with worms or flies. When Bob caught two more salmon, we ate our piece (sandwiches) and drank tea. On our return, Helen gave us fresh salmon boiled with newly dug Derry potatoes, a dish fit for kings.

For years I had seen brown trout and salmon in Poll an Eisg, a pool below the Geusachan entry, and had caught trout there with worms. On my visits, I saw salmon clearly above the mainly sandy bottom, and doubtless they saw me. Bob and Willie knew it well and said that fishing with fly suited it. On 8 August 1950 I walked to Corrour with my brother Stewart. We fished Dee, he with fly, I with worm, catching a few small trout. At Poll an Eisg I waded barefoot to a big boulder and caught a big trout that dashed into a hole where the gut became stuck, so I guddled it (caught it with fingers). *Stewart hooked a salmon but it got away. About a dozen lay where they had cleared small stones off the bottom with their tails. Thunder rolled up Geusachan as we tramped to Corrour, and midges hellish outside the bothy.* My diary for Wednesday 9th ran *fished again, small trout.*

Stewart and I returned to Poll an Eisg on 12 August with Bob, Bill and Andy. The clear low water did not suit Bob's sniggering or us with worms. *We went up in a heavy rainstorm but it cleared later, bright sun and only a little cloud. At a rapid in Poll Sgeir Dhearg, Bob got a fine salmon, turning a bit red. We fished almost down to Chest of Dee, grand scenery with bright sun and flashing light on the river. Home for miles over the Sgor Mor with low sun on the wide moors.* Willie and Bob caught many fish by snigger at the Linn of Dee in the early hours when nobody was about. Both ran sure-footed on the wet rocks and often leaped across, though Bob could not swim a stroke.

Both of them excelled as fly-fishers. I often watched Bob catch salmon with a fly. He maintained of a fly: "The colour disna maitter avaa (at all). If it's the richt size the fish'll tak it". Bob and Willie walked miles to lochs and rivers for fly-fishing. Willie had fished Loch Mhairc in Atholl and had caught trout in Loch nan Eun of Gleann Taitneach, Loch nan Stuirteag and Loch Etchachan. It was interesting that he called Loch Mhairc of the Ordnance Survey maps Loch Marg-ridh, emphasis on Marg. He had never fished the Pools of Dee and showed keen interest when I said I had often seen and fed trout in the biggest pool. Once we walked to fish Loch Tilt, a fertile loch that held good trout. After 1950 I gave up fishing as a sport, but enjoyed walking with Bob and Willie on fishing trips.

At low water in June 1950, Willie showed me the Ey gorge. I wrote: *thirteen big salmon swam in quiet water at the Cave, nine more in another pool, and two dead ones lying without a mark at the bottom in the Cave.* He looked longingly. After being in the wartime army, it angered him that local folk had fought and many had died or been imprisoned or wounded, only to return to a pittance, whereas lords, lairds and factors commanded wealth and power over them. Local folk for generations had taken salmon and deer legally for the pot, only to have it made illegal by toffs.

"Ae (One) day", Willie told me that day at the Cave, "I'll be back". He had no respect for bumbling Braemar policeman 'Smiler' Florence, and said, "By God, Adam, ae mornin I'll hae some fish in my MG an awa ower the hill to Glen Isla afore Smiler has even waakened up" (his friend Heather, later to be his wife, lived in Glen Isla). One day he did, too. He and Bob disliked agent Somerville at Corriemulzie and factor Munro. Willie wanted to get away from them, and moved to Attadale and then Ardchullerie where I visited him in the mid 1970s not long before he died.

Bob shot an odd red deer or roe for the pot, and often I went with him. In winter he took a yeld hind without a calf at foot. A few deer removed selectively did not reduce numbers, which had risen high anyway, preventing tree regeneration. Usually we dragged a hind to the road, and took it by vehicle or pony-sledge to Derry Lodge for skinning. When he shot a roe deer, he split the carcase and we carried half each. I once carried a hindquarters round

my neck from the east end of the Quoich wood, a load that kept bobbing forward to drop blood on my head.

On 13 January 1951, Bob decided we should skin a hind in the Luibeg barn because nobody was likely to come. *Bob got 13 rabbits and I skinned them with him. He also got a hind, which we skinned in the barn. Then I spotted hikers approaching. We rushed to the meat safe with haunches, locked the barn and cleared up.* Bob generously gave heart, liver and cuts to friends and relatives, and never sold fish or venison. In taking the odd fish or deer for the pot, he was like most of the deerstalkers or grouse gamekeepers that I knew well. As Jenny put it, on the many times when a Glen Esk keeper's wife asked her to stay for a meal, venison or salmon was the main dish, whereas the keepers used hares and rabbits for feeding to their dogs. This has been the case wherever I have known keepers and stalkers well, from Perthshire to Sutherland. With Jenny and me present, a Sutherland stalker's wife before dinner would say to her husband "Go and get a fish", and he duly came with one 20 minutes later, time after time!

AW and Bob with fox skins at Luibeg bothy, January 1952 (Tom Weir)

From 1949 onwards I increasingly made lone trips on ski or foot, day or night, and often arrived at Luibeg at dusk or in the dark, unexpected and without telling anyone I was coming or going. On such occasions, Bob and Helen welcomed me with delight. They became more used to it as I grew older and tackled bigger trips. So, when I called at dusk on 14 April 1951 after skiing from Gaick, it surprised them no more than on a morning in September 1949 after I had bivouacked in the Lairig Ghru. Willie often recalled that morning, "By God, Adam", with Willie's strong emphasis on "God", "that was some day, you comin aifter us to the tap o the Derry Cairngorm aifter waalkin doon Strathfarrar fae Monar an spendin the nicht at the heid o the Lairig".

Helen occasionally walked as far as Derry Lodge but no further, save once when she, Bob and I strolled on a 1949 summer evening to a footbridge erected in November 1948 by the Cairngorm Club in Glen Luibeg. She asked me about the nearest houses on Speyside. One autumn day when my father came in a new car, he suggested I take her there while he and Bob walked round the fox traps. We went by Pitlochry to Kingussie where she stood me tea at the Gordon Arms Hotel, and I pointed out Gaick and Feshie. Then I drove to Tullochgrue and the start of the path to the Lairig Ghru. Over the Lecht I pointed out the hills including those at the edge of Bob's beat, the Braeriach, Ben Macdui, the Cairn Gorm, Beinn Mheadhoin, Beinn a' Chaorainn, Beinn a' Bhuird, Ben Avon. What a roll call!

In 1951 the Cairngorm Club took a lease of Derry Lodge as a club hut. Some of the Club's office-bearers irritated Bob. He disliked President W.M. Duff and Mrs Duff because of their pettiness. Outside the larder at the lodge, Bob stretched inside-out skins of butchered stags on a wire to dry. Coal tits cleaned the skins by feeding on fat, and Bob eventually sold the skins, a traditional stalker's perk along with tusk teeth and cast antlers. Mrs Duff, staying at the lodge, asked why he put "nasty smelly skins beside the lodge". He answered "I've aye pit (always put) them there. I hing (hang) them to dry". She asked "Could you not hang them somewhere else till we go back to Aberdeen?" Bob said "My advice is to pack yer bloody case, ging back to Aiberdeen, and come back to the Derry aifter aa ma skins hiv dried".

When the outside toilet needed repair, Bob asked Dr Taylor of the CC if the gillies could use a toilet in the CC part of the lodge, and the ever-helpful Dr Taylor agreed. However, Mrs Duff saw gillie Stewart McIntosh about to empty tealeaves in the toilet and said he should not use the CC toilet. After Bob told Stewart this, Stewrt emptied them on grass outside, which annoyed her further. Mr Duff next walked to Luibeg to ask Bob to order the gillies not to use the CC toilet at all, but Bob replied that Dr Taylor had given authority. Duff then wrote to the factor in Banff, complaining about Bob, but the factor backed Bob when Bob told him about Dr Taylor. The row between the CC and Bob rumbled for weeks. Eventually Leslie Hay of the CC committee came to see Bob, bearing Christmas gifts for Bob and Helen, and wishing to discuss the Duff issue. Leslie said Mr Duff was very awkward and should really stay in a hotel, not at the lodge. Bob asked how many members the club had, and Leslie said about 300. Bob said "Div ye let an aal mannie like Duff rin three hunner o ye aboot? You tell Duff if he comes back to the Derry I'll brak him into three bits and drap him into the burn in three different places". Mr Duff did not return!

On an evening of heavy snowfall, Bob spoke to two lads at the lodge whose booking ended that afternoon. He advised them to stay overnight and not go down the glen in the dark. Later they asked him at Luibeg if they could stay in his bothy. Bob said yes, but why had they left the lodge? They said a CC committee member had found that their booking had expired, and ordered them out, saying they should go to Luibeg bothy. Bob hastened to the lodge to confront the CC man, "Fit wye (Why) did ye pit oot the twa lads? God Almichty, this is nae a nicht for a beast to be oot in, let aleen twa young loons. I tellt them to bide (stay) in the lodge on sik a coorse nicht (such a bad night). There's plenty o room in the lodge. Fit if there had been nae bothy for them? Ye'd hae landed in a richt mess if ye'd forced them oot and they got smored to death in the snaa on their wye doon the glen. Ye widna pit your ain loon oot on a nicht like this. Ye should be black burnin ashamed o yersel".

Bob condemned unfairness. The father of the CC's Ada Adams lodged for a week at Bob's house and was a busybody. One afternoon he told Bob he had seen two lads at a tent up Glen Luibeg. He waded across the burn to tell them that the stalker would have to eject them. Bob said he would go up later, but over the next few hours Mr Adams twice asked him to go. In due course Bob walked up and asked the two when they intended to leave. When told it would be two days, he said "Jist you bide, but mak sure ye tidy the place up when ye leave. If that aal mannie wides (wades) the burn again and tells ye to clear oot, jist ye tell him to mind his ain bloody business". Bob told me, "If aal Adams hidna interfered I micht hae gotten the lads to shift, bit he was sik a cantankerous aal bugger that I let them bide".

A Canadian booked at the lodge one winter evening. Bob advised that he leave the tap running slowly to prevent frozen pipes. The visitor said "I come from Canada, with much harder frost than here", to which Bob replied "I dinna care a damn faar ye come fae. I bide at the Derry and I ken aboot watter here". Bob told me, "An affa hard frost set in that nicht. When I gaed ower (went over) in the mornin, the tap was dry. I gaed up the stair and the Canadian was still in bed. Bob said "Fit the hell are ye daein still in bed? The watter's dry". The Canadian said "Oh, as the frost got harder last night I just turned the tap on more until I had it full on". Bob said "Ye silly bugger, I tellt ye to leave a smaa flow. Ye've teemt (emptied) the bloody cistern dry".

Isabel Duncan, who published an article in 1972 about Bob after being a gillie with him, told of his relationship with the kirk. When the minister came to Luibeg and mentioned Bob's "infrequent attendance at Sunday worship", Bob replied "Bidin awa up here at the heid o the Derry I'm nearer Heaven than in ony o yer kirks". He never attended except at weddings and funerals.

Bob plays with terrier Jiffy in January 1952 (Tom Weir)

In the late 1940s and early 1950s, Hugh Welsh often went to the Cairngorms and eventually lived in Braemar. A craggy-faced stalwart of the Cairngorm Club, he believed in the supernatural and told me of hearing fairy music coming from rocks in Coire Sputan Dearg. One winter evening at Braemar I came off the last bus and had just taken my cycle from a shed when I met him out for a short walk along the street. He asked "Where are you going at this time of night, Adam?" I said "Luibeg". At once he begged me to stay in Braemar. With quivering voice and grave expression, he asked if I knew of the spectre that haunted the Black Brig at night. I said no, but was going to Luibeg in any case. Realising I would proceed despite his warning, he said, "After you cross the Black Brig, don't look back till you reach the Splash. The spectre appears if you look behind, but can't follow once you've crossed the next water".

I cycled up the road on a cloudy dark night with a wild wind roaring. As I went up lower Glen Lui I reflected on Hugh's face and compelling words, for he certainly made an impression. When I heard a loud squeak, I knew the wind must be rubbing a branch against a tree, but looked twice to make sure. Mounting the bicycle to skim to the Black Brig, I did not look back until I had passed the Splash burn! Even beyond, I felt slight apprehension until reaching Luibeg. It showed the power of suggestion from a powerful mind. As I told Bob the story he laughed with a great bellow and gave an excellent imitation of Hugh's quivering voice.

Aberdeen Water Department paid Bob to read a rain gauge monthly on the Beinn Bhreac, and I often did it for him. In spring another task was that the stalkers spent days burning heather. The beat stalker usually lit the fire and left, having chosen a place where the fire would die out. On a few occasions it did not, whereupon other stalkers and

I helped extinguish it. In Glen Luibeg I recall Bob starting a fire which soon raced among trees, and we had no beater. However, Bob said it would die when it came to a wet bog, and it did. It ran so fast that it merely blackened the bark and did not kill any old pines.

One autumn day, Bob, Helen and Margaret left for a week's holiday, staying with Ronald at Craigellachie. A man named Corbet in the bothy had befriended Bob and told him he would go to the Corrour Bothy after a week. Bob left him to feed the hens and pony, and told him when they would return. On the evening of their return, they arrived at Luibeg in the dark but saw no bothy light. Margaret was first into the house. Seeing the ransacked kitchen, she shouted "Michty, we've been burgled". Their possessions lay strewn everywhere. Corbet had broken in, burgled the house, taken Bob's unlicensed .22 rifle, stolen a bag of coal and shot Bob's tame white hen. Shattered, Bob drove at once to Braemar police station.

Before dawn next morning, Bob and Constable Florence hurried to the Corrour Bothy. As they approached it, Florence said "Robert, ye'll swear I had my policeman's hat on when I put on the handcuffs". Bob said "I'll kick his bloody airse first". Florence said "You can't do that. He'll have to appear in court", whereupon Bob retorted "They're nae gaan to look at his airse in coort (court)". As they approached the door, Florence warned "No violence, now, Robert". When Bob flung open the bothy, it stood empty. Bones and white feathers lay in the fireplace with the remains of a coal fire. Bob told me "The mannie had killed my big white hen and taen it up to the Corrour Bothy to eat". Bob and Florence returned empty-handed to Luibeg.

Then they checked Bynack Lodge. Entering the porch, Florence told Bob to take the left passage while he took the right. Bob opened a door quietly to find no one, and then "I heard the helluvanest roar fae Florence shoutin 'If you're in there, come out' but of coorse there was naebody. Florence was an affa excitable craiter (creature)". Later Bob heard that the police caught Corbet near Fort William, after he had burgled other homes. The sentence handed down was only three months in jail. Bob said "The fizical (fiscal) in Inverness should hae got a year in jile for that".

Constable Florence came to Luibeg with Willie Grant one summer evening to report a lad missing on Beinn a' Bhuird and asked Bob to help. Bob thought it daft to leave at 10 pm, but afterwards told me "It was a grand nicht up on Beinn a' Bhuird. I mind (remember) comin on a dotterel's nest as we come aff Beinn a' Bhuird in the mornin. The sun was het, and I mind Smiler takkin aff his socks and beets (boots), and dancin aboot on a great wreath o snaa to cool his het feet. Fit (How) Willie and I laached".

In winter snow, Bob fed hay to stags at Derry Lodge, but in a severe winter it did not prevent starvation. I vividly recall 15 April 1951. On the previous dusk I arrived at Luibeg after skiing from Gaick, before an all-night blizzard. The lodge wood next morning was a pathetic sight. The storm had been the last straw. Scores of emaciated stags lay dying, unable to rise or feed. One staggered to its feet and threatened us, crunching its teeth in aggression, but soon had to lie down, exhausted. Bob returned to Luibeg for his rifle and shot them. I helped him drag them on snow to a pool behind the lodge, as Jenny and I did again with him in the snowy spring of 1955.

Bob used his dark brown pony Punchie for carrying deer. One afternoon in Glen Derry, after a stag had been tied on Punchie's back, Bob asked me to ride Punchie to the larder while he tried to shoot another stag. I jumped on Punchie's back behind the stag. All went well until an antler tip broke a twig. Punchie hated a twig cracking above, and went into a fast trot which I could not stop. It is risky for a horse with a stag to do more than walk. Fortunately Punchie knew the area well and chose a good line, while I clung on and eventually coaxed and managed to slow him down to a slow walk.

Once when Punchie grazed near Luibeg I jumped on his bare back and we went for a walk, which he liked. I had read that you can alter direction by putting fingers in a pony's nostrils and moving its head. Punchie would have none of it. He neighed, raised his back legs and flung me through the air to land in a heap. Waving his tail triumphantly, he turned to resume grazing.

In later years when I was a gillie, the ponies supplied by Ewan Ormiston of Newtonmore surpassed Punchie for quiet temperament and deer-carrying, but Bob swore by Punchie for other reasons, his ability to know the way home in a bad snowstorm. Luibeg is in the snowiest part of Scotland, and Bob and I often knew how easily we could progress in a snowstorm with the wind on our backs, and how hard and weakening it was with the wind in our faces. Later he told Isabel Duncan: *The only thing to dae in a blizzard is to pit yer back to it and get aff the hill*, a wise piece of advice.

Bob sits with his tame white hen at Luibeg, June 1954

In snow, he used Punchie to sledge to Inverey or the Linn of Dee, and then back home, often arriving in the dark. If deep snow filled the road, he would guide Punchie to shallower snow on the moor. Punchie knew the way. At night it is easier to see slopes, woods and hills with snow lying than without, but in a thick storm you see nothing but whirling flakes or drifting snow. Using a torch worsens visibility because you peer into a narrow tunnel of light and focus on nearby flakes or spindrift rather than on ground ahead. Nonetheless we had no difficulty on the many nights when I accompanied Bob.

However, on 18 January 1952 he told me that on the previous day, which I described in Aberdeen as *a very wild day, NW wind and snow squalls*, "it was the worst storm I've ivver been oot in, on my wey hame fae the Linn in the aifterneen. The drift came on sae thick I couldna see the horse's heid as I sat on the sledge. I couldna have got hame if it hadna been the horse". A gale battered his face with suffocating drift. He judged that he must be near the Derry wood, but the storm now became violent. He had to turn his head away and let Punchie take over. Suddenly the gale dropped and the drifting stopped as a dark wall loomed yards away, the lodge wood! Snow still fell thickly, but he had shelter and knew where he was. Punchie had come right to the narrow gap where the road entered the wood.

An old wooden seat stood at the east wall of Luibeg Cottage, good for watching folk passing Derry Lodge. James Beattie often sat on it, lifting a telescope to see who might be entering his domain from the low ground. Bob followed suit. On a day when he expected John Munro, factor from Fife Lodge at Banff, Bob and I sat there well before the scheduled time. A black car came slowly past the lodge and Bob lifted his telescope. "Christ, Adam, it's Munro the bugger. He's early. Ye'd better mak yersel scarce and haud awa up the wid afore he gets here". Rushing into the house he announced, "Wife, the bloody factor's here gaan aboot. He'll seen be walkin ower fae the lodge. Pit the kettle on and mak a cup o tea for the devil".

Before a general election in the 1950s, Bob remarked "By God, aa the lairds'll be shaakin in their bloody sheen if Labour gets in". He voted Labour in 1945, and although he worked for a feudal sporting estate he had scant respect for factors, lairds and royalty.

When I was in Norway during late summer 1951, Alick Sutherland at Gaick phoned Turriff asking to speak to me, and my father answered. Alick had an eyrie with young, and wanted it verified so that he could get an RSPB reward. Having arranged to stay at Luibeg in the coming few days, my father told Alick he would go from there. Bob had heard me talk of Alick and Gaick, but had never been there, so when my father asked if he would like to go, he came like a shot. My father said they had a memorable day, with Bob in top form. When they met Alick, the two stalkers spoke of their deer and their factors, and Bob excelled in conversation and wit, laced with oaths, keeping the party in fits of laughter as they drank tea and walked to the eyrie, and then back to Gaick Lodge for a meal with Alick before driving home to Luibeg.

While at university in the winter of 1951–52, I studied ptarmigan on Derry Cairngorm as part of my Honours degree in zoology. Usually I left Aberdeen on a late bus, and walked or cycled from Braemar, depending on whether I had left my bike with Constable Florence or not. Sometimes I skied. If a light was in the Luibeg window I called at the house. If no light shone, I made tea in the bothy and slept there or in the barn, and next morning Bob asked me in for breakfast, but often I breakfasted in the bothy and was off in the dark for dawn observations on the high hill. On 1 April 1952, I returned from watching ptarmigan on Carn a' Mhaim. My diary runs *April Fool's Day and I was really fooled, told by Helen that Eric Hosking had been up, hoping to see me, and would look for me in Glen Lui. I biked down Glen Lui on the lookout for him.* Seeing nobody, I cycled to Luibeg, where Helen admitted her trick. I had completely forgotten the date.

On the hot weekend of 5–7 July 1952 I ran in gym shoes to catch the last bus from Aberdeen, carrying a plane table for practice in surveying before an expedition to north Norway, and no other equipment apart from binoculars and a hunting knife. Dismounting short of Braemar, I pulled a turnip from a field and walked to the Derry. The turnip, in slices cut with a knife, kept me going over two long days working on my study area, and I slept in the heather without sleeping bag or anorak. On the way down I called at Luibeg, where Helen gave me tea and wished me luck in the far north, before I walked down to Braemar for the bus to Aberdeen.

Before I left for Canada in September 1952, Bob made a perceptive remark. Aware of my growing responsibilities at the University of Aberdeen and in Montreal at the Arctic Institute of North America and McGill University, he said he thought the years of my full freedom had already passed. He knew I would return as often as I could, and told me always to think of him and his house and family as home. But he said the years when the Cairngorms were my playground and home, and when I crossed them freely, without telling anyone where and when I would come, and usually without telling where and when I would go, had ended. He had appreciated my unannounced arrival at his house or bothy or barn, by ski or foot or cycle, day or night, heat-wave or blizzard, sun or moon, snow or thaw. He had enjoyed part of that freedom, through our close association.

When I returned from Canada at the very end of September 1953, I bought a US army Ford jeep for £100 from Turriff banker and farmer Niven Paterson, who had converted it into a long wheel-base shooting brake. Now on the staff of Aberdeen University's Zoology Department, I had registered for a PhD study of ptarmigan on my study area at Derry Cairngorm. No longer with all the time in the world, I needed to drive to Luibeg at any time of the day or night. Snow often blocked the road, but the jeep could go through small drifts and avoid deep ones by being driven on the moor. It proved a godsend for Bob and Helen. We could drive to Braemar for provisions and call leisurely at houses from Braemar to the Linn of Dee, knowing that we would return safely.

Sometimes I drove Helen and Eileen to Aberdeen or back, and on 5 February 1954 went from Aberdeen to Luibeg with ski-mountaineer Sandy Russell, Jimmy who was Helen's brother, and Eileen. Sandy and I spent the next six days ski-touring. He and I were the only climbers that Bob trusted absolutely, and only we were asked to help carry hinds that Bob had shot.

After a week of heavy snowstorms and drifting, on 10 March 1954 I *went up to Luibeg to try and open the road, but stuck just before the Black Brig. There has been a thaw, followed by frost, calm, and high cloud. After I had skied to Luibeg, Bob and I returned and dug the jeep out with shovels. A great spotted woodpecker flew past near the Black Brig. Then we drove to half way between Clais Fhearnaig and Derry by dusk, facing a big wreath. Next day was quiet, with sunny blinks at noon, and thawing during the day. Song thrush and mistle thrush were singing at Luibeg, two peewits in Glen Lui, a golden plover in song there, and skylarks singing. Snow was melting fast everywhere and a real touch of spring in the air, with a hazy blue sky beyond snowy hills. Bob and I walked to the jeep, dug out the snow wreath with shovels, and eventually got through to Derry Lodge by 3 o'clock. Then we drove to Mar Lodge and back to clear the road properly on a lovely afternoon, sunny and warm.*

That night I felt ill, and next day wrote: *Foggy in morning, but a warm sunny day. First chaffinch cock arrived at Luibeg.* Though still feeling unwell, I drove Bob and Helen to Braemar for shopping. Helen persuaded me to go with her to the doctor, who diagnosed bronchitis and strongly advised bed. Helen and Bob told me to drive straight back

Bob and Punchie about to sledge to Inverey, February 1954

to Luibeg, without the usual social stops, and I followed their advice. At night I felt bad again, and wrote on this. *I had to go to bed and was in bed all weekend.* Helen insisted I use a warmer bedroom above the kitchen, and I had meals and fly cups with her and Bob as I sat by the fire, wearing a warm Inuit blanket jacket from Baffin Island. It was tantalising on such calm warm sunny days, for I had hoped to study ptarmigan on Derry Cairngorm. On Monday I enjoyed walking with Bob to feed stags at the lodge, even though my legs wobbled. Colours were rich on the bottle-green pines and the faintly blue hills with creamy coloured snow. Later I took Helen and Bob to Braemar, the jeep now easily smashing through the remaining snow in warm sunshine.

On the Tuesday I returned to Aberdeen, but still did not feel strong enough for the hills on the Friday night, so I drove to Turriff and stayed with my parents. My father in his car took me bird-watching on the Moray Firth. I drove the jeep to Luibeg on Monday evening, *mild, dark and windy. The tame stag dropped its first horn yesterday, Bob says.* Next day came *showers, turning colder and strong wind, with snow at night. At Luibeg, 67 stags grazed. The tame stag has lost both horns.* To Braemar I drove Bob and Helen for shopping, and we spent hours visiting folk in Braemar and up to the Linn of Dee Cottage. On the Wednesday I had a long wintry day watching ptarmigan.

John Morgan of Inverey was nicknamed by Bob "The Provost o Inverey". John had a part-time job as the postman to Luibeg, and also took up milk and other provisions. He used a bicycle and later a motor bike, but in deep snow he walked and I often skied to meet him. Over tea at Luibeg, he would talk about local folk and events. He kept a diary. Sometimes I tricked him by coasting my jeep past his house Concord. Although Concord stood on a hillock hard by the tarmac, I judged the acceleration and the moment to switch off, so that I passed quietly. Next morning he would see the jeep at Luibeg and say "I see ye're up again, Adam. I nivver heard ye come by last nicht--ye maan hae teen (must have taken) the back road". This was the shortcut by Victoria Bridge, Mar Lodge and Claybokie.

In those years the estate allowed a car to Derry Lodge on payment of ten shillings for a key to a locked gate. Mr Gordon at Victoria Bridge held keys and received payments. Locally called Gordon the Brig, he travelled in a motorbike and sidecar. He hailed from Deveronside, where my father and he knew many old folk. I got on well with Mr and Mrs Gordon, and had many a cup of tea in their little house while we spoke in broad Deveronside Scots. If I had come to help Bob or had any of Bob's relatives as passengers, Gordon the Brig waived my fee for the key.

In 1954 the Nature Conservancy declared the Cairngorms Nature Reserve and appointed Malcolm Douglas warden on the Mar side. An ex-stalker, he liked to watch deer. Bob respected his fitness, "Malcolm can ging oot the hill like a bloody hare". However, Bob was so much the king of the Derry that conflict was likely. After the estate signed a reserve agreement, the rules irritated Bob. Soon the words Nature Conservancy and warden were a red rag to a bull.

On 21 January 1956 my father stayed at Luibeg, and with Bob walked to Derry Lodge in the evening to see Prof V.C. Wynne-Edwards and Pat Baird. VCWE produced a whisky bottle for a "New Year" dram for Bob. Soon Bob let fly with complaints about the "Conservancy Board", knowing that VCWE sat on the committee. Bob criticised the Board repeatedly because of events on Mar. My father's diary records VCWE saying, "Bob, I'm willing to listen. If it's a solace to you, when I retire from the board, I could nominate you as my successor to put your ideas into practice". Quick as a flash, Bob rose, and making for the door, exclaimed "I widna file ma sheen (foul my shoes) waalkin alangside the buggers." Bob got on well with most folk, but suspected some, and never became close to anyone who was not open or who stayed silent. He had no time for patronising, which he would put down instantly by quick-witted remarks in Scots.

When Bob and I checked his fox traps in Derry on 21 May 1954, two crows flew around a tree for 20 minutes. After going there, we could see nothing, but the crows still flew, calling excitedly. I climbed the tree, standing on Bob's shoulder to reach the lowest bough, but saw nothing higher up. About to descend, I suddenly noticed a wild cat's brilliant yellow and black eyes three feet away as it crouched on a branch! I exclaimed "wild cat", whereupon it leaped off to run through heather, vainly pursued by Bob's dog.

Albert Wiseman from Aberdeen courted Bob's daughter Margaret and once came to Luibeg for a few days. He knew nothing of the hill and Bob did not take to him at first. I remember once coming into the kitchen with Bob, and seeing Albert lounging on Bob's favourite armchair. Bob gave him a withering look and did not need to say a word. Poor Albert leaped to his feet and went slinking across to a wooden chair. One fine morning, Albert unwisely decided to accompany Bob to the hill, and, lacking hill clothes, wore his usual suit and shoes. The weather turned bad and rain poured. On return, Albert was soaked. Removing his wet clothes, he saw that his whole body had become bright blue from the dye in his suit. To Bob, this was heavenly food for hilarity. Loud and long did he laugh, "My God, a blue Albert, fit a bloody sicht that is, ha, ha, ha".

When Margaret married Albert in 1954, I drove Helen and Bob to Aberdeen, where we stayed the night with Helen's father and sister Dolly in Great Northern Road. Down Union Street, I easily drove the wide jeep through narrow spaces between trams and other vehicles. Bob, who disliked urban driving, was surprised at this. In a house full of relatives, I stretched my sleeping bag on the carpet. Next morning, Margaret made cooked breakfast for everyone before getting ready for the big day. Bob and I forsook hill togs for suit and tie, and Helen had a frock, coat and hat. After a reception in a Dee Street hotel, I drove Bob and Helen back to Great Northern Road and then home to Luibeg.

A hard winter came in 1955 with snow down to the coast. Huge drifts blocked Bob's road and a severe frost gripped the burns. In February and March, skiing conditions were superlative. Bob had a pair of old skis and sticks, but never persisted with them. However, in 1955 the snow was so good that my father persuaded him to try, and wrote on a photograph: *Bob Scott on skis just before he and I set off to meet John Morgan the Post. I met Morgan before the Black Bridge. Bob got on unusually well, and chose an outstanding day for his first outing. It was Saturday 12 March 1955, without doubt, the finest conditions for skiing I have ever seen or may yet see, a sparkling sun on an almost fairy colouring of snow, with low temperature. The skis made a swishing noise.* He wrote in his diary: *I arranged to give Bob some ski lessons and we decided to meet Morgan the Post. I went fast over the flats and hailed Morgan.*

A week later, Jenny and I became married in Aberdeen on Saturday 19 March. After picking up Bill Jenkins, who had come from southern England, we went in my jeep through a snowy countryside to the Udny Arms Hotel in Newburgh. There my father had arranged an afternoon party, attended by more climbers than relatives, and with Bob and Helen well known to everyone. They had offered us Luibeg Cottage for our honeymoon while they stayed with Helen's relatives in Aberdeen. Bob gave me the key at the party, telling me he had asked Freddie Malcolm, who had come to the bothy for the weekend, to keep the kitchen fire going in the cottage. Bob and Helen would return on Monday forenoon by pony and sledge.

Bill soon had to catch a train south, so Jenny and I left early to take him to the station. Also, she and I had 80 miles to go on icy roads and four miles to ski in the dark in yet unknown weather, for I could see from the hotel the snow

At Margaret Scott's wedding, grandpa Dickie, Helen Scott, her sister Dolly and AW chat on an Aberdeen pavement in 1954 (courtesy of Margaret Wiseman nee Scott)

clouds to the west. As Jenny, Bill and I left, sitting on the wide front seat, everyone cheered us before continuing the party. Bob shouted "That's the first time I've seen a honeymoon couple gaan awa as a threesome. Ha, ha, ha". Leaving amid much waving and smiling, we went to Pat Baird's house at Inverdon to collect skis and don winter clothes, took Bill to the station, and drove up Deeside in the dark on icy snowy roads.

From the Derry gate in severe frost, Jenny and I skied on perfect smooth snow under a star-studded sky to beloved Luibeg. As we passed Derry Lodge we could see a distant light in Luibeg's scullery window. Freddie had a good fire going in the kitchen.

However, as I went to the scullery to get fresh water for tea, I noticed with dismay that he had turned the tap off. I had long known that in hard frost it must be left slightly on, to prevent freezing. Alas, when I turned the tap, not a drop came. Freddie said Bob told him to leave the tap on, but because he had a good fire in the kitchen, Freddie had unwisely decided it would not be necessary. I said we must try immediately to thaw the pipe where it went underground at the outer wall of the scullery. Otherwise the water would freeze in the underground pipe all the way to the distant well in the wood. I knew that the deep snow outside would insulate water in the pipe for a time, but not for long.

Opening the scullery door wide to let heat in from the kitchen, I lit a heater in the scullery. Fortunately a big kettle of hot water stood beside the kitchen fire. I asked Jenny and Freddie to soak cloths in hot water and I put them in relays on the very cold pipe where it left the scullery wall. After five minutes of this, a tiny drip appeared at the tap, slowly increased, fell off, and another formed more quickly. Yes, we've done it! We had been just in the nick of time,

Bertie Duguid, Elspeth McMurtrie, Mac Smith and Jenny Raitt at Luibeg Bothy, 19 December 1954, Jenny wearing AW's Inuit sealskin mitts from Baffin Island

as it took another few minutes of gradual increase before the water flowed normally. With relief I saw no crack or hole in the pipe, again just in time. Now we could relax, and a cup of tea was welcome with water from that tap. Then the much-relieved Freddie went to the bothy, well aware of the rightful tonguing he would have received from Bob if we had arrived later and the water had frozen.

In hard frost next morning, Sunday, sunlight flooded the glen, and hoar-frost crystals like flat soapflakes on the snow sparkled like diamonds. The Luibeg robin sang as Freddie and I fed the hens and stags, and crossbills called in the pines. Monday morning dawned with hard frost and cloudless sky. Bob and Helen arrived from Mar Lodge on the sledge with Punchie in the late forenoon, delighted to see us and find a warm kitchen fire. I told them about the tap, and Bob laughed loudly but also shook his head about Freddie.

After tea with them, Jenny and I left on a perfect ski-tour down the glen's west side. In lower Glen Lui the sun felt warm, reflected with intense brilliance by boundless deep snow, and it was a joy to skim effortlessly downhill among the old Scots pines. Above the jeep a mistle thrush sang loudly from the top of a tall spruce, a good sign that spring had come at last.

After Malcolm Douglas left for New Zealand, the Nature Conservancy appointed Braemar resident Davy Rose as warden. Davy had the gift of the gab and impressed newcomers, but disliked going to the hill. Once he told me of a young eagle in a nest, but later I saw two. When I asked him he admitted, "I jist spied wi a telescope fae the bottom o the glen". Bob liked to tell stories about Davy. "His father got saiket (sacked) aff o Balmoral for poachin and his grandfather drooned in a puil (drowned in a pool) in the watter o Dee at Coilacriech. Davie wis nae staalker. He wis jist green keeper at Braemar golf course. When Davy was on the Mountain Rescue Team, ye should hae heard him

Bob skis at Luibeg on 12 March 1955, wearing his 8th Army sunglasses from the desert war (Adam Watson senior)

blaa (boast). He nivver went to the hill. He wis supposed to stan with the waakie-taakie at the end o the wid (wood), far (where) there wid be a good signal. Div ye ken faar he wis? Drinkin tea in the kitchen faar there wis nae signal, wi the waakie-taakie sittin on the table. The wife and me nivver saw the like o't. He telt folk and wrote aboot bein on the tap o Ben Macdui or Braeriach, but he's nivver even been at the fit o them."

On a rescue search to Loch Etchachan, Bob found Davy standing 100 yards from Derry Lodge. He asked "Fit the hell are ye daein stannin there, Davy?" Davy said "Well Bob, ye aye need somebody to stan at the bottom o the glen and hurry aabody else up the hill". On one occasion a Braemar man saw Davy in Braemar on a summer noon. Looking at his watch, Davy said, "I should be up at Etchachan by this time o day". Bob said "Ye ken this. He's nivver been at Etchachan in his bloody life".

Helen had diabetes for years but kept going with pills, which Bob described as "the wife's sweeties". Isabel Duncan in 1972 wrote how he helped rescue a man who collapsed on Cairn Toul. "*We carried him a' the wey doon to the hoose and then he said something aboot diabetes so we gied him some o the wife's sweeties. He sat up richt as rain a few minutes later and gobbled tea and scones. If we had kent his trouble in the first place we could hae taen the sweeties up the hill and lat him waalk doon himsel*".

On the morning of 27 October 1963, Helen suffered a heart attack. Three times Bob drove to Braemar, but the doctor had gone, leaving no message. At 6 o' clock next morning, Bob drove down again, this time seeing the doctor, who phoned for a helicopter to go to Luibeg and take her for urgent treatment at Aberdeen, but fog prevented it from landing. The doctor drove up and gave Helen an injection, but she died 15 minutes later, aged only 57. Often over the years, ironically, she had wanted to be in a helicopter one day as a special treat. When the Cairngorm Club hired one to carry a footbridge, she asked if she could get a brief trip, but the operators refused because of her lack of insurance. Soon after her death, the fog lifted enough for the helicopter to land, and it carried her body to the hospital. The funeral at Braemar on 2 November drew many relatives and friends as far as Lincolnshire. I wrote: *Went*

Bob and Helen Scott approach Luibeg from Inverey, 26 March 1955 (Sandy Anderson)

to Mrs Scott's funeral at Braemar, a dull day with mist and showers on the hills. A cock and hen adult eagle appeared over Creag a' Chleirich while we were at the churchyard, a common buzzard over Braemar Castle, and stags roaring. Sam van Den Bos was at the funeral. Sam from Lincolnshire had stayed with Bob and Helen in May and June of several years to search for birds with the bird-photographer Harold Auger. After the funeral, the estate paid for a phone line to Luibeg, and on 16 November 1965 my father wrote in his diary of phoning Eileen at Luibeg to tell her he was coming up.

In later years, Bob became more confident when talking in the bothy. I recall him standing while Mac Smith, Kenny Winram and I sat on chairs. He castigated the Nature Conservancy, punctuated by laughs and by oaths so colourful I dare not type them. His china blue eyes sparkled and he stamped his tackets on the floor to emphasise points. It was quite theatrical.

When telling a story, he liked to exaggerate, which added punch. In 1964, factor Calum Macfarlane-Barrow, called 'Barra' by Bob, persuaded owner Gerald Panchaud to put cattle up to Geldie and Bynack in summer, and for a few years Bob stalked there as well as on the Derry. In December 1966 he said to me, "The gents they winna come back in a hurry, Adam. They could hardly get moved for coos' shite". When Barra put cattle to Glen Derry one summer, Bob thought it sacrilege.

Mr Pilkington of the glass firm was tenant for a few years. When I asked if he was a good shot, Bob said "He couldna shoot a bloody rabbit wi horns on. He couldna even hit the bloody hill ahin the stag". In 1966, Bob told

Jenny on a ptarmigan count at Lochan Uaine of Derry Cairngorm, 24 April 1955, wearing AW's Saami mitts from Swedish Lapland

about "a Belgium". He said "I tellt Barra I got three stags ready for the Belgium, een at thirty yards, een at fifty yards and een at a hunner. Ye ken this. The bloody mannie missed the lot!"

Isabel Duncan wrote *He has never stood in awe of rank or riches and foreign titles impress him not a bit, as he showed once when a certain wealthy Italian Count was under discussion. "Coont?" he demanded, "He canna even speak"!*

Some Deeside stalkers were jealous of Bob and his many friends. One told me that Bob was Deeside's greatest salmon catcher, who caught fish in the Linn of Dee and hid them in the pram underneath baby Eileen until Helen reached the house at Woodside. Some gamekeepers on grouse-moors miscalled him and the other deerstalkers for protecting eagles, and complained that Mar eaglets flew to their moors. In retrospect, I think the stalkers fitted international views on wildlife conservation, the keepers not. Andy Brown of Aboyne told me in 1999, "Some folk thought Bob was mad, but he was no fool". He will be remembered long after his detractors are forgotten.

On retiring in March 1972, he and Eileen moved to a cottage at the Quoich. With Mar Lodge bar nearby, he became the frequent occupant of a chair facing the door, and regaled customers with stories. Drink could make him dogmatic. In January 1970 my father and I met him outside the bar while we spoke with Malcolm Slesser and his wife. An unnecessarily rude remark by Malcolm about Swiss owner Panchaud annoyed Bob, who launched a tirade of angry remarks without his usual humour. After Malcolm replied with even more vigour, Bob glared like a fighting cockerel, and Mrs Slesser and my father looked worried. Only when I went between Bob and Malcolm did Bob walk away, silent. But Malcolm was also at fault in being rather arrogant and thoughtless.

When Willie Forbes became Luibeg stalker, it irritated Bob that someone else ran his former kingdom. Worse, he could not go to his former beat. Walkers who roam freely can seldom realise that nearly all hill land is forbidden to stalkers and keepers. By convention they do not visit one another's ground unless invited by the home occupant or by a third party who is well known to both. This convention continues after they retire, so Bob did not go off his own bat to his former beat, but was pleased when I asked him to go there with me.

Later he suffered a stroke, but recovered almost completely. With BBC producer Chris Lowell I presented a broadcast featuring him at the Quoich on 18 April 1980. He knew he must speak English, and not swear or laugh loudly. Despite these curbs, he rose to the occasion by speaking well about his life as a Mar stalker. In December 1980 he fell ill and thenceforth until his death spent twice as many days in hospital as out. He stayed at two Aberdeen hospitals, and when I visited him there he recognised me but kept forgetting my name. When Jenny visited him later at a hospital in Banchory, she found "a thin peer craiter" (poor creature). With a wee smile, Bob said to a few close friends: "I'm jist like an aal deen hind awa oot (old done hind away out) on the Glas Allt. They should just lat me dee" (die). It was a telling phrase, lightened by his brilliant wit. Yet he picked up, enough to leave hospital and stay with Margaret and husband Albert Wiseman at Oldmeldrum. Suddenly, though, he fell ill, to be taken to Inverurie Hospital, where he died soon afterwards on 26 July 1981 at 77 years.

His funeral on 30 July drew hundreds of people, including scores of climbers. From the cemetery, crowds filled the road and street. The family had arranged for drinks, tea and sandwiches at a packed Fife Arms lounge, where folk stood or sat at tables on a memorable social occasion.

Bill Brooker, then editor of the *Scottish Mountaineering Club Journal* and an early user of Bob's bothy in the late 1940s and early 1950s, asked me to write an obituary. The journal carried obituaries only of Club members, but Bill wanted this exception. It appeared in 1982. I wrote: *Bob Scott was not a member of the Club but the appearance of his obituary in the Journal is certainly justified. He put his stamp on Scottish mountaineers if not on mountaineering and a proper record for posterity would not be right without him.*

Bob was an extraordinary contrast when he took over from Beattie in 1947. He welcomed everybody, provided they stuck to the fair rules that he laid down for litter, fires and other aspects of his countryside code. He laid down these rules with a unique mixture of wit and sarcasm, combined with enough aggression to enforce rapid compliance from even the most pompous and status-conscious naval officers, professors or judges. In doing this, Bob used the Aberdeenshire dialect to good effect. There is no tongue more expressive than Aberdeenshire Scots, and Bob was the best exponent of it that I have ever come across. Even at his most aggressive, though, he always had such a deep wit and such a marvellous turn of phrase that he could make everybody laugh and appreciate his abundant sense of humour. That, along with his outgoing personality and the great welcome he gave to visitors, made him outstanding with people.

It was partly because of this that Luibeg and the Derry became the main base for mountaineering in the north-east. It stayed that way for over a decade of remarkable advances in exploration of new routes in summer and winter on the crags. The place was such a good base that the keener climbers tended to go there, and mutual stimulation then forced the pace even faster. The excitement of exploration at that time was tremendous. The stimulus of a gathering of the right number of people, as happened so often at Luibeg, the Fife Bar or the Bruachdryne tea room on the way up to Luibeg, helped greatly. Much of this was due to Bob's marvellous personality. Although he had no wish to climb the crags, nonetheless he greatly appreciated what was being achieved. Bob was proud that this was happening on his beat, which he regarded as the finest part of Scotland. And he was delighted that it was being done by north-east loons with whom he could communicate most easily in the rich tongue of Aberdeenshire. Into the 60s, the wave of general tourists became so great that Bob had to impose more restrictions on everybody, for the sake of maintaining the marvellous area around Luibeg without serious damage.

Bob was rightly and rightfully Bob Scott o the Derry, in a way that Highland lairds can never be. Nobody can really own land in the sense that one can own and carry around a book or a suit. All one can do is have the right to have use of land. In that fundamental sense, Bob clearly had pre-eminence in the Derry beat and it was truly his kingdom. Both it and he were never the same after he left. Those of us who were privileged to know and use the kingdom under his stewardship will not forget that.

Chapter 6 With Tom Weir

Tom Weir influenced my attitudes to hill-walking, mountaineering and skiing more than any other person. Only 17 when I met him, I was youthful enough to be learning and developing rapidly on the hill. One might say that at such a young age I would be too easily influenced by a strong personality such as Weir. On the other hand I was already thinking along similar lines before I met him. So maybe two minds met and reinforced each other. Certainly we encouraged one another to greater adventure, appreciation and effort. We believed anything was possible if we set our minds to it and appreciated the results. Also we realised that although you needed to be physically fit, psychological aspects were more important, indeed crucial.

It was at Luibeg near Braemar that I first met him, on Saturday 20 December 1947. I had travelled from Turriff by train, bus and bicycle, to spend my first winter week in the Cairngorms, alone. Since July I had known Bob and his wife Helen well, and already they treated me like a son. She often gave accommodation to climbers, and Tom had arranged for fellow Glaswegian climber Allan McNicol and him to stay a week.

In early afternoon I arrived, and in the late evening wrote of the day in my diary. *Then I cycled right up to Luibeg, which I reached in good time, and it was difficult to believe the date was 20/12 – it was more like 20/5! The hills were sharp and clear, but there was no unbroken snow anywhere, even on Ben MacDhui. I had the usual stimulating view of Luibeg from the Lodge, the smoke from the lum waving in the strong breeze, and then I was over at Luibeg, looking at about 20 stags which were fairly tame and feeding at the corner of the field. After a cup of tea, I went out to the bothy, where two climbers are staying. Bob Scott and I had a long crack with them round the fire in the evening, and then two Glasgow mountaineers arrived to stay in the house for a few days, and it was quite laughable seeing their skis! One of them is Tom Weir, a keen ornithologist and mountaineer, and incidentally a brother of the girl who does Ivy MacTweed in the MacFlannels and Tattie MacPherson in ITMA* (BBC radio shows popular in Scotland and Britain respectively). *He's a member of the Scottish Ornithologists Club. Quite a gale was springing up in the evening.*

Tom and Allan arrived from Braemar long after dark, by taxi to Derry Lodge and then on foot across to Luibeg. I was sitting at the kitchen fireside with Bob and Helen when Tom knocked at the front door. Bob ushered them to a sitting room with a fire and Helen gave them tea there. They had taken two ice-axes and three pairs of skis and sticks, which stood in the porch. I wrote about this. *It was laughable seeing their skis!* They would get the last laugh, and I would thank my lucky stars over and over again that Allan had taken a spare pair of skis and sticks and later in the evening would offer them generously to me for my first days on skis.

Late on during that first evening, Tom knocked on the kitchen door. Then he and Allan came in and Bob introduced me to them. Allan sat down, but Tom stood beside the kitchen door, facing us with his back to the wall. At once he held our rapt attention with his story-telling and sense of humour.

Though small in height, he more than made up for it with his bright eyes, infectious smile and laugh, and brilliance as a conversationalist. I had never met such a confident and experienced all-round mountaineer. For many years he had walked and climbed in every part of Scotland, knew hundreds of local folk, and had skied in the previous winter with Allan in the Telemark county of south Norway. They hoped to ski in the Cairngorms before the week was out.

I found it enthralling to listen to him. He dominated the room, doing more talking than the rest of us put together. Far from typical conversation, it was more a form of oratory, but oratory where he presented himself in such a way that he raised us above our normal levels. We learned about his background as a child in Glasgow, his early trips to the hills, his staunch friends from those days, the Scottish Mountaineering Club which he joined in 1945, his climbing friends in the SMC such as Douglas Scott, Tom Mackinnon and Bill Murray, his job in the Ordnance Survey, and his relatives. His sister Mary was the Molly Weir of radio and stage.

Later he told me he had been surprised by how much I as a 17-year-old knew the Cairngorms and knew about the Cairngorms, and by how keen I was on the hills and on snow. He soon found that, like him, I was an ornithologist and member of the Scottish Ornithologists Club.

Towards midnight, he took leave with Allan, and asked if I would like to join them hill-walking tomorrow and later. At once I replied yes. Allan said that if snow came during the week, I could use a spare pair of skis that he had

Tom Weir leaves Sgor an Lochain Uaine to ski to Speyside, 18 March 1948

brought. It was all like a dream come true. After they left the kitchen, I thought how lucky I had been to arrive on the very same day. My excitement leaped unbounded, for this was grand adventure. Bob and Helen were pleased for my sake and also because they liked Tom. Now they had another good friend who would come to see them at Luibeg, by the name of Tom Weir.

On that evening he told us to call him Tommy and Allan was calling him this. Later on that 1947 trip and over the next two years he usually called himself Tommy, and always when I was with him. When speaking to me, Bob Scott used to refer to him as "Little Tommy Weir". This was not derogatory, but matter of fact. Indeed, Bob had huge respect for Little Tommy Weir on the hills. Tommy was small in size, but without par for confidence and boldness and enthusiasm.

By the time of our trip to Norway in 1951, he had changed to preferring Tom. I do not know why, but subtly he let it be known that he preferred the change. His early books *Highland Days* and *Camps and climbs in arctic Norway*, showed Thomas Weir as author, but later books, articles and TV broadcasts had Tom Weir. An exception was that in 1968 he wrote some articles by a pen-name Ward Clarke. He told me that it included his mother's maiden name.

After that first evening at Luibeg in December 1947, several mild days with gales or strong winds followed, when we walked to Derry Cairngorm and Loch Etchachan, Beinn a' Bhuird and Stob an t-Sluichd, and Ben Macdui. On the wildest day, with a severe gale, I suggested we search for eagle eyries in the old Caledonian woods. Tommy and Allan had never been there, and enjoyed the day. I recommended that we walk separately about a quarter of a mile apart so as to search more trees, but the roaring gale and thick trees prevented easy contact. Despite shouts and whistles, we kept losing contact with all of one another, but eventually came together as a trio for the walk up to Luibeg.

At Christmas the snow came, and by the 27th six inches had fallen. In my diary I wrote that *Allan and Weir were going skiing and I accompanied them – my 1st time on skis. Walking was easy but climbing uphill into the Carn Crom wood was more difficult and I fell all over the place, also falling going downhill. Then we crossed to the Lairig hillocks and though it was frosty and snowing hard the sweat was pouring off my face. Skiing certainly isn't a cold sport! I went further and further on the slope every time without falling.* I recall Tommy shouting "Bend your knees" repeatedly as I took off downhill, good advice indeed when I as a beginner tended to lean back. While shouting, he had a broad grin and often he chuckled. Also he demonstrated how to do it.

Next day *We set off early on ski and went up to the shoulder of Carn a' Mhaim at about 2000 feet.....Got a lovely slope of velvety drifted snow and practised turns on it....soon we came down to the bridge. I had some lovely long runs on the way down (without falling this time!). Conditions were hopeless for walking without ski as you went in to the knees at every step. Allan and Tom went up Carn Crom and down to the Lodge, but I came straight back to Luibeg in a run downhill most of the way. I enjoyed this run best of all so far, and at the Sands of Lui the sun came out brilliantly for a few minutes and I took a snap in sparkling snow.*

On 29 December we carried skis up to the skyline edge of Sgor Dubh and *then skied along to the top of Sgor Dubh. There was a long straight run of a mile to the south from here over grand snow and you got up quite a speed.....The snow was in perfect condition and Weir said the run was the best he'd ever had, better even than runs he had in Norway. Then Tom and Allan skied towards Sgor Mor, and I decided to ski down towards the Black Bridge over Feith nan Sgor (a shorter trip than Sgor Mor)....I came to Luibeg from the S.E. after a long, fine day on ski, one of the most enjoyable I've ever had.* Next day we headed back home. I said goodbye to Tommy and Allan in Braemar *and then got the 5 pm bus to Ballater, the end of the best holiday I've ever had in my life.*

My father and I bought skis in Aberdeen during January 1948, and shortly after met Weir again at Luibeg. Soon Tommy and I formed an unstoppable pair, sharing memorable days at all seasons. In 1948 and 1949 I was with him during many days on ski and foot, and less frequently but annually thereafter. We went out whatever the weather.

On 28 December 1949, Tommy and I skied on A' Chailleach of the Monadh Liath on a grey day of snowfall that turned to heavy sleet. In the late afternoon we reached the bothy in Glen Banchor. *We were soaked to the skin and after coaxing a fire into action, we stood side by side with nothing on for a few minutes, backsides to the fire. Then we had a fine meal. Our clothes steamed happily while we thrashed out the problems of life and the universe and their bearings on religion. Outside it was a foul night of rain, with the snow very mucky and falling off the roof. We cursed Scottish weather.*

Next day, Thursday the 29th was *Tommy's birthday. We expected a hell of a day. Instead, when we got up at 7.30 a.m. there was severe, crackling frost – I think about 20 degrees of frost – and not a cloud to dim the sky.* There followed a magnificent ski-tour across the high tops of the Monadh Liath in brilliant sunshine. At the end of it, we came *rattling down right to the bothy in great style over hard frozen snow. A memorable meal followed and our chief talk was of today's tour. Somehow the views and impressions were so fleeting on this ever-changing ski-tour that we found it hard to re-live them again. We seemed to have done and seen a tremendous lot in the space of 6 hours....It's been one of the finest days of my life.*

The memorable meal would have been cooked by Tommy. Although I was used to cooking in bothy and tent and bivouac, he was a master. On arrival at a camping spot in Norway during our trip in 1951, Douglas and I would erect

At shepherd Archie Anderson's house at Glenballoch, Newtonmore, Tom Weir holds the dinner goose, AW next to Archie is bearded, whisky bottle a present from Tom, 1 January 1952 (Tom Weir)

the tent. As soon as it was half up, Tom would be under it, already starting the stove and preparing a meal. He had good ideas. A superb one was to make a dumpling, put it in a pot with water, raise the water to the boil, and then immediately put the pot inside his sleeping bag. On return from a climb, we would find the dumpling well cooked and hot, ready for eating. He admired and encouraged efficient labour within a team. I was good at catching fish, gutting them and preparing them for cooking, while Douglas brought all equipment into the tent and laid out plates, mugs and cutlery.

In Scotland, Tom followed the same routine. I was good at finding tiny bits of dry twigs or leaves for starting a fire, and would do this and start the fire while he would be already preparing a meal. Another good idea of his for a Scottish day-trip was to take dry resinous sticks up to bothies such as Corrour. I would then make a fire, on which he boiled a pan of water for tea. Tom always used the words *drum up* or *drummed up* when he boiled water for tea. To him, a *drum-up* was a cup of hot fresh tea. I found myself often using the same terms. Later, I followed his idea of taking resinous sticks to the hill as well as to bothies. I remember sometimes making a fire on boulders or in the roofless Sappers' Bothy when Sandy Russell, my father and I ski-toured to Ben Macdui in spring or spent the night in a bivouac there.

More than half a century after our first meeting in 1947, I asked Tom if he would write a Foreword for this book, and said how I felt when I first went with him. He replied "We believed there was no situation so bad that we could not get out of it safely by our own efforts". A close eye we kept on terrain and weather because of interest in them for their own sake, in summer sun as much as in winter storm. If anything, I tended to keep a closer eye on terrain and weather than Tom. Ever since I have kept an eye on them and still do, even if just shopping with my wife. Neither Tom nor I in 1947 or since filled up a route-card or left a note about an intended trip. Further, we disagreed with, and disputed, the assertion that parties are necessarily safer than singletons.

He was the toughest man on the hill that I have ever known, apart from arctic explorers Pat Baird and Fritz Schwarzenbach, and also Tom Patey, who were all in the same league. Steady in ascent, he was not fast, but had great stamina. An all-rounder, he was happy and confident on rock, snow and ice, on foot and ski, on glens, moors, woods, sea-cliffs, beaches, estuaries, fields, farms and towns.

During our trip to north Norway in 1951 he was a bold climber. Douglas Scott had the reputation in Scotland of being an outstanding rock climber and also very proficient on steep snow and ice. In Norway, Douglas led the hardest rock pitches, with one exception. On the massive rock pinnacle of Svolværgjeita, Douglas had led our first attempt on the bottom wall from the shoulder behind the pinnacle, and failed. Then we tried a different route which he led easily, up to an astonishing stance where one suddenly looked outwards to the south, down to the town and the sea far below. With Douglas belayed at the neck, he brought up me and next Tom. Then Tom led the pitch above the stance, up to the neck between the two horns of the pinnacle. Though only very difficult in grading, it was a bold lead. I found it the most exposed place that I had ever been on, and they later told me they felt this also. The feeling came not from great technical difficulty, but from the immensity of space, sea and the town with its fishing boats far below, beyond our boots.

Tom was superb at reconnoitring mountains if maps were small-scale and poor, as in the best maps available for north Norway in 1951. On the 1951 trip, Douglas also excelled at reconnoitring. Discussions with the two of them together, both using binoculars, resulted in even better understanding of the mountains and the potential of different routes. I learned much from this. Only once in Norway did I think they had misunderstood the layout, on Jiekkevarre, a complex mountain more like a small mountain range. I gave my opinion, but deferred to their greater experience and majority view. As a result we climbed the wrong peak, a smaller one to the north. When we trod the summit and looked down the far side, it became evident beyond doubt that we must descend south to the glacier below us and then climb the much larger ice-capped mountain yet further south.

In Scotland as well as Norway, bad weather did not put him off. Often he started the day in bad weather, hoping optimistically that it might clear and then produce sudden wonderful light and clarity. I have seen no one enjoy a sudden change to good weather or snow or views as much as him. He became ecstatic and would shout with joy, infectiously.

On Braeriach plateau in March 1949, I recall leading on skis into very poor conditions near the Wells of Dee,

AW at Aberdeen University, January 1952 (Tom Weir)

laborious deep snow mixed with water and slush, added to dense fog. As we reached the summit of Braeriach, we suddenly saw blue sky and immediately the sun poured forth strong light and the snow began to turn firm in the frosty air. Just as we began to see extraordinary views of snowy slopes and cliffs leaping out of clouds, a flock of 30-40 snow buntings flew past, with their tinkling contact calls. Tommy shouted "Great stuff!" and on hearing this I felt like leaping into the air with excitement. Another of his sayings on such occasions was "Man oh Man", delivered with emphasis and exuberance. Hearing that and seeing him look so happy made me agree and appreciate the scene more, which in turn added to Tommy's feelings.

He had other good Weir sayings: "That was a home from home" for a good bothy or lodgings such as Mrs Macdonald's at Coylum or Mrs Scott's at Luibeg, and the ironic "That was the best ski- run we never had" if we had intended to go skiing but turned back before reaching the snow because one of us felt out of sorts. In his thoughtful obituary of Tom, Douglas Scott in 2007 wrote of another Weir classic. *The best times were rewarded with his ultimate praise: "That was a day of days".*

On several occasions in the late 1940s, Tommy told me he was fed up with poor snow or bad weather, but these feelings soon passed, to be replaced by enthusiasm again. Only once did I see him really depressed. On the above trip across Braeriach from Luibeg to Coylumbridge, we had a fast descent on skis off Braeriach on frozen snow, and then a skim along Sron na Lairige, where Tommy discovered that he had lost his wallet. It contained £100. There followed an extremely fast run down the Coire Gorm, but he had a bad fall at the bottom. He *had wrenched his ankle, so with this added to the lost wallet he was more downhearted than I've ever seen him. Not even the wonderful peace of the evening could bring him out of it.* We walked, stumbling in the dark, down to reach Mrs Macdonald's house in Coylumbridge at 9 p.m. Next morning, *Tommy was unable to walk at all today because of his sprained ankle.*

Soon, however, his determination and good humour took over, and in a single day I walked to Luibeg and back, and handed over his wallet in triumph that night at Coylum. My father drove from Turriff to meet us, and a few days later at Aviemore station we saw Tommy off on the train to Glasgow. As the train pulled out southwards, he leaned out of the window with a grin *from ear to ear and held it until the train disappeared.*

He had an instant sense of humour and quick wit. At Mrs Macdonald's in Coylumbridge, I shared a double bed with him in an upstairs bedroom where we had the luxury of a fire lit by the kindly and motherly Mrs Macdonald. I recall after a long day on the hill falling asleep quickly. I slept soundly that night. When I awoke next morning, I said, "I slept like a dead man last night". Instantly he quipped "I've never known a dead man kick so hard!"

In the early 1950s he told my father and me that he felt inferior in the company of George Waterston, the then Secretary of the Scottish Ornithologists Club. An articulate well-educated Edinburgh man of great charm and enthusiasm, George organised a larger, more effective Scottish Ornithologists Club, started Fair Isle Bird Observatory, and had become a leading figure in Scottish ornithology. Although very influential, he was no snob, and indeed he identified and nurtured good talent among inexperienced bird-watchers, whatever their background or accent. He and Tom were both great Scots. My father and I reassured Tom that he should not feel inferior in the slightest. Both George and Tom could enthuse in different ways.

Like many Glasgow folk, Tom would readily talk to total strangers and have good conversations with them. However, he had outstanding ability to go further than this with total strangers, inducing them to talk about themselves and their lives as if he and they had known each other well for years. In this he certainly surpassed George. Tom later developed this with great skill when he wrote about people all over Scotland in a monthly article in the *Scots Magazine*, called *My Month*. This flowered even more when he came to present people on television, as in his series *Weir's Way*.

Sometimes I told him I was thinking of going alone to a part of the Highlands I had not visited. Usually he had been there often, and knew the local deerstalker or shepherd or gamekeeper well. He would tell me their names and say, "When you go there, Adam, tell them I suggested you speak to them". I found it better than a passport! At Gaick Lodge he told me of Alick Sutherland, at Monar Lodge in Glen Strathfarrar it was Fleming with his ingenious hydro-electric scheme run off a little burn, at the Reay Forest it was head-stalker John Scobie at Achfary by Loch More, and so on.

When I went there and knocked on the door, I said who I was and then that Tom Weir had told me to be sure to call. In every case the reaction was immediate. I would be asked to come in, sit down and have tea, and be invited to use a nearby bothy or lodge, or in one case to stay with the family. These folk had a great liking for Tom and respected what he did on their hills. Their liking extended to me, a total stranger to them. Mentioning Tom Weir did the trick.

He had an unusual trait of liking to walk in the dark without a torch. Already used to this around Turriff on short winter days when I watched birds going to roost, I followed by walking in the dark to hear owls, and to see and hear wild ducks flying on the river Deveron. When Tom worked with the Ordnance Survey, for some months he lived in Birmingham. I had gone by rail to Bristol to do a radio broadcast at the BBC natural history studio there, and called to see Tom on the way back north on 7 October 1949. He met me at the station and I stayed for two nights at his lodgings. After a meal on the second evening, he suggested we walk across fields and woods in the dark. We listened to tawny, long-eared and little owls calling, for me the first little owl I had ever heard, a remarkably loud high-pitched yell. Tom also had a great ability to distinguish bird calls from just hearing them. At this he surpassed me and evidently had a more musical ear. I tended to forget songs or calls of species I had not heard for some time, but Tom remembered them exactly.

On a later overnight visit when he lived at Gartocharn, I had gone to the Scottish Game Fair near there with Raymond Parr, to demonstrate an exhibit about our research on red grouse. Tom asked Ray and me to stay overnight. After a meal, Tom suggested we take a walk. It was midsummer, so not completely dark. We walked miles along unfrequented tracks and roads, seldom seeing a car and nobody on foot or cycle. We looked at stars and planets, listened to tawny owls and long-eared owls hooting, and had excellent conversation.

At New Year 1952 on a brilliant sunny day with deep snow, several of us enjoyed marvellous skiing on Carn Liath at Laggan. We had travelled in several cars, some of whose occupants changed to different cars on the way back. Only on return to Newtonmore did we realise the absence of one of us, Muirhead Moffat. A friend of some Glasgow climbers and skiers, Muirhead did not climb or ski. He had just gone walking while we skied. By the time we realised his absence, darkness had fallen. His friends discussed this and that, but Tom cut short the dithering by taking charge and instructing a search party. On return to Laggan we found Muirhead walking along the road in the dark, none the worse. He had been disorientated by strong light off the snow. This event clearly identified the most decisive person in our large party. We followed the natural leader without question.

AW and Tom Weir on Beinn a' Bhuird, 15 October 1967 (Adam Watson senior)

Supremely confident, he was bolder than most in stamping on domineering behaviour or bullying. My wife Jenny and I recall a remarkable occasion when Tom, Jenny, my parents and I were in my father's car on the north side of Glasgow. My father had driven to a petrol station to fill his tank before driving to Inverarnan beyond the top of Loch Lomond. He had just stopped when a large car swerved to park in front of us, blocking us from the pump. Out jumped four large Glasgow men, one of whom walked smartly to the pump. Tom leaped out of our car to confront the tall intruders. Despite his puny size compared with them, he immediately said "We were here first". The tall Glaswegian replied aggressively "But we're gonnae go to Aberfoyle". Not to be outdone, Tom responded "We're going to Aberdeen". It was so quick that he took the wind out of their sails. The tall man shrugged his shoulders, went into his car with his three passengers, and moved away until we had filled up and left for Loch Lomond! Eventually we would go to Aberdeen, but not till two more nights and a day's climbing in the west.

Tom was forever generous, but on rare occasions showed a selfish unbecoming streak! When he, Douglas and I went to Lofoten in July 1951, the three of us got on very well on the ship, in our tent, and on the peaks. He and Douglas had been climbing companions for many years in Scotland and during 1950 in the Himalayas, and the Lofoten trip followed with both of them even more enthusiastic. During one of our first days, however, Tom showed something different. On a warm sunny day we strolled around the main town, Svolvær, taking photographs and talking with local folk. At one street junction, Douglas walked ahead of Tom and me, and turned left to go towards the harbour. At the corner, Tom whispered to me and grabbed my sleeve, saying "I'm fed up with Douglas' company, Adam, let's go right and give him the slip and enjoy ourselves for an hour". We did. I disliked this, but as the youngest and most inexperienced of the trio I demurred. In later years I would not have agreed and would have gone after Douglas. After an hour we came upon Douglas looking for us and pleased he had found us. No more was said!

I had already spent a month in Iceland in 1949 and a month in Norway during 1950, on both trips trying to understand local languages. I found Norwegian the easiest foreign language that I had ever tried to learn, because so many words resembled my own northern Scots tongue of Buchan. By the time we went on the 1951 trip, I could already speak some Norwegian and I knew many Norwegian words when I heard them or saw them on signs. A sign that used to amuse Tom greatly occurred frequently on posts at rocks near harbours, *Sagte fart*, meaning *slow speed*, for ships. Tom liked the play of words with the different meaning of *fart* in English. Every time we came to a harbour and he saw the sign, he would exclaim "Ah! Here's old sadgy fart again" and then chuckled infectiously. It would have been impossible for Douglas and me to keep straight faces even if we had tried.

Both Douglas and Tom were experienced photographers who later made a living from this. Excelling at taking photographs, they also had great skill in the darkroom, achieving the best out of a negative. They took great care and time when composing a picture, and I learned much from listening to them discussing this. Often I waited five or ten minutes after taking my own photographs, while they moved around to reach a better position or wait until a cloud passed. Tom liked to use me as a figure to give scale, and often asked me to walk and then stand on a cliff-edge or near a snow cornice, while he waited for the best light. Then I would feel more

Tom Weir and Bob Robel hear signals from a transmitter on a blackcock at Glen Dye, December 1967

exposure than usual, simply because I stood or sat so long on one spot, with great depths below.

In his obituary of Tom, Iain Smart (2007) recounted story after story, and then wrote *I could go on reminiscing about Tom for pages and pages.* I feel the same. Indeed, I could go on reminiscing for a whole book. I have little doubt that Iain could also go on reminiscing for a whole book and that most of his stories would not overlap with mine.

Iain wrote an excellent paragraph about Tom's opinions on Scotland. *Tom was dedicated to Scotland and like so many of us he hoped that Scotland would grow strongly from her own roots into an independent, self-respecting country with its own individuality. None of us suspected that in the end we would founder in the morass of a global sub-culture in which the chief end of man is to maximise profit.* Iain, this was brilliantly written.

Since a child, I wanted the same as in that first sentence about Tom. Back in the 1940s and since, Tom and I often

Tom Weir, AW senior and AW near Ballater about 1976 (Tom Weir)

spoke of the need for Scottish independence. I do not know if he became a member of the SNP, but after he gave a lecture in Perthshire the SNP Constituency Association there asked him to stand as prospective MP. At the time, Perthshire was a safe Conservative seat, if I recall held by Sir Alex Douglas Home. Tom declined. He told me that he feared he would win, and would then have to be an MP and leave Scotland and its hills.

In 1974 I became an SNP member and later political organiser of the West Aberdeenshire Constituency Association and the successful Marr Branch. In the late 1970s they wanted me to stand as prospective MP. Although willing to work in my spare time, I did not wish to give up scientific research, or, like Tom, living in Scotland and going to the hills.

In recent years I have been dismayed by the SNP's foundering in the morass. This culminated during 2008 in appalling behaviour by First Minister Alex Salmond and Finance Minister John Swinney. They stooped to nauseating kowtowing to the bombastic Donald Trump, bias and domineering interference with the planning systems of Aberdeenshire Council and Scotland, smirking arrogance when criticised, and craven silence for months about Trump's wishes for compulsory purchase of homes whose innocent owners just wanted to stay where they were.

Iain's perceptive sentence about the morass reminds me of another incident with Tom. A friend of Tom's from early climbing days was Bob Grieve, a planner who gained high promotion and helped to create new towns near Glasgow such as Cumbernauld. This attracted skilled people from Glasgow and left Glasgow worse off. If they had paid attention to prior experience elsewhere, they might not have needed to re-invent a bad wheel. However, the

Tom Weir and three generations of Adam Watson below Craigencash, Glen Esk, October 1975 (Tom Weir)

notion that planners and public bodies and the state know best was something that thrived under a UK Labour Government. Secretary of State for Scotland Willie Ross then created a Highlands and Islands Development Board and appointed Bob as first chief. I got on well with Bob, but as he soared towards official heights I found him becoming too arrogant for my liking.

Once in 1962 a colleague David Jenkins and I gave a paper on the economic value of game to a conference in Edinburgh, run by the Scottish Council for Development and Industry. As we entered the hotel, Bob walked in behind us with a group from the HIDB, also to give a paper. By then he knew me well from SMC meetings and informal gatherings of SMC climbers at Inverarnan and elsewhere. But with his coterie of HIDB minions beside him, he said with a sneer, "Oh, the wildlifers are here!" An expression of arrogant contempt, it deserved a response of disdain and silence, which I showed without a word or a nod. At coffee-break he came up to me on his own and acted as the old friendly Bob as if nothing had happened. I could not respond in like measure to such insincere double standards.

A few years later, Tom saw Bob and asked about his work in the HIDB, and shortly afterwards an article by Tom appeared. Tom left out the prize sentence, which Tom told to me. During the conversation with Bob, Tom had asked about the damage done to scenery and wildlife by poorly controlled development in the Highlands and Islands. Tom had become an early conservationist, acting as trigger to prevent a hydro-electric scheme in Glen Nevis and to protect Loch Lomond. In his interview with Bob, he wondered what Bob thought of this. Bob replied "Tom, I would sell the Highlands to the highest bidder". Tom told me of his profound dismay and disappointment at this attitude from one who had been an early companion going from Glasgow to the hills. In due course, Bob became Sir Robert Grieve. Tom got an OBE. Tom will be remembered long after Sir Robert has been forgotten.

Tom and Rhona married on 22 July 1959. I drove along loch-sides to Callander on a brilliant day and then to

AW sits on a pinnacle of Lochnagar cliff, 6 August 1977 (Tom Weir)

Aberfoyle kirk. Many Glasgow climbers thronged the kirk outside and in, almost like a New Year meet apart from the resplendent clothes and hats. The setting was superb, the scenery the finest I had seen in the southern Highlands. After a hotel meal, we all stood at a loch-side in warm sunshine under blue sky, with spectacular woods and hills reflected in the still water. As Tom, Allan McNicol and I chatted, I said almost 22 years had passed since first I met Tom and Allan at Luibeg and they gave me my first lessons on skis.

When he married, Tom had reached the age of 44 and had long fitted the term 'confirmed bachelor'. For many years, Rhona had been a hill-walker winter and summer, and a member of the Ladies Scottish Climbing Club. As a school-teacher she excelled, devoted to educating children and getting them to shine. Typifying her outgoing nature, she showed far more interest in my own children than Tom did.

Years after Tom married Rhona, in the company of my father and me he occasionally found her continual conversation tiring, and would make an exasperated comment. One day when I drove my father's car on a fairly unfrequented main road from Crathie to Ballater, quite slowly so that they could enjoy the scenery, Tom sat in the front passenger seat and Rhona in the back seat with my father. Suddenly she became agitated and said she feared we might crash, until Tom spoke sharply and she desisted.

During another day when we came near Loch Lee, my father parked his car and took some time getting ready, while Rhona talked to him. Meanwhile, Tom started walking and I went with him, expecting the others to catch up. But Tom shot off at speed, and I with my long loping stride could always walk quickly and easily. Then Tom laughed and told me his ploy, to leave Rhona behind with my father so that Tom and I could walk without her! My father evidently disliked this arrangement, as his diary later showed, complete with a transcript of her complaints and what he called "indelicate remarks" about Tom and his relatives!

On one ski-trip with my father, Tom felt near death. It was a warm day, Wednesday 8 April 1969 to judge from my father's diary. He and Tom had arranged to meet north of the Cairnwell pass, after my father skied to Glas Maol, Cairn of Claise and Carn an Tuirc. He wrote: *Left Layby at 8 am and was back at 1 pm after a very fine day. After a sleep and a meal I waited in Car and Tom and Rhona came down at 3 pm.* Tom and my father went up Allt Coire

Fionn, donning skis only 150 yards from the cars. While my father returned, *Tom skied up to Glas Maol Cairn and had a super run down – he said the best for many years.*

Later, Tom told me that as he neared the bottom end of Allt Coire Fionn on the way back, skiing along the edge of a steep snow-bank above the foaming burn, a ski slipped and he fell upside down. Both skis had firmly jammed into the snow above, one arm and ski-stick lay unusable under his body, the other arm and ski-stick free but on the wrong side for using a stick to raise his body by pushing the stick on to a boulder or on to the bed of the burn. There was no point in trying to shout above the roar of the burn, and in the unlikely event that my father and Rhona heard him and came to rescue, this would be several minutes away and too late. As he weakened, his head came nearer to the rushing water, only a few inches from his mouth as cold water sprayed his face. He decided he must make a mighty effort, and with all the strength and determination he could muster he bent his body upwards like a spring, at the same moment thrusting his free hand to grasp the nearest ski binding and release the catch. Now with one foot free, his ordeal was over, and within a few seconds he had freed the other foot and scrambled upright. He had been out of sight of the cars, but within a minute he saw the cars with Rhona and my father standing outside, chatting in the sunshine. I do not recall whether he told Rhona or my father but I think not, for my father made no mention of it in his diary.

Rhona did not fit easily into the male-dominated groups of the Scottish Mountaineering Club, which in those days was

AW senior in the 1970s (Tom Weir)

a male-only club. A conspicuous element of the male hunting-group occurred in Tom and a few of his best friends in the SMC. I understood this completely natural result of man's evolutionary history. Politically correct attempts to change it by decree and to impose feminism by rule are unnatural and lead to tension.

Maybe when Tom and I shared wonderful comradeship in the hills, we re-enacted male hunting-bonds that helped form the origin of man. At any rate, the best comradeship I had with him, or Bob Scott, or Pat Baird, or Fritz Schwarzenbach, or Tom Patey, or my own father occurred with just two of us on the hill. I spent more days climbing and skiing with Tom Weir than with any of the others apart from my father.

Even if Tom and I had never met, I might have gone on to climb and ski in Scotland and the Arctic, and might have had my best and biggest days on the hill when alone, as I have done. Already when 13 I enjoyed lone days on the hills and wanted to go to the high Scottish hills in winter, and the Arctic excited me more than the Himalayas by the time I was 17 and met Tom.

Tom Weir in upper Glen Gairn, June 2002

However, I have no doubt whatsoever that Tom Weir raised my confidence, enthusiasm and knowledge rapidly to a steep new peak at the end of 1947 and through 1948 and 1949, and to a lesser extent in 1950 and 1951. These were not gifts, but he certainly was gifted and I a thankful ready recipient.

I know that he benefited from some of my enthusiasm and knowledge, for he told me so. Nevertheless I am sure that the net benefits went largely one way, from the older and far more experienced hand to the younger. For all those benefits, I was and am abundantly grateful. To me they were priceless, beyond anything that all the money in the world could buy.

Some writings by Tom Weir about our first meeting

Tom had a big influence on my life. In his semi-autobiographical books he wrote about meeting me and describing some of our early trips. Douglas Scott and I featured in his book *Camps and climbs in arctic Norway*, and he wrote about me on many later trips in the *Scots Magazine* within his monthly article *My Month*. Below are a few examples.

In the *Scots Magazine, My Month, From the Cairngorms to the Eildons* in 1992, he wrote of a trip in early summer 1992, *When I arranged to meet my old friend Adam Watson in Braemar on a misty evening we wasted no time in driving up to Inverey to take a walk on the Mar Lodge estate.......Adam Watson was a schoolboy at Turriff Academy when we met for the first time in Luibeg Cottage in January 1948* (actually late December 1947), *a red-headed loon whose knowledge of the Cairngorms amazed us when he joined our party of three.*

His book *Weir's World* (1994, p. 187) reported on Nell Macdonald and Bob Scott, *The love that Nell had for the Bynack, Bob had for Luibeg. It was in his house I met a red-headed schoolboy by the name of Adam Watson.*

In the *Scots Magazine, My Month, Adam's Eden* (1994, p. 309) he wrote about Adam Watson, *his early days discovering the Cairngorms and the influences which shaped his life, Seton Gordon who aroused his interest in the hills, and meeting me with a climbing pal in Bob Scott's house at Luibeg at New Year 1947* (really late December 1947). *It was Adam's first time in the Cairngorms in winter* (in fact my first solo winter trip there, not my first time in winter). *There was lots of snow. We invited the schoolboy to join us, and quickly discovered he had as much stamina as we had ourselves. Until then he had not thought of skiing as a dimension of travel. He proved to be a quick learner. In 1948, the year when he became a zoology student at Aberdeen University, I spent a week with him in December, climbing and skiing. V.C. Wynne-Edwards, the Professor of Natural History, had confided in me that Adam was an exceptional student. He had known him since he was 16 and suggested Adam should make the biology of the ptarmigan the subject for his Ph.D. and that his enjoyment of solo skiing would make study possible even in stormy weather – the ptarmigan being the hardiest of birds. Success in this led, in 1952, to a post-graduate scholarship with the Arctic Institute of North America. I knew Adam to be an ideal expedition man, for Douglas Scott and I spent the summer of 1951 with him in Arctic Norway, beginning in the Lofoten Islands.*

Following Tom's death on 6 July 2006 at the age of 91, the *Press and Journal* carried a news report and asked for my view. *Deeside environmentalist Dr Adam Watson, of Crathes, was a lifelong friend of Weir's and met him while walking in the Cairngorms. He said "I was 17 when I met him. He was a brilliant conversationalist. When he came into a room he was a small man but had great confidence and a great look and people just stood listening to him. He had a knack of speaking to total strangers and putting them at ease."*

Kevin Howett, Editor for the Mountaineering Council of Scotland, asked me for a short appreciation. Here it is.

Tom Weir. Appreciations. Scottish Mountaineer (2007), November, p. 72.

I first met Tom on 20 December 1947 at Luibeg. I'd come alone from Turriff for my first winter week in the Cairngorms, Tom from Glasgow with Allan McNicol. I was 17, Tom 32, a man of bright eye, infectious laugh, and brilliant conversation. I'd never met such a confident all-round mountaineer. He asked me to join him and Allan, and I took to it like a duck to water. After that week, I wrote "the end of the best holiday I've ever had in my life".

Within a few weeks Tom was back in the Cairngorms, the first of many trips when he and I went out in all weathers. We were determined, so anything was possible. In 1951, we and Douglas Scott spent six weeks climbing in north Norway. And for decades since, Tom and I continued frequent trips to hill, glen, and coast.

With his passing, Scotland lost a son who cared deeply for Scotland, its folk, landscape, and wildlife. I have met nobody who knew Scottish regions and their local folk so well. A naturalist as well as mountaineer, he was a brave pioneer in conservation, long before organisations brought safety in numbers. He stimulated Tom Patey and other young climbers greatly. That enthusiasm lives on in TV's "Weir's Way". A natural interviewer even when there was no microphone, he had a rare gift of abounding curiosity. I count myself fortunate that I met him 60 years ago and shared his company so often.

Adam Watson

Chapter 7 The traivellin gillie, or once in a blue sun and moon

In 1948 I helped stalkers Bob Scott, his older brother Frank, and Willie Grant with stag-shooting on Mar. They shot the stags, and I helped gralloch them (remove entrails), drag them downhill, load them on pony or cart, and skin them. Bob taught me to take safe routes for a pony to pull several shot stags by a dragging tackle. In 1949 I tried to get a gillieing job, and Bob would have taken me, but had engaged a man the day before I asked. So I worked unpaid.

On return from Norway in summer 1950 I looked for a job as a gillie. Bob knew of one at Fealar so I called there on 13 August, writing, *Dad and I went there today, first by car to Bynack, then walking almost to Tarf Bridge and up the path. There was a shortcut much nearer but I did not know it then. We saw an eagle north of Tarf Bridge and had interesting views of the Cairngorms from here, with Creag an Leth-choin showing as a distant rocky point far through the Lairig Ghru. Rain had been threatening, and as we climbed up the slope it came on heavily and mist wreathed the hills. We had no map or compass but I won a bet of 30 shillings that we had come on the right route, and at last the white buildings of Fealar Lodge appeared in front.*

First I saw the gamekeeper and the wife of the laird, who is a Tory MP in Yorkshire. She asked me to drive her and Dad out the Gleann Mor road in a jeep, which was easy. However she said I would have to drive her and do odd jobs taking in coal and driving sheep in a float, and we did not like her, so I decided not to take the job. They get three months' food at a time in winter. On return we took a shortcut over Meall na Caillich Buidhe and Allt Garbh Buidhe, going fast as we were late, then home to Turriff. In 1998, retired stalker John Robertson told me he heard of the same job in 1950, went there, drove the jeep, and turned down the job for the same reasons!

Bob decided he wanted me as a paid gillie in 1950, after Newtonmore game dealer Ewan Ormiston took the lease. On 20 August *Ormiston has fixed me up at Derry for the season. I went from Turriff to Braemar today by bus, had a meal at Braemar, and then up by taxi to the lodge, as instructed by Mr Ormiston who said he would pay.* Later I had a job with Bob in the stalking seasons of 1951 and 1952 too, for six weeks annually. Ormiston, a breeder of Highland ponies, arranged that each gillie had a pony. He sent a van to take deer from the larder, and occasionally to give us free sausages and other meat from his shop.

Two other gillies came in 1950. Jimmy McCartney, a stocky 22 year-old from Kiltarlity near Beauly, also got a job in 1951 and 1952 too, like me. Later he married Inverey girl Morag McDougall, raised a family in Braemar, and for years drove the county snowplough. The other 1950 gillie, a student named Whitehouse, liked the hill, but his pony sometimes got the better of him.

We lived in a wing at Derry Lodge with sitting room, kitchen and bedroom. An outside hut had a flush toilet, and a larder and stable stood nearby. Shooters Sir George and Lady Schuster liked to come in their car. Other shooters wished to be driven by Jimmy in a land-rover. Stalkers speaking to a guest called him 'sir', and used 'gentleman' when referring to another guest. When talking to stalkers or gillies, they called the guests 'toffs', 'gents', 'mannies' or 'gent mannies'.

Bob appointed me 'traivellin' gillie in 1950, 1951 and 1952. Scots traivellin means walking. My appointment had *primus inter pares* more responsibility with equal pay. Bob knew I could walk fast, navigate in mist, and spot distant deer. Also I knew his beat well, some parts better than him. Like other gillies I had to tend a pony, load stags, and skin and butcher them.

The traivellin gillie had two tasks not shared by other gillies. Sometimes Bob asked other gillies to wait while he walked with the toffs and me. Once a stag had been shot, Bob and I looked to see if the gillies had moved. If we saw no sign, Bob lit a heather tuft to raise smoke, hoping they would see it. If this failed, I returned to the gillies. Then we walked to load the stag and I caught up with the stalking party. Later, radios and then mobile phones removed the need for this.

The other task still applies. When stags were on Moine Bhealaidh, a plateau too open for stalking, the traivellin gillie drove them. Out of sight of the deer, I walked fast to a hill dominating the Moine, and then towards the deer, which ran into corries where they could be stalked. The stalking party, other gillies and ponies often went to the

Frank Scott and AW in Glen Derry, 30 September 1948

Stoban Biorach at the west edge of the plateau. I walked to Beinn a' Chaorainn via the Lairig an Laoigh path, and ran to the plateau. If the stags moved towards Glen Avon, I headed them off by running east. Such driving had been done on Mar for decades.

In the first two seasons, Sir George and wife tenanted for two weeks, followed by Col Benton Jones for a month, but in 1952 Benton Jones took all six weeks. Old and weak on the hill, Sir George or his wife rode uphill where possible, so we had only two ponies with deer saddles. If they shot three stags in a day, we could take only two back, and returned in late afternoon or evening for the third, but if it lay far out we could not do this before dark. So, occasionally a stag lay all night, to be lifted next day by two of us. This reduced venison quality and disrupted stalking for next day.

On the day before each toff's first stalking day, Bob arranged target shooting. I recall Jones being so excited that he could not hold the rifle steady. American hunters later told me about "buck fever" on the season's first day. A professor of game biology saw "a great rack of antlers" on a mule deer, and was about to pull the trigger when the antlers vanished, revealing a doe's smooth head; he had imagined the antlers! Unfit at the start, our toffs sweated much on ascent, but gradually became fit enough to appreciate the long walk and the scenery. It is changed days now, after decades of bulldozed vehicle tracks and widespread use of landrovers.

Ormiston left little hay in the first two years, saying we could leave the ponies out at night to eat grass, but the Derry offered poor grazing. The ponies ate unpalatable heath when we stopped on the hill, but soon learned where better grazing lay. When we stopped to sit and wait, they would look towards home. Sometimes they began to walk home and we had to run to catch them. When we returned to the lodge we let them loose. Next morning we usually saw them on the fertile grasslands of lower Glen Derry or Glen Lui, but sometimes they had gone miles to Inverey or Allanaquoich. To get them home we tied them in line, and one of us rode the front pony back to the Derry.

After pleas from Bob, Ormiston on 18 September 1951 brought hobbles to prevent them wandering far. That very morning, we had to go to Allanaquoich to get the ponies, after a windy night with a full moon and flying drizzle, and a bright white lunar rainbow spanning Glen Luibeg. Even with the ponies hobbled we still had to go a mile to find them on some mornings, down Glen Lui. In the next season, Ormiston sent enough hay to stable them all night, a decision of good management for nights of cold rain and strong winds. We let them out to graze on fine afternoons and evenings, but liked having them dry in the morning. Most of them were touchy in 1950 and 1951. When we sidled past them in the stable to check hay or harness, they occasionally tried to squash us against the wooden compartment wall.

Whitehouse once had diarrhoea, and used so much newspaper in the flush toilet that it became blocked. Bob liked using it, for Luibeg lacked this luxury. Finding it choked, he spoke to us, and Whitehouse admitted. Bob ordered him to clear it and Whitehouse did, but later choked it again and defaecated under trees nearby. Telltale newspaper gave the show away. When Bob came next morning he found the toilet choked and noticed the paper in the wood. He raged, "I tellt ye to clean that shitehoose, but ye've choket it again and ye're shitein ahin trees and spreadin a mess o newspapers. Whitehoose, clean that shitehoose, and if I catch ye haein anither shite ahin a tree I'll kick yer bloody airse". Whitehouse crept away and caused no further problems.

In 1951 and 1952, the gillie besides Jimmy was Sandy Gunn in his early 20s, from Uist. Although a reliable gillie, he took too much whisky at Braemar. One night he raved when Jimmy and I helped him to bed, so we drove to Braemar, where the doctor treated him for alcohol poisoning. We acted just in time.

On 24 August 1951 I returned to Turriff from Norway. Next day my father and I drove to the Derry. On the way we called to see my elder brother Stewart at the Knock bothy in Inverey, where he had been a gillie for grouse and ptarmigan shooting in Glen Ey with Willie Grant. Jimmy McCartney said "our three ponies arrived over a week ago and have been running nearly wild, and nobody has been able to catch them". Along with Sandy, Jimmy and I caught them early next morning.

While Stewart lived at the Knock, I cycled down on a few evenings and we went to a Braemar pub for a beer with local folk. Cycling back in the dark, we had no lights, but our eyes became adjusted. At Mar Brae the road descended among Norway spruces, so dark that we could not see the road as we cycled down. Stewart knew what to do from earlier trips. He said "look up", and sure enough I could then see a dark grey strip of slightly lighter sky between the blackness of trees on either side. He skimmed down and I followed, looking straight up. We came round bends easily, because the light sky above each bend followed the road's curves. Stewart would then kindle a fire and brew tea at the bothy before I left to cycle the five miles up to the Derry.

Often the Derry gillies felt cold while waiting on the hill. Once I returned after three hours to find Jimmy and Sandy asleep, huddled together. On a day when the stalking party had walked miles out of sight, Jimmy suggested we ride. We trotted and galloped over Moine Bhealaidh, hooting like cowboys, and Jimmy tried to get his pony to make ours throw us. The ponies enjoyed the fun.

Ormiston sent new ponies in 1950. I chose a white pony Queenie and had her for three seasons. Jimmy chose a brown one with a white forehead flash and Sandy a black mare. In the Dubh Ghleann on 3 September 1951, *Sandy and I tried to load a stag on the black mare, but it was no good. She is as round as a barrel underneath, and the stag kept slipping.* Queenie took it home.

Queenie and I got on perfectly. She persisted on difficult ground if I led her. I taught her not to be scared if a stag's antler broke a twig above her head. Also, ponies dislike the sight and smell of stag's blood during the loading of a stag. The trick is to put a jacket over the pony's head during loading. Queenie seemed phlegmatic when Bob and I began to lift the first stag on to her, so I decided to remove the jacket and hold her head while Bob and Jimmy lifted. As they raised the stag, I spoke softly to her and stroked her head. We never needed a jacket on her again. At the end of the season I sang her praises to Ewan Ormiston and he sent her again in 1951 and 1952.

An erratic shot, Jones sometimes fired badly and missed one stag after another, disturbing the beat as we moved from one failed stalk to another, the corries resounding with loud echoes. I recall up to three blank days in succession. On other days he was in top form, killing every stag he came across, usually with a single shot. In September 1950 he shot ten in one day. By early evening we had eight in the larder after three relays of carrying. Jimmy and I loaded the last two at dusk, and darkness had fallen by the time we reached the larder. We had all ten skinned and butchered by midnight.

Next morning, 26 September, was the worst I ever saw on the hill. Rain poured in sheets, driven by a strong cold wind. The gillies thought we should not go out, because we could not see well and the stags would be sheltering in gullies where they would be hard to find. However, excited by their previous day's record, Bob and Jones hoped to raise it to at least 12 in two days.

Bob Scott and Sir George Schuster on Derry Cairngorm, 4 September 1951

Shooting 12 in two days was not to be. As we walked up the wood in eastern Glen Derry, the entire hillside was awash with running water, and hundreds of little burns raced down in places where we had seen no burn before. Within a mile the downpour soaked us. Even with waterproofs, the rain ran down every opening, especially round the neck. When we reached the burn from Beinn Bhreac, a raging torrent faced us. It would have been risky to cross on foot, hard to persuade unladen horses to cross, and crazy to attempt a return crossing with a laden horse. The rain battered so hard that the roaring burn visibly rose as we watched. Also the rain had turned cold, and we could see and feel sleet. We retreated beside the Derry Burn, now a raging brown torrent.

Sandy and I took the ponies to the stable and fed them, while Jimmy drove Benton Jones to Braemar. Sandy and I lit a fire and put on spare clothes while our wet ones steamed. We ate packed lunches and drank tea as Jimmy arrived from Braemar. He said the river Dee at Linn of Dee thundered down as a brown foaming mass of water with no sign of the usual falls and pools. Torrential rain fell all day, and by afternoon the main burns had burst their banks. However, no flash floods occurred because the rain fell as snow above 2000 feet. By evening we had dried wet clothes and equipment, and the now dry horses rested comfortably, the first night they had been inside this season. It still rained when we walked to Luibeg for dinner.

Next morning at 6.30, Police Constable Florence of Braemar called at Luibeg, saying, "Excuse me, Robert, for being so too early, but there's been a terrible tragedy in the Lairig Ghru, with two hikers dead". Bob retorted "Christ, I thocht there wid hae been six", whereupon Florence said "Now, Robert, don't speak like that". He asked Bob to come with a pony to the Pools of Dee. Bob said "No, I'll hae to go on the hill wi Colonel Benton Jones the gentleman, he pays a lot o money to staalk here, but you go to the lodge and ask Adam Watson the gillie to go to the Pools wi ye an tak his pony. He kens the Lairig like the back o his haan, better than me".

At 6.45 a.m., Florence woke me, whispering "Adam, there's been a tragedy in the Lairig Ghru. Can you help?" As I swung out of bed and put my bare feet on the floor he said excitably "My goodness, watch yourself Adam, you'll get a chill". He had come with Willie McDougall of Inverey, a 54-year old with experience of stalking and the hill. Florence I had known as a policeman in Turriff, where folk called him Smiler because he smiled so often. The nickname had spread to Braemar. On the previous morning, he said, a party at Corrour Bothy left for Aviemore. The swollen Dee swept James Mackay off his feet and out of sight. The rest, in shock, turned up the Lairig path, in a gale with torrential wet snow. Soaked and cold, they sat to rest near the summit. William Pinkerton died of hypothermia where he sat. The others reached Aviemore, where they reported the death. Because they possessed rail tickets from Aviemore to Glasgow they had ignored the easy walk from Corrour down to the Linn of Dee or Luibeg. The body lay inside Aberdeenshire, so the Aviemore police phoned Smiler to arrange for the body to be lifted.

Once I had risen, Smiler said Mrs Scott would give Bob and me breakfast, and I walked to Luibeg to eat, next to the stable to prepare Queenie, and then walk up the Lairig path. The weather had been dry overnight and with relief I saw that the Luibeg Burn below Carn a' Mhaim had abated, though still far higher than usual. I jumped on Queenie's back to guide her at a place with few boulders and a wide shallow crossing. It looked like a fine day to come, dry and almost windless. Grey cloud covered the sky but a pale yellow sun shone dimly, and fresh snow lay to 3000 feet.

When we came opposite Corrour Bothy, Smiler walked towards it and blew his whistle. The occupants came out and he waved his arms in sign language, but they could not understand. He had to go to the river and shout to them on the far bank, finding that they knew nothing of the tragedy. This wasted 20 minutes. South of the Pools of Dee, Smiler told Willie and me to stop while he went ahead, because he must be first to see the body. At first we did, but I decided it was another daft delay, so we started again. When Smiler criticised us, I said we must stop wasting time, for we still had much to do. I warned that Queenie would be slow on the way back, carrying a body, and we must move so that she could cross the Luibeg Burn well before dusk. At this he relented.

In July 1959 *The Scotsman* carried a story about a rumour that the Scots Greys had ridden on horseback through Lairig Ghru about 20 years previously. The editor published my letter stating *I do have first-hand experience that it is by no means a great feat for a good Highland garron. During September 1950, when I was a gillie at the deer-stalking on Mar Forest, a man died of exposure in the Lairig, and the body had to be taken back to Derry Lodge. I was using one of Ewan Ormiston's fine garrons from Newtonmore for deer-carrying at the time, and we had no difficulty in getting as far as the Pools of Dee. Between the Pools and the summit, the pony had to be coaxed and led gently over the boulder field, and even through one of the Pools at one very bad place, a job that the average garron would never have begun to tackle. But meanwhile I had spotted what looked like a feasible route for the return journey some way up the hillside on the Brae Riach side of the Pools. Our return by this route proved to be easy. From the spot where I turned the pony, a good pony track leads in the opposite direction all the way down into Rothiemurchus. After this experience, I would say that any competent horseman with a garron or an Iceland pony could easily go through Lairig Ghru.*

I led Queenie slowly through the water at the east edge of the biggest of the Pools of Dee. Large rough boulders lay below the water surface, though easier for a pony than the impossibly large ones on the bank. She came through slowly while I coaxed her, but I knew that this would be harder with a load. Then I noticed the easy return route on

AW with Queenie at Derry Lodge, September 1951

the west side of the pass. Meanwhile we neared the summit. Smiler asked, "Do you think we'd be approaching the dead man now, Adam" and I said "Yes, we're nearly there". Smiler then said "I ought to go in the lead now", and Willie and I followed shortly behind. In another 30 yards, Smiler stopped as he came to the dead man, and blew his whistle loudly, another pointless act.

The body lay near the Spey march. Plump and unfit, Smiler looked at the body and said wearily "My dear friend, if you had walked another 100 yards, the Aviemore constable would have had to deal with you and we would have been saved all this bother". Pinkerton still sat upright on a boulder. He seemed lifelike until I saw his dead-white face and hands, and felt them cold and stiff. Willie and I had to drag the body over the boulder field to where Queenie stood, and then lift it on to her deer-saddle and tie up. Because Pinkerton's boots dangled below the level that a stag's legs would reach, we tied his legs so that the boots did not kick Queenie.

Later, the story became embellished. Richard Paterson of Aberdeen, often seen in Mar Lodge bar at weekends in the late 1960s when the Lodge had become a hotel, used to tell young hikers with emphatic emphasis on "break" and "bloody", "When they reached the dead man, Adam Watson and Willie McDougall had to break his bloody arms legs and ribs to get him on the horse, because *rigor mortis* had set in".

We returned on a boulder-free deer-track on the west side and then to the Lairig path. Two snow-patches in Garbh Choire Mor stood out prominently to the west, and I suddenly noticed that the sun, still shining through diffuse cloud but with stronger light, had a pale metallic blue colour. I called the others to see it, for they had not noticed it, and it stayed a pale electric blue for the rest of the day. We stopped to rest Queenie at Clach nan Taillear, where we had our last sandwich and tea. At a green spot further south I halted longer to let her graze on a wee patch of smooth green grass, for she had not eaten in a long tiring day, over by far the roughest ground she had ever walked on the Derry.

On Sron Carn a' Mhaim we met a Ballater constable who said "the second body's been located on the east bank of the Dee opposite Geusachan. I called at Luibeg and asked Mrs Scott to tell her husband when he comes off the hill to come with another pony. But there's no sign of Bob Scott". I said "It's time we were all off the hill with a laden horse now, it'll soon be dark. Bob won't be coming so late". When Bob returned in late evening, Helen told him what the constable said. Bob told the gillies to refuse if anyone asked for a pony.

When our party reached the Luibeg Burn, I jumped on Queenie's back behind the body and guided her across, glad to see that the depth of the burn had declined since morning. On the far bank I noticed that the body had slipped to one side, unbalancing the weight. Willie said "Just gie the airse strap a good rug (pull) up, Adam, and that'll dee fine". Smiler said "Now, William, don't use such coarse language. Mr Pinkerton will have his dear ones". This silly comment mistook plain Scots, which Willie used, for coarse speech. The 'airse strap' was the right technical term.

As we passed Luibeg, Smiler walked to the cottage to ask for a sheet to cover the body after it was put in the lodge, and Bob joined Willie and me walking to the lodge as darkness approached. I told Bob what happened during the day. After Willie and I unstrapped the body, Smiler and Bob took it off the saddle. Bob pulled the man's legs, ready to let the body drop to the ground, when Smiler said "By God you want to be careful, Robert", whereupon Bob asked "Fit wey?" (Why?). Smiler replied "My jove if there's any blue marks on him they'll see them". Bob said "Blue marks? Ye've pulled the bugger ower the bloody boulders. Adam tellt me he and Willie had to tak an airm each and pull him oot ower the boulders to get him to the pony". Next, Smiler and Bob carried the body into a room on the ground floor, and Smiler covered it with the sheet. I led Queenie to the stable for hay and a rest, and then walked with Bob to Luibeg to eat supper and tell what happened. Bob roared with laughter when I recounted what Smiler said to the body.

Surprisingly, the stalking party had not noticed the blue sun. That night a bright moon shone, also a pale metallic blue. A few days later, newspapers and radio reported that smoke from a huge forest fire in Alberta had moved with a westerly wind and caused the blue sun and moon. Newspapers continued discussion till February 1951. *The Observer* reported smoke as the cause, but some thought a mother of pearl cloud had caused the blue sun. When I first saw it, it shone through a mother of pearl cloud far above high stratus, but when it shone later outside the mother of pearl cloud its colour remained a cold blue. The journal *Weather* carried a factual account by Elseley about the fire, the wind carrying the smoke over eastern North America where many people saw the blue sun, and then moving the smoke over Newfoundland to Britain. 'Once in a blue moon' now had real meaning to me, and indeed 'Once in a blue sun and moon'.

Next day, Bob wanted me to go with him to take in shot deer. Mackay's body lay on the east bank of Dee, a far easier task than we faced with the first body. Jimmy McCartney took his pony with a police inspector from Aboyne, Smiler, Willie, and a forensic doctor. The inspector said to Bob "We're going up for the second body and wondered if you could give us another sheet to cover it at the lodge". Bob said "Surely to Christ ye maan (must) think I'm a bloody undertaker noo, fit the hell div ye think I am? I'm jist a staalker". The doctor stupidly told the party to return with the body to Glen Luibeg, a trackless climb of over 300 feet on peat-bog, whereas the easy safe route lay by the Glen Dee path to the road at the White Bridge. Bob criticised this when he heard. Had I been in charge of the pony, I would have refused to return by any route other than down Glen Dee, but Jimmy had never been there.

The two bodies lay at the lodge for another day and the police then removed Mackay's body for cremation. Pinkerton's body, to be put in a coffin, remained another day. A policeman came to Bob and asked for a volunteer to help him remove Pinkerton's clothes, and Bob agreed. Taking his gralloching knife to cut the laces, he pulled the boots off, held the heel of a sock and whipped the sock off quickly. The policeman said, "Now, now, I went through a medical course, and I'll show you how to take a sock off. He slowly rolled it down to the back of the heel, as the body lay on the floor with the head on a sandbag. As he rolled the sock down the foot, the man's head moved off the sandbag and banged on the floor. The policeman jumped as if shot, and shouted in fright. Bob said "I'm bloody sure he thocht the mannie was to come up and look at him. Ha, ha, ha, ha. He was so feart that I had to tak the bloody sock aff in the finish".

Sandy disliked bodies being in the lodge, and apprehensively passed the door at night while climbing the stair to our bedroom. Humorous as ever, Jimmy called through "Mackay, you lot stay where you are and don't disturb our

Gillies asleep after waiting hours on Beinn Bhreac, 20 September 1951

peace and quiet". Bob gave a hilarious account in later years. When asked "Bob, what was your best day at the Derry", he said "My best day at the Derry wis ten stags and twa Englishmen." It was poetic licence, for we shot ten stags the day before the men died, and I recall that both the dead men came from the Glasgow area.

In 1951 and 1952 we paid Helen to give us breakfast and dinner with Bob at Luibeg. This helped unite us as a team. However, the team came close to ending on Saturday 22 September 1951. Bob decided to go to Beinn a' Chaorainn, but its corries held no deer. He and Benton Jones walked to Beinn a' Bhuird, leaving us on Moine Bhealaidh. Later we rode the ponies to the top west of Allt an Aghaidh Mhilis and scanned Beinn a' Bhuird. We watched the two men in an unsuccessful stalk which alerted all the stags and moved them to the Dubh Ghleann face below An Diollaid. The two of them then walked east out of sight. For hours we waited on the exposed top, becoming cold, and then walked into Dubh Ghleann nearer to where they had vanished. About to start climbing to An Diollaid, we noticed them on An Diollaid, facing us but making no sign. Next they walked south out of sight, towards home we surmised. We went home, arriving at 7 to find they had not returned. In the dark they came at 9, after waiting two hours for us beside two dead stags in the Coire Gorm of Beinn a' Bhuird.

An angry Bob did not accept our explanation. Jimmy drove Jones to his hotel, and later all three gillies walked to Luibeg for a late dinner. Bob said we had deliberately left them in the lurch. This went too far. Jimmy had a quick temper under unfair treatment. He snapped. "I've had enough. We've told you what happened. It could have happened to anybody. You could have given us a sign, but didn't. I'm not enjoying this dinner and would rather be at the lodge. You can look for another gillie the morn, because I'll be down that glen and home to Kiltarlity to look for another job with decent folk."

Leaping to his feet, he headed for the door. Bob ran after him, followed by Sandy and me. Outside the house, Bob apologised to us and asked us to come back. We did. Despite long silences, we finished our dinners. When we left, I said "See you at breakfast", and Bob smiled in relief. In later decades, radios between stalker and gillies prevented such misunderstanding.

Next day was Sunday, usually a day off, but two stags lay on the hill. Still smarting, Jimmy would not go, but Sandy and I offered. Bob did not need to come, as I asked for detailed locations and he knew I would find the stags. *Sandy and I rode up to the Coire Gorm of Beinn a' Bhuird to get the two stags shot yesterday. Southeast wind, still dry, very cloudy but clear, clouds lower later, turning to rain and mist at night. We went out and back in three and a half hours. The Bucker (Jimmy's horse) had been seen at Inverey and we went in the van to get it. Jimmy rode it back to the lodge.*

In the evenings we left Luibeg in the dark and walked to the lodge without torches. We could see the footpath's pale gravel, and even with an overcast sky could discern the hills' shapes. On one moonless overcast night, however, we came into pitch darkness. Once we had gone past ground lit by the cottage window, we saw nothing. Not a wind stirred. Blind, we kept together by voice, staggering towards the footbridge. Hearing water near, we crawled on hands and knees to avoid falling in, for Ian Grant had removed boulders in earlier decades to make a deep swimming pool. Soon we heard water very close, and on hands and knees we reached the bridge. Now we could return for a torch, but decided to walk to the lodge, using our memory. Reaching the Derry bridge, we walked to the stable, larder, and lodge, and felt the stonework to the back door and then along the inside walls as we moved to the kitchen. Jimmy felt for a box of matches. Suddenly came light.

Bob, Helen and the gillies went regularly to Mar's weekly social occasion, an evening dance at Inverey hall, and many came from Braemar. John Morgan played a piano and Jockie 'Stuffer', whose father had been Mar Lodge taxidermist, a fiddle. Then we had tea and cheered Jockie's singing: *Little brown jug don't I love you.*

We got a day off on Braemar games day. After jollity, drinking, and a late night, Bob and the gillies next morning found the first slope stiffer than usual. However, to sweat on the climb and then walk miles in a fresh wind soon had everyone fit. All local estates gave staff the day off. However, Ballochbuie stalker William McGregor, locally called Aal (Old) Mac, told me in 1949 that King George VI changed this. Aal Mac said "He has a mania for grouse-sheetin (shooting). There wis only one day fae the third week o August till the start o October that he didna sheet grouse, the day he'd to ging to Harewood's wedding. But he shot the morning he left for London for the wedding, he shot on the evening o his arrival back at Balmoral, and he shot on Braemar games day till 1 o' clock, so we got only the aifterneen aff". When I asked where the king is now, he replied "He's awa doon at Sandringham noo amon the pertricks" (partridges).

Once I crawled in mist behind Bob and Jones as we approached stags whose heads projected above the horizon, outlined against the sky. Bob decided which one to shoot. I raised my binoculars to see better, and suddenly noticed that the 'stags' were red grouse with their heads up. Instead of stags 100 yards away, we had stalked red grouse 20 yards away. I told Bob and Jones. We laughed, whereupon they flew off with a whirr of wings and loud cackling.

Bob, Jones and I once crawled towards a big boulder between us and four lying stags. As we reached it, Bob said Jones would be within shot, but should wait till the mist lifted. When it did, Bob gave a high-pitched shout, whereupon the stags stood up and Jones shot all four dead through the lungs. They collapsed in a heap together, their feet almost touching.

One day on Beinn a' Bhuird, Bob decided to go to Moine Bhealaidh. He led and the rest of us followed. We started from a high-walled stone shelter. In dense fog, hardly an eddy stirred. After 45 minutes of fairly flat terrain, we expected to turn west on to Moine Bhealaidh, when suddenly in front rose the stone shelter. We had returned to where we started, after more than two miles in an anti-clockwise circle. Bob now asked me to go in front. After making sure of directions by walking round the shelter and noting ground and vegetation carefully, I walked ahead. After half an hour I turned west and we came out of the fog on the edge of Moine Bhealaidh.

Queenie asleep, 20 September 1951

If the toff wounded a stag, we followed it, and tradition allowed stalkers to go on an adjacent estate to kill it. One toff wounded a stag on Carn Crom. Lying on the slope below, the gillies saw the stag being wounded and then walking down into Glen Luibeg, after it had gone a short distance northwards. Assuming that it had continued northwards, the stalking party walked north and passed out of our sight, a mile away from us uphill. We followed the stag downhill until it stopped in Luibeg Burn, where it turned at bay to face us, bleeding. While one gillie held the ponies, Jimmy and I took our knives out and waded into the burn. Slippery boulders covered the bottom and swift water rose to our knees. We had to struggle to hold the stag and slit its throat, but it died quickly. Then we hauled it out and lay on the bank to rest, tired and soaked in water and blood.

On another day, a toff wounded a stag on Beinn Bhreac. Bob had asked me to watch from Meall an Lundain and return to the other gillies before coming with ponies to lift the stag. The stag started towards Dubh Ghleann, but then turned towards Meall an Lundain. By then, Bob and the toff had gone out of sight beyond Beinn Bhreac's east corner. Watching the wounded stag lie down, I went there to find it bleeding and breathing heavily. I stretched my left hand to hold an antler so as to steady my aim with a knife in my right hand. As soon as I touched the antler, the stag tossed its head and flung me through the air. I had not realised how strong a wounded stag can be. Then I lunged at its throat with my knife, and soon had it dead. After gralloching it, I walked to tell the other gillies where to find it, before racing up Beinn Bhreac to look down the east slopes and wave to the stalking party.

The stalker decided when to have lunch. Bob showed the toff where to sit and took the toff's lunch bag from my rucksack. He then sat with me in a different hollow within sight of the toff but out of earshot. If the whole party arrived together, Bob and all the gillies sat together. Over lunch, Bob would say what he thought of the toff's poor stalking or shooting, and we would laugh together. Then Bob returned to the toff to prepare for the afternoon's stalking.

Occasionally a stalked stag ran out of shot, after disturbance by something unseen by us, and on looking down we saw distant hikers. On as many occasions, however, a stag ran to us, without our seeing it earlier, whereupon Bob took the rifle out and Jones shot the stag. Usually, stalkers at leisure select a stag and shoot it after a stalk, but a stag's unexpected appearance excited them. I realised that disturbance of stags which appear suddenly must result from hikers not seen by us. Hence for every stalk spoiled by a hiker, an extra stag appeared suddenly.

Mar's policy in the 1950s was to shoot old stags, switches and hummels, but Bob often chose stags with good heads. A royal had 12 points, ideally six on each antler, a symmetrical top trio, and a tiny flat part in the trio. On a perfect royal, a tiny whisky glass could sit on the flat part. The stalker asked the toff to pour a nip, a gillie would hold the head up, and the stalker put the glass on the flat part. If it passed the test, the toff drank the nip and then poured one for the stalker and one for the gillie. I had several nips like this, and others when a toff shot a 13 or 14-pointer. In another tradition the toff gave the stalker a bottle for each royal shot, whether symmetrical or not.

On 12 September 1949, Mr Forshall shot two royals and a double celebration followed. Bob told Tom Weir this, and an article by Tom mentioned three in a day. Tom told me that Bob said three, and certainly Bob often exaggerated to enrich a story. Factor John Munro read the article, saw one royal noted in the game book and asked Bob to explain. Munro said not even one should have been shot. Bob escaped by saying Weir must have erred, but it was a close shave.

Most stalkers known to me would occasionally suggest that a toff should kill a stag with a good head. This pleased the toff, who would tip the stalker and gillies better. Bob did not differ from this. Years later, Mr Pilkington of the glass firm had the tenancy and asked Bob about good heads. Bob told me he said to Pilkington "Sometimes you just canna get past a royal, and if you've one or two, or maybe three or four on your beat and a gentleman wants a good head and he's a nice man, you just give him a good head". Pilkington, a man in his late 70s who had stalked Dalnacardoch and other deer-forests, said, "You know, I've never really killed a right good head, Scott, and I wonder could you get me one?" Bob obliged.

At the larder we skinned and dressed carcases, helped by Bob. Blood covered the floor, tables, knives, saws, and our hands, arms and boots. Once, two Aberdeen medical students in final year looked in, but left hurriedly. Later they said they felt sick at seeing so much blood. Their medical training had not prepared them for it. After the dressing, we hosed the floor and equipment with tap water, removed skins and feet, and wiped the carcases clean.

Before skinning, we weighed carcases while Bob noted weights. After the hard winter of 1951, stags weighed below the average for past years. If our toff shot a small stag of 10 stones or less, Bob said "We'd better nae include that shargar (runt) in the game book, because it wid tak the average doon"! Sometimes he added a few lb before noting a weight, but did not reduce the weights of big stags. Of a very small stag he said to Jones "it would be best if this one went to the bothy, sir", so excluding it from tally and gamebook. Jones agreed, as it gave him an extra stag to shoot for the same rent. Then Bob and we cut the stag for Helen to use for our dinners. We ate like kings.

Chapter 8 Skiing alone through the Lairig Ghru at New Year

<u>Sunday 2 January 1949. To Coylumvbridge</u>

Another bad day came to the Drumochter hills, snowstorm and strong wind. Dad and I went up the road on skis but a blizzard sprang up, so we packed up at Dalwhinnie and drove north in the early afternoon. It was snowing when we left, and plastering all the house walls and telephone poles thickly with driven moist snow. Dad dropped me off at Aviemore on his way home to Turriff. Conditions were really filthy, with dirty slush from yesterday's thaw, and now snowing heavily. Two ravens flew over the village.

I pushed off on ski and by the time I reached Coylum the skies had begun to clear and it had turned frosty. Then I had difficulty getting a doss and wandered about, vainly knocking on doors, until a man offered a barn and asked me to come in to the cottage for tea. I joined a family gathering at a warm fire. The man said that bird-photographer John Markham stayed there on his Speyside trips. The man's brother in law was Moormore gamekeeper when George Yeates photographed blackcock there, and recently was deerstalker at Coire Bhachdaidh Lodge on Loch Ericht, a place with no road access. I told him I skied at Loch Ericht yesterday and had seen roe deer on the moor. He once saw 21 roe in birches at Coire Bhachdaidh in a hard winter, and said many roe at Drumochter lived far from any trees. Later an old lady said to the first man "Show the gentleman his quarters". He ushered me to the barn and told me to leave anything I would not need tomorrow, for collection later. Then he bid me good night and good luck for tomorrow.

Tonight was really grand. A severe frost had set in and a lovely ghostly light from the new moon lit the snowy firs and pervaded the earth. I crawled into my sleeping bag at 9, and thought about the trip I planned through the Lairig Ghru to Luibeg in deep snow tomorrow. It was the biggest undertaking I had yet attempted in my life.

<u>Monday 3 January. The Lairig Ghru on ski</u>

Waking at 7.30, I melted snow on the stove, ate a big pot of porridge and cups of tea, thawed my frozen boots, left some spare equipment, and at 8.30 set out on ski into a severe frost with not a cloud in the sky. Away far back stood the line of the Cairngorms, blue and cold like stone domes, a sea of hills hard-edged against the lightening sky. Eastwards a red glow merged into the duck green of the sky, and away over the Monadh Liath a fan of purple and red clouds spread ominously to the zenith. Not a breath of wind stirred in the old wood, and deep silence reigned. Six inches of powder snow on the firs made Rothiemurchus a fantastic world of beauty, although the sun had not yet appeared. Hinds grazed in the wood, their winter coats looking warm brown against the snow. A few coal tits moved and a crested tit, but otherwise the land seemed devoid of animals.

As I reached the footbridge, an indication of how the day would go appeared in the extraordinary colours on hills north of Carr Bridge. They glowed golden against a black sky, a wild vivid effect with omens of impending storm. And now from every hill in the Cairngorms, snow plumes began to stream, trailers that swept in fury hundreds of feet from the corrie edges. The plumes had the same inky-blue colour as the shadowed slopes, but as they whirled above the tops like great waterspouts the sun caught them to warmest flames, rosy against the pale sky.

I skied up the wood into ever deeper snow and soon a biting west wind arose, tearing snow off the trees and flinging it in drift storms so thick that I might have been in a blizzard. Towards the last trees, conditions became appalling. In the light powdery drifts my skis sank ten inches at every step, and every few steps one ski would stick and come off as my climbing boot kept slipping off its binding clamps. Staggering to the conical little top above Allt Druidh, I stopped to look back over the wood, now a haze of grey from snow blowing off the trees. Already, heavy falling snow obscured the Monadh Liath and the Sgoran Dubh. The Lairig looked a fierce place, dim and gloomy, with storm clouds racing across blue sky. Three men from Glasgow appeared on foot, floundering to the waist and very cold after a night in a tent by the burn. One joked about Dunoon in high summer. They said the Lairig was insurmountable and "You will die if you try to cross it", but they had no skis and I decided to give it a try.

In deep snow among the last trees my speed fell to a crawl. When I passed the moraine I made for a big cairn half a mile ahead. An exhausting plod followed with head bent down. Every time I looked at my watch I could see that the minutes were flying and the cairn seemed remote. When at last I reached it, I had taken 50 minutes to cover the half mile. The skis ploughed in a foot at every step, in snow of average depth two feet.

After a rest I skied heavily to the burn and spent 20 minutes climbing a hillock 150 feet above. By now things looked pretty grim. The wind rose to a gale and a blizzard of fine hail cut visibility to ten yards. Ptarmigan were down at 1750 feet. With the pass summit still miles away, I fell into the snow to weigh my chances. At this rate I would reach it in mid afternoon, and to climb to Ben Macdui seemed madness in view of worsening weather, although skiing would have been better there on harder snow. However, I knew I could reach Corrour Bothy before night, so I pushed on.

An exhausting plod at less than 1 mph followed to the summit, with the hours seeming to race past. Never was I gladder than when I reached the top. I sank into the snow with quivering knees and wept with frustration. It was so frosty that my fingers stuck to the ski-bindings. For miles back, the slope I had ascended faded into distant Speyside, and with interest I picked out the rocky gap of Beum a' Chlaidheimh where the road goes from Duthil to Nairn. I already felt good, knowing that the uphill grind was over. I ate some sardines and glucose, and felt a new man.

On snow that suddenly became firmer and wind-packed, allowing much faster progress than in summer, I skied on the flat past the Pools of Dee. Ice and snow covered them except for a square yard at one end of the big pool, where water bubbled up, a good place for a drink. The time was 2.30. I had taken five hours to come five and a half miles from the footbridge.

But now for two glorious miles I floated down effortlessly on perfect hard-packed velvety drifts. Snow fell heavily again and the Garbh Choire looked wilder than I had ever seen it, its cliffs plastered and half hidden by falling snow. Snow covered the whole course of the river Dee and no one seemed to be in Corrour Bothy, for a drift lay against the door. The snow was still hard-packed and easy going as I passed Clach nan Taillear, and I took a straight line to cut the distance. A plod in softer snow followed as I climbed to the shoulder, and then I skied more quickly round the south side of Carn a' Mhaim. Snow had stopped falling, and the high tops looked blue and cold. Darkness fell with a ghastly light on the snow, but the firs of Glen Luibeg were a grand sight, only two miles now to Luibeg.

Skiing in the dark down to the Luibeg Burn, I crossed a small cornice which I had not seen, and tumbled into deep powder. Both skis shot downhill out of sight because I had loosened my bindings in case of a bad fall. After a fruitless search I stuck a ski-stick in to mark the place and staggered to the footbridge through waist-deep drifts.

The time was 5. The walk to Luibeg was utterly exhausting in the dark. At every step I sank to the knees, often to the waist, twice to the arm-pits, and twice through soft snow and up to the knees in water. I staggered on with gritted teeth, though it was no more exhausting than it had been earlier from Rothiemurchus to the Lairig summit. When only 300 yards from Luibeg I came on a continuous track left by a big party who had walked to the bridge earlier in the day, but I had missed it in the dark. I heaved a big sigh of relief when I saw the lights of Luibeg at 6.30. Never were they more welcome and cheery after by a long way the toughest and most exhausting day I have ever had. Yet I felt elation about coming through the centre of the Cairngorms in deep snow and bad weather on my own. I had seen and learned much.

Bob and Helen Scott got a surprise when I knocked on the cottage door at 6.40, just over 10 hours from Coylum. 'Smithy' (Edwin W. Smith, Meets Secretary of the Cairngorm Club) is staying at the cottage, and doubts if the Lairig has ever been crossed on ski. Snow is very deep here. Fortunately the first four miles after the Pools of Dee gave good skiing, or I would not have passed Corrour Bothy tonight.

Tuesday 4 January. Glen Luibeg

What a perfect morning! A severe frost, several degrees below 0 F, cloudless skies, no wind, and sunshine were good after yesterday's poor weather. I set off up the Lairig Ghru on Bob's skis. How easily I skied to the footbridge in sunlight compared with floundering on foot in darkness. Glorious sunshine made the tops look their very best. A soft satin sheen rippled on the head of Beinn Bhrotain, and everywhere I saw delicate shades of silver and deep blue shadows. Ben Macdui, Carn a' Mhaim and even Carn Crom looked a shining creamy white against an almost purple-blue sky, darker and more vivid than I have ever seen.

Mack Graham skis on to Luibeg footbridge, 4 January 1949

Thick ice covered the Luibeg Burn, where a shrew ran along the ice. Snow buntings flew in small flocks with tinkling calls, and a twite rose with one flock. My loose skis yesterday had left slight marks, which I followed until I found them safe and sound, stuck in drifts. I vowed to fit the binding clamps better to my climbing boots on return to Luibeg, and thenceforth to ski with a lace attached from each boot to its ski binding. Slipping my skis on, I had the best skiing I have yet experienced, on beautiful velvety powder above a packed base. After a few runs on the slopes west of the bridge I skied to Luibeg, skimming in my tracks and with a rope pulling Bob's skis like a sledge behind me.

By 2 p.m. the sun still shone hard and brilliant, turning frost on the grasses to sparkling diamonds. From Meall an Lundain one might have imagined the Cairngorms to be moon mountains, waves of snowy hills white and rigid, and throwing great blue shadows. The trees too looked fantastic under their heavy load of snow. Gradually the sun sank and the hills turned from cream to soft gold and then to a flush of crimson. Long after the sun had left the glen, the summit of Beinn Bhreac glowed with a spectacular red, its lower slopes inky blue. Snow plumes waving from Beinn Bhrotain turned a dusky pink, and an utter silence brooded amongst the black and white tracery of the firs. I skied on the hillocks north of Luibeg on lovely hard powder snow till 5.30, when it grew too dark. Soon after, Allan McNicol arrived from Glasgow with his brother Ian. Just over a year ago on these very hillocks, Allan and Tom Weir had taught me my first ski-lessons.

About eight years ago, when our enthusiasm was always able to get the better of our caution and inexperience, we started to think about how to get to Spitsbergen. It was good to get letters headed importantly "Store Norsk

Pat Sellar and Robert Shepherd at our Grenivik camp, mid July 1949

Icelandic schoolboys at Grenivik

Spitsbergen Kulkompani" but alas! they had clearly decided that we must be unreliable types with no money and they were not to be taken for a ride. Nowadays you can book a passage to Spitsbergen by luxury steamer, shoot your own polar bear by the light of the midnight sun, and probably meet there Americans "doing" the world for the nth time as one more means of getting even with those Joneses. But eight years ago Spitsbergen was still recovering from the war and there was no room for tourists. We knew no string-pulling patrons who could wangle room for us, so we chose north Iceland instead.

Aberdeen was an ideal start then, and we waited expectantly for a trawler. At last came late June, and one night Pat came rushing to say -- unbelievable luck -- there was an Iceland trawler in with a record catch. Wartle and I had still a full day of botany examinations ahead, and next day Pat was given special permission to tell us, in great excitement, the latest news. It may not be a coincidence that Wartle, mentally thinking of skis and pemmican instead of seeds and pteridophytes, had to re-sit his botany in September.

Once through the Pentland we were into rough seas that kept us sick or dull till the third day, when a streak of

Peaks east of Kaldbakur, mid July

barren snow-streaked coast loomed out of the fog. A few hours later, with a clearing of the sky, a range of snow-white peaks rose like a great curtain out of the grey seas. Sea birds in vast numbers fluttered noiselessly about the water. South lay a land of utter desolation, snow-streaked, flat, bare, treeless, with not a house or sign of human on its sinister dark surface. Nearer and nearer to the mountain wall, and then the dark cliffs rose beside us, straight from the sea to snowy heights. Suddenly there was an entrance, and a fjord, and late that night we docked at a windy bare town below the great hills: Akureyri.

The scene at the quay would have satisfied the most exacting of Hollywood producers. Great crowds thronged the place for this important event, and as soon as the boat touched the side, men swarmed aboard, like a mad race of Hamelin's rats. Somebody in uniform, the customs man, was ushered safely below to the skipper's cabin. By then, kitbags, crates and sacks were being marshalled on deck with incredible speed, and a human chain delivered them in rapid succession to the crowd on the quay. There seemed to be everything, from fur coats and cameras to children's toys, bicycles, sweets and whisky. We stood gaping. By the time the customs man came up again the lot had gone.

The customs man drove us in a jeep to his office. Where were we to stay: the....Hotel? We didn't know. But we must know and as aliens he had to have an address where the police could contact us. At last he jumped up: the forms had beaten him. He announced he would drive us to a camp site, and in the jeep we raced away out of the town, to set up tents on a rolling moor above the fjord. Here the whimbrel and golden plovers sang through the night and the ptarmigan croaked, like their fellows of the Cairngorms, while we waited to see the northern night sun on the mountains.

The first plan was to go to a lake 50 miles away; Myvatn, the fly lake, well-known as one of the great world haunts of wildfowl. The road had only just been cleared of snow and no buses ran. We went in a car, sharing it with two others. Myvatn was one of the strangest places imaginable, a green oasis surrounded by barren wastes of volcanic hills and lava deserts. Though we had planned for a short stay, we became completely fascinated by the place.

The only problem was food, as we had very little money. At Myvatn the finding of a nest of scaup duck with five fresh eggs was therefore hailed with shouts of delight greater than those of the keenest ornithologist, and we were so elated that we fried and ate them on the spot. This was only a beginning as the place teemed with wildfowl and nest hunting was a simple matter of walking round the shore and flushing the ducks off their nests. We tried scaup, scoter, teal, merganser and others, a motley assembly. They formed our basic diet for several days, fried over fires of dwarf birch and pony dung. Later we learned that the local people collect them in vast numbers. We used to draw the line at the sight of the embryos, but the locals, less fastidious than us and so better at the same game, ate them with or without the young birds, and even stored them to eat later on in the winter. Then we were told they "smell very bad but are very good, like cheese".

Thumbing for lifts and walking, we made our way back to Akureyri with a diminishing stock of eggs. Prices there were extremely high as result of leaping inflation, and this decided us to live cheaply. Salted cod was the answer, so we bought a good stock of the stuff and usually had some at every meal. Economy was the usual order. We boiled cod and eggs in the same water, and then used that water, now of the right salt concentration for making potato with 'Pom' powder. We even used the water once for porridge, but only once.

From our Akureyri camp we climbed the glaciated 4800 ft high Vindheimajökull, skiing for a long way up the glacier to the final rotten ridge in a position like A' Chir. The next move was to one of the northern peninsulas where the snow came in vast fields almost to sea level. Skis were essential for mountaineering there and the steep descents to the sea were tremendously exciting on perfect spring snow.

In the little hamlet of Grenivik here we had some entertainment with the local doctor who seemed to be perpetually tipsy. He wanted a fur coat for his wife; fur coats were unobtainable in Iceland but could be bought in Britain, so could he not have just a little British kronur? The sight of some loose change sent him into rapture, reaching for his wallet and a thick wad of Icelandic notes. Had we not been honest men the title of this article might have been *Iceland Mountaineering with a Profit*. Later in Akureyri, men offered us three times the bank rate for a pound note. In Iceland even policemen hinted delicately that they couldn't get spare parts for their cars, or tents, or binoculars. Of course, the trawlermen could buy all these things in Britain with the help of pound notes.

In mid-July we went south again to the 5000 ft Kerling, and it gave a good climb by difficult glazed rocks above a glacier, on a wild day of gale and snow squalls. Now the others had to go home, and I stayed another week to climb in another northern peninsula where the peaks seemed finest of all. Three wonderful days followed in that lonely range. There was tremendous joy about climbing alone there and just being alone in sunny weather in such a beautiful place. The peaks gave easy or moderate climbing and some thrilling long glissades up to one of 2600 ft down a steep couloir.

At last I had to tear myself away to the reality of getting home again. I was back in Akureyri, waiting for a trawler. I camped beside the police station, and the first night was offered a bed in the jail. It was good to get a soft bed in a warm cell and have coffee brought there in the morning, and to sit up with the night-shift police and race about the town with them in their jeep in the early morning.

At last the trawler came, then days of sea sickness to Faeroe, and finally Grimsby. I was broke and the rest of the memories that now stand out relate to this fact. Breakfast in a Grimsby workhouse; the Grimsby policemen, less human than their Iceland fellows, repeatedly asking for my identity card; a lift to Glasgow, then trying to spend the night in the Central Station there with many other local vagabonds who had the same idea, till the police finally showed me a train to spend the night in. Some day I'd like to get back to Akureyri, this time with £100.

(1955, *Etchachan Club Journal* 2, 79–83)

Wartle in the two chapters on Iceland was our nickname for Robert Shepherd, brought up at Wartle in Aberdeenshire.

Chapter 10 Lonely days

What is it that grips people and makes them go to the high places of the earth and explore the far North? Public opinion will say they are mad but a few know better. In the last *Alma Mater* you read of the fulfilment of a climber's dreams. Last summer I was in Iceland and fulfilled some of mine.

From the age of eight, mountains and then wild life have always thrilled me. With them grew the spell of the Arctic lands. Climbing and skiing in the Scottish hills served only to quicken the appetite for the Far North. At university kindred spirits meet and that was why Pat, Wartle and I got together last winter and planned to go to Spitsbergen in 80° latitude north. This year we hope to pull it off but it was impossible to reach it last year so we swallowed our grief with Iceland as second choice.

June passed quickly. It was the last day of the term and there came a last-minute offer of a lift on the trawler Kaldbakur. Though our food had not all arrived this was an opportunity we could not afford to miss. At 5 o'clock Wartle and I were staggering out of a Botany degree examination; at 11 o'clock, after a frenzy of packing, all three of us were on the boat. At 2 a.m. we left heading for a land about which we knew very little.

Excitement never failed when we went up on the bows in the now rapidly lightening midnight hours and watched our little ship plunge ever onwards into the dull grey of the sea and sky to the north. At last after three days the Promised Land was at hand, a colossal landfall of snow peaks dropping right into the sea. Iceland was just getting under way after the hardest winter for 60 years. We docked at the fishing town of Akureyri in north Iceland, and set up our base camp 5 miles away on the slope of Vindheimajökull (wind-home glacier).

Later, more than a fortnight had passed when we celebrated our last night together in Iceland. We had just that day climbed a 5000-foot glaciated peak in trying wintry conditions, so it was a double celebration. Nothing less than the famous concoction Mummery's Blood with boiling Bovril, brandy and sugar was of any use. At once the cold became less bitter and fierce Kerling that had nearly beaten us took on an almost benevolent look. Our spirits rose to a high pitch. Yet as we turned in, I am sure each one of us was a little sad. I know there was a pang in my heart at the thought of what tomorrow would bring.

1 can remember that afternoon as if it were yesterday. It was a queer feeling to climb up to our base camp and see that view by now so familiar of the big peaks Kerling and Vindheimajökull straddling the moors. Dismantling camp was easily done and then we spread out all the remaining stores on the grass for a share out of food and fuel. As we tramped downhill for the last time and listened to the ring of wader song sweeping over the moor, we could not help thinking of all that had happened since we arrived here for a start -- so much that it seemed months and months.

Pat and Wartle were now to proceed to Akureyri, camp there, and eventually go to Reykjavik by bus the next day- and eventually home to Scotland. I was to go to the Bægisa mountains in the Dalvik peninsula, a set of wild peaks that had fascinated me since the first time I set eyes on them. A lorry appeared coming my way; we shook hands, wished the best of luck, and then I was off and away in a cloud of dust with a last shout from Pat, "All the best, take care of yourself". It was a short awkward farewell. From afar off I waved through the dust to the two little figures on the long white ribbon of road. I felt intensely sorry to go.

I got a lift for 30 kilometres, and then after many weary hours, evening found me at last in Bægisardalur, sweating my way uphill with a 65-lb. pack whose straps had long since snapped in rebellion. The mountains were all hidden in gloomy clouds and a drizzle of cold rain fell. It was a pretty dismal night, but at last I picked on a fine camp site, and soon had the tent up and a meal of pancakes, cocoa, and salted cod. By now it was bitter and the mountainsides under the clouds were grey with new snow. I turned in, hoping fervently for decent weather but feeling strongly that nervous elation that comes only with anticipation of unknown adventure on the grand scale.

Sunlight flooding the tent woke me early next morning and I crawled out sleepily to find a real dream world outside. Over everything was the icy jewelled breath of the Arctic. Hoar frost sparkled on the flaming cushions of moss campion, the peaks looked incredibly near and sharp in the clear air, flaunting snowy crests against the blue sky, and nearer at hand the sweet tinkle of a snow bunting rose defiantly above the roar of the river.

For the first time I could see all my surroundings. They were pretty much as God made them. Glaciers had gouged out the U-shaped Bægisa valley in the ice ages and now the sides of the valley rise in a straight 4000 feet of shattered basalt rock and snow. Not far up in Bægisardalur behind my camp was the present-day glacier, still so big that only the tips of the rock peaks breathed freely above it. But this was only one dalur or valley, and there were plenty more lonely snow-filled valleys and frozen skylines wherever one cared to look.

But the turfy moors, rich with Arctic flowers, and the vast green bogs along the river spate-flats teemed with life. I remember being struck this first day by the wealth of life in these lonely glens. The carpets of flowers were a riot of vivid colour in contrast with the dark shining green of the crowberries and scrub birch. Among this vegetation, insects, particularly flies and moths, lived in fantastic numbers, and on them in turn a heavy and varied population of birds depended for its existence. Down here you were never out of hearing of the whinnying bubble of whimbrel, the shrill whistle of the dunlin, the thrumming drum of snipe, the mournful pipe of the golden plover as it flapped over in its courtship flight. Rich song poured from the heavens, and down below the broods of downy young ones scuttled about in the grass and snapped at passing flies. In a few weeks, with the onset of colder weather, the season would be over, the birds and their young would all be gone, away far south thousands of miles to Britain and even warmer lands. The wilderness would be a largely dead place, unutterably harsh and bleak, deprived of most of its birds. Just now, though, it was vibrating with life.

Above a certain level there was no vegetation or animal life of any kind at all. It was real Nature in the raw -- nothing but naked shattered rocks, dust, ice, snow and the immense blue bowl of space. Some people abhor this but others find it a welcome change from the type of controlled Nature so often evident in city parks like Pittodrie and the Duthie Park.

On this first day I went a long way from camp to a peak above Svarfaðardalur, unnamed on the map. In contrast to the last few snowy days, it was easily the hottest day of the whole trip and barely freezing even at the summit. As a result the silence -- so real that you could almost feel it -- was broken frequently by the grumble of snow and mud avalanches all day. Boulders crashed off the tottering basalt cliffs every other minute. One couldn't help feeling that the whole land was falling very rapidly to bits. Here was a perfect example of a country undergoing extremes in climate with disintegration and erosion proceeding at a really frightful rate. At the time I thought of those people who worry over the shortness of the human life-span on this planet and like to think of the never changing, everlasting hills. I wished they could have seen the fast changing hills in action that day to find out how wrong they are.

What a view opened out from the top of that peak. This sea of snowy mountains seemed to go on, wave after wave, to the very ends of the earth. There was only one opening out of it, with a glimpse of blue Eyjafjorður, and many miles away, over the brown desert to the east, the mountains round Myvatn and beyond, where the cumulus clouds hung top heavy above their own blue shadows -- it was all a climber's dreamland. I thought of Pat and Wartle in the hot Reykjavik bus and wondered if they knew what they were missing.

Trollafjall (troll mountain), was my aim next day. Thick mist filled the dale as I ate breakfast but there were rainbow halos, so I knew the sun would win the battle. Soon I was above the mist, looking down 300-foot sheer walls to where the Bægisa grumbled angrily through the narrow gorge. I tried to cross many times, jumping from rock to rock, but it was no use. The jumps were too long and the roar of solid walls of water thundering past on every side did nothing to help clear thinking. A slip would mean perdition.

So I gave up Trollafjall and climbed Landafjall instead. Another grilling day followed; already I was climbing minus my trousers. Late afternoon found me crossing the great swelling breast of the glacier of Bægisarjökull, so deep under snow that the glacier ice was nowhere visible. The lower slopes for 1500 feet were ideal for a glissade and I schussed quickly down to the glen, lying leisurely full length on the snow. A quick plod followed down the valley to that little green speck of a tent that was so much a home to me.

The finish to a fine day in the hills is reckoned usually to be a fine evening meal and some good company round a bothy fire. These evenings in Bægisardalur I had the roar of the river and the tame snow buntings that fluttered about my tent. Always I used to lie while waiting outside among the flowers and watch the peaks turn blood-like in the midnight sun. It would be queer to go home and see a dark night again. I hadn't heard the news for ages but somehow I couldn't care. It seemed ridiculous almost to think of it. The natterings of UNO sound pretty small in the vastness of the far north.

Peaks at top of Bægisa valley

One's dreams were intriguing, too. At Myvatn, where we lived on wild duck eggs for four days, we used to dream of feasts of fruit and meat, and sometimes we even got to the stage of eating them. In Bægisardalur I used to dream of home, not the bare summits but the beauty of the Scottish glens, the heather and the green of pines that were so lacking up in this treeless land. But though I pined subconsciously for the sight of trees, I never felt alone or cut off from the world as I thought I would when I left Pat and Wartle. Instead I was enjoying myself as never before. This was the very essence of adventure.

Another day dawned fiercely cold and foggy, and I was glad because I wanted an off day from painful snow glare. But, no! Here was the sun again wrestling with the clouds. It was irresistible. I found a way across the river low down and started up Trollafjall by a great rock ridge. What a battle the sun and the clouds had! I can remember the mountains jostling like boats above the white vapour, columns of cloud rushing out of the valley and disappearing in the blue sky, the weird halos and Brocken spectres. It was like walking on a tight rope to climb that arete with the bottle green ice of the Vindheim glacier far below on the left and the emptiness of the clouds close by on the other side. I have never seen such rotten and dangerous rock as on the tricky pinnacles and rock walls of that ridge. Whole ledges would collapse if you put a hand hold on them. But at last-the top of Trollafjall was there, edged by enormous snow cornices. The view went out to Vatnajökull (water glacier), largest ice cap in Europe, 100 miles away, and far out over the fog of the Arctic Ocean to unseen lands further north that whetted the appetite even more.

I turned for home. Below, 4000 feet down, the Bægisa river wound like a thread through the gorge. There was a choice of a fierce 2600-foot snow slope or a steep scree ridge-- no doubt which was safer but no less doubt which was the finer way down. It was a time for quick decision and of course I decided to glissade it, after a little hesitation as the risk involved for a lone man was a very big one if things went wrong. But I felt only a trifle nervous as I clambered over the cornice and gingerly schussed forwards on the first part of this colossal slope. Things went well and I had a tremendous swoop, standing on the first part but sitting down to it on the last part to get up a really fast speed. At the bottom I looked back at the peak, seeming miles above and the long track that pointed out the most thrilling glissade of my life.

AW at Fort William on return from Iceland, July 1949 (local photographer)

It was glorious fun, and though I was soaked through with melting snow I stripped and soon had my clothes dry in the warm sun. And so I came back to camp for the last time, dead tired after three tough climbs. The spell of lonely days was nearly at an end.

It was almost sacrilege to pull down the tent next morning and pack up. I was very, very sorry to go. Curtains of sleet and rain hid the peaks again -- how lucky I had been. Time passed and I was in Akureyri again, waiting for a trawler to take me to Britain.

At last the boat came but it seemed ridiculous to go home. It seemed so long since I had come and the time before I had come seemed so short-lived and far away that it was as if I had been in Iceland all my life and Scotland was just an interesting dream. I couldn't have cared whether I returned or not. As we headed down the fjord and I looked from the stern of the trawler up to the Bægisa mountains fading into the distance I admit I was in tears. The Arctic fever had truly claimed another victim.

Since I came home, Wartle suggested that if anything had happened to me on those three lonely days, the chances were that not even my tent would have been found let alone my bones, because even he had no idea where I was making for when we took leave of each other that afternoon. This may be true, but I am sure the experience was well worth the risks. I think I enjoyed at least trying, as Dave Thomas said (in an earlier *Alma Mater*), "to see beyond the hill". And Wartle, I think, when he said these things, secretly wished he had shared in these lonely days too.

(1950, *Alma Mater* 61, 2, 21–24, Aberdeen University students' literary journal)

Chapter 11 North Scandinavia in July 1950

Monday 9 July 1950. Approaching Lofoten

North from Bodø rose queer skylines and great cliffs, quite fantastic. Then far away appeared the mountains of Lofoten, a misty jagged skyline above a grey sea and mingling with clouds. Nearer views became spectacular as clouds broke and the sun shone on massive cliffs, showing every crack and gully. In the west the sunlight poured weakly through watery grey cloud, silhouetting a weird black skyline.

The ship came to Stamsund, a village nestling beneath a gigantic rock pyramid, where a few common eiders had broods in the harbour. Herring gulls up north have quite dark mantles. The thirty miles to Svolvær left me in tears. How lucky I am to see this. Vast shattered peaks drop into the sea, and huge rock fingers rise behind contorted ridges.

At 22.00 the boat docked at Svolvær in a harbour as calm as a lake. Spectacular rock peaks ring the town, and late sun shone on the cliffs of Store and Lille Molla islands. Later we left, heading for Stokmarknes, the finest part of the journey. Now higher and snowier, the peaks soared brilliant and clear in red sunlight.

As we moved up the Raftsund, glaciers high up shone like gold silk. Dozens of vast rock mountains passed, so many that my memory is in a whirl. They dropped more steeply, and in the narrows where water lay smooth without a ripple, the walls rose 3300 feet. Light puffs of cloud around the ridges turned to fire in the midnight sun. Once, brilliant gold searchlights burst through a cloud to fire a mountain in patterns of misty shade and light. A turnstone crossed the bows. Snow patches lay almost to sea level among scrub, and here and there stood a house. As we came into Hadselfjord it is Monday at 00.30 and the midnight sun shines full on the boat.

Tuesday 18 July. Climbing at Abisko in Swedish Lapland

After breakfast at my camp in birchwood by the lake Tornetrask, the shade temperature was 70° F and sunlit thunder-clouds towered over the mountains. Intending to climb the highest nearby peak, the 1743-metre Coamuhas, I walked up a path towards Abiskojaure seven miles up. The valley had birch wood, pines and marshes. Half way up I made tea on a fire of birch sticks in a grove, with the peak showing dimly at the back. Some birches of great age stood a foot or more in diameter. Sometimes the river flowed over shingle, but mostly thundered in rapids or great falls. Birds were exciting. I saw many fieldfares and redwings with fledged young, a willow tit, and red-spotted bluethroats and a redstart carrying food to nests. A pair of rough-legged buzzards had a nest in a birch, and the big young stood up as a parent swooped in with half-closed wings, carrying food.

I reached Abiskojaure, a lake hemmed in by craggy peaks. Away to the south, higher mountains rose, heavily snow covered and mostly glaciated, with great rock fingers sticking through black thunder-clouds and rain. I walked up a thick wood, intending to climb a gorge, skirt the first hill, and climb the high one beyond. The wood had only a few willow tits, one of which fed fledged young, a willow warbler, and some wheatears and meadow pipits.

The air was hot and clammy. Instead of mosquitoes vanishing as I climbed, they abounded more. When I stopped a few seconds they buzzed in front and bit me. They became so bad that I had to move, climbing fast up a steep birch grove. I sweated hard and was thirstier than I have ever been. I thought of the fine drinks I would like. My mouth became parched and saliva thick. At last I reached a stream shaded by willows, and in eagerness fell in to the knees to enjoy a wonderful drink.

So up the gorge I climbed and out over the col, into arctic vegetation with moss campion, snow patches, and bogs. Even though I moved as fast as I could go, some mosquitoes flew in front, buzzing and biting. When I turned to look back, I could hardly see for them settling on my eyes and face. They bit through my shirt and trousers, and soon would wear me down. At 1200 metres I decided to get out of the bogs and run down rough bouldery ground covered with birches and scrub. A willow grouse flushed, calling 'go back' like our red grouse, and a raven pair flew over.

Eventually I came to the path. Hundreds of mosquitoes still abounded but it seemed like heaven compared with the buzzing hell of the bogs. A sudden cool breeze sprang from the south, shaking the birches. Up to the south the sky turned black and a crash of thunder echoed. Others followed, then the black clouds tumbled low on the mountains and heavy rain fell. I was glad I had turned, for the storm might have been nasty on that high peak. I rose to walk down the woods to camp. Under the dull skies during and after the storm, few birds called in the woods, a

View north from Higravstind in Lofoten at midnight, late July 1950

deathly hush. It is the same during a solar eclipse.

For fishing though, dull weather is good. After a refreshing cup of tea at camp I walked to the river to fish from a rock where spray from the dashing torrent kept mosquitoes away. I caught a small salmon. Putting head, tail, fins, liver, and two steaks into a small bag, I kept the rest cool for tomorrow in a river pool, with boulders on top to prevent it being washed away or eaten by a fox. At camp I lit a fire of birch sticks, used the head, tail, fins and liver to make tasty soup, and grilled the steaks on the red embers while a pot of water boiled for coffee.

<u>Saturday 22 July. Climbing Higravstind</u>
At the milk boat in Svolvaer I met six local climbers, a surprising number for such a small town. Magnar Pettersen, a cheery hero of the Norwegian resistance, had great mountaineering experience. Also I met Emil Olsen, Lars Hansen, Wilhelm Hoier, and girl-friends of Emil and Magnar. The milk boat went up Austnesfjord. Under a cloudless sky we cruised in and out of hamlets delivering milk cans. On the west side the hills resembled Arran, but on the east rose much higher, culminating in the massive rock peaks Geitgaljartind and 1161-metre Higravstind, highest mountain in Austvaagøy. Between the peaks, steep rocky valleys ran down to the fjord.

After a few hours we arrived at a village at the top of the fjord and then climbed a few hundred feet to camp on a knoll. Birches clothed hillsides to below 1000 feet. I saw many redpolls, a few fieldfares, and willow warblers, the last still singing slightly. Higravstind rose steeply at the back, a rock peak with snow-filled gullies. After coffee and cakes, Magnar said we should start.

We left at 20.00, Magnar leading fast up steep grass to a gully with waterfalls, rock walls, scree and snow. We saw wheatears and meadow pipits up to 700 metres, three willow grouse, and at 800 metres a cock ptarmigan. Eventually we came to a ridge where a great cliff dropped to the south. The late sun shone through thin cloud to light up the buttresses and gullies. We ascended quickly, unroped but taking extra care when others were below, to avoid dislodging stones. Another climb ensued by steep snow, scree and rock walls, and then Magnar announced, "And now, Adam, you will soon see one of the finest views in Lofoten", as we approached the narrow neck of the summit ridge. And it was, too. Below a big drop from dark granite cliffs and past a deep bergschrund, a huge bowl of snow led to a glacier with blue ice at its bottom end. Beyond were the Raftsund, the narrow Trollfjord and the lake of Trollfjordvatnet with floating pans of ice.

The route gave moderate climbing and easy scrambling with no need for a rope, but required care because of the exposure and steep precipices at times below our feet. At 23.00 we stood on the summit, a narrow high airy pinnacle with big drops all round. To the north the sun shone low above the Arctic Ocean, which reflected it like a vast pool of golden liquid. Islands appeared jet black, with fantastic mountains stretching mysteriously into haze. To the north-east rose Moisalen, highest point in Vesteraalen, a magnificent glaciated peak that now burned red in the sun, especially bright on the snowfield leading to the summit.

We stood in the sun on Austvaagøy's highest peak, and between us and Moisalen stretched the finest mountain land I have ever seen, weird and fascinating in the red midnight light. On the mainland, snow peaks and icecaps north of Narvik glowed with a soft rose colour above lines of haze. A cool breeze blew from the east. South-westwards, thick weather brooded over the Atlantic.

Down the peak we climbed unroped, and along the ridge to the east, up and down pinnacles and rock walls. Wilhelm Hoier and I went ahead. At an exposed spot that required both hands for a delicate move, he decided to drop his axe to a gully 10 feet below and suggested I do the same. Mine rebounded to crash down the cliff. Wilhelm spotted it and shouted "OK". A miraculous escape or I should say a great axe by Simond. It fell 200 feet, leaving only a scratch in the wooden handle.

Magnar had found an easier way for the girls, who were less experienced and slower, and we all arrived on a col. After a rest here till 23.45, when the sun shone close above the sea, Magnar asked me whether we should descend to the glacier or to the corrie to the south. He said the glacier would be more difficult and he knew nothing about the big drop from the glacier tongue to the fjord. I said the glacier would be more interesting but left the decision to him as leader. He chose the corrie, because the glacier might be too difficult for the girls. We climbed down crags, interesting as none of us had been here before, to a standing glissade on snow for 300 feet.

Now we gathered to brew tea on a stove. After feeding to repletion, we descended the vast corrie over rock slabs and snowfields, down by a waterfall where we stood in the spray to cool off, then into the birch wood and so to the camp. At the nearby Post Office, about 50 starlings were roosting on the roof, juveniles and adults mixed. They showed much activity at 03.00, clucking, stretching wings and shaking themselves, for few slept in the bright sun. After coffee and food we went to bed at 04.00.

I felt like the starlings. With bright sunshine on my tent, very warm air inside, and the continual clucking of the starlings, I found it hard to sleep. The eight hours since yesterday evening seemed more like eight days. My mind was in a whirl, thinking of a near-endless array of fantastic rock peaks rising from the sea, glaciers and snowfields, vast ocean and sky, and good comrades, after the most exciting night of my life so far.

Chapter 12 Three mountaineering incidents at Aberdeen

I am going to tell you about three unorthodox "routes" all lying within the boundaries of the city of Aberdeen. I dare not call them climbs and I use even the word route with some trepidation. If you read on, you will see why on this occasion I prefer that much vaguer term "incidents" so beloved to journalists.

The first incident was an ascent of the Mitchell Tower at Marischal College in February 1951. At the time I lived in digs near Clifton Road with a fellow-student of zoology called Bill Jenkins, who was another of these wild Welshmen. He was always thinking up some wonderful, idealistic scheme, and as a debater prize-winner he would argue about each one with great skill till the early hours of the morning. His latest idea was the ever-recurring one of how to put an end to student apathy. All these medicals at Foresterhill knowing nothing about culture, and the science men from Marischal and the arts men from Kings just as antagonistic, and looking down their long noses at each other. The students were split into three irreconcilable blocs. So Jenkins thought what a great idea it would be to bring back the red gown or toga that used to be compulsory wear at one time, and persuade all the students to wear it once again. All red-gowned together, at last the medical, science and arts men would first of all recognise each other as students of Aberdeen University, and so would mix much more freely again. Of course it was a daft idea. First of all, the gowns were expensive. Then they were at best only second-rate substitutes for coats if the weather was bad. Again, nobody could imagine a red-gowned science or medical man mixing chemicals or dissecting intestines in the laboratory. Finally, it pandered to snobbery and uppishness, like most other uniforms, old school ties or club badges.

Still it was a great idea for Jenkins, and he pursued it with unimaginable vigour. Unfortunately the result of his campaign was a damp squib. Nobody cared. What was he to do? The eleventh hour had come; the situation was desperate. Though I had shown contempt for the whole thing right from the start, Jenkins now implored me to help. If only we could do something spectacular, like draping banners from the Mitchell Tower or hanging a red-gowned body from the Rubislaw Quarry, and so I got interested.

We tried the Tower first. It looked formidable. But there was a story that Ludwig had climbed it in the early twenties and had tied a skeleton to the topmost spires, so we were full of hope. As Jenkins had never seen a climbing rope or climbed a crag in his life, we spent a couple of hours that day at Cove. After ten minutes instruction he was moving up and down the cliffs without a rope and without any feeling of exposure. That afternoon, two days before our planned ascent, we went up the Tower to have a look. From the last tiny platform in the final tower, the route didn't look too bad, and the chief problem seemed to be how to get into the Tower at night. Lower down, where the side roofs abut against the Tower, there were several windows and in place of one window was a small wooden door locked on the inside. We undid the catch, and went out the usual way down the stairs along with a few sightseers.

Two nights later we boarded a Seafield bus dressed in old clothes and carrying a rucksack with climbing rope. We clambered over the wall near Queen Street, then up to the quadrangle. This was the danger moment, but there was nobody in sight. We walked as if to go into the Physics Department, but at the last moment turned swiftly into the bell-tower. Moving very carefully past the big bell, we were at last on the side roof. Up a short steep wall where Jenkins' shoulder came in handy for a push up, and there I was looking along a short stretch of roof to the Tower. Through the unlocked window we crept, then up the stairs to the trapdoor leading to the final platform. From here we looked out of glassless windows arched in fancy granite patterns, which gave excellent holds. Reaching up for the topmost arch, we then simply leaned out below the overhanging edge above, and grasped upwards and sideways to get into a cavity alongside one of the four subsidiary towers. After short pull ups, we were beside the subsidiary towers.

It was quite comfortable to sit there, and the view that night was magnificent. The sheer walls below us were remotely bathed in a pale ghostly light from the street lights far below. I remember a wild wind moaning through the arches and beating loud against the walls, and the starlings, disturbed at their roost, chuckling and fluttering below us. The sky was clear and it was cold, and the North Sea was roaring in the distance above the hum of the city. Immediately below, a few people were coming and going around the library, and a car moved out of the quadrangle. Not one of them looked upwards. But then how few people ever do look upwards from the throng, in daylight let alone at night?

Marischal College, 15 February 2006 (courtesy of Aberdeen City Council)

While I was sitting there, Jenkins had nipped smartly ahead up the final steep section, and already he was tying his banner to the metal spike at the top, singing joyfully in the face of the north wind, and waving in victorious abandon. In fact this final section (done alongside the lightning conductor just in case an extra hold was ever needed) was easy as there were plenty of big granite knobs giving holds almost as good as a ladder. Marischal College has often been criticised as a granite monstrosity with its over-ornate towers and countless granite knobs, but no climber criticises a place for having plenty of good holds. We climbed down, not bothering to abseil. Negotiating the overhang back into the platform I found easy, but Jenkins with his much shorter reach found it harder. However, at no point was it ever more than difficult.

Elated, we sped down the stairs, locked the window on the inside to cover our tracks, and opened the Yale lock at the bottom from the inside. Then we tip-toed in stocking soles through the hall, eyed we imagined with disfavour by some of the crustier-looking old characters on the many paintings lining the walls. From there we gained access to the Zoological Museum, after removing a great pile of chairs and replacing them all as carefully and noiselessly as if they were old china. Once in the Zoology Department, we could relax, change our clothes, and then walk out in suits and shoes, saying good-night to the night-watchman as we went out! Next morning the *Press and Journal* had photographs of the Tower with its banner. Unfortunately the wind had increased during the night and had wound the banner round the spike, so that the motto was barely legible.

But now we were for the Rubislaw. A reconnaissance that afternoon was shattering; the place really looked grim. But we were full of hope as Jenkins that night made a man-sized dummy, painting in eyes and leering mouth, and sticking on an old hat and a red gown on it. The problem that now arose was how were we to get from Clifton Road to the quarry in the early morning, without paying for a taxi? The answer soon became obvious: phone a journalist! And so early next morning, while it was still dark, a car drew up for us, with a journalist and photographer from the *Bon Accord* newspaper. In luxury, we sped on up to Rubislaw, enjoying the warmth of the car. It was a raw, foggy and frosty morning, and there was a glaze of ice on the road. We walked straight to the main wire, and at once climbed up a ladder to the platform at the south end, where the cable quickly brings you over the depths down below. We decided to tie ourselves separately by karabiner and rope-sling to the main wire, which is unmovable, and use the movable two thinner cables below for an occasional seat or for foot rests. (The two bottom cables are part of a continuous cable running over pulleys at both ends of the quarry). At once we were up against difficulties. The main wire was thick with grease, and covered with a glaze of thin ice and hoar frost. Our clothes stuck to the wire as if they were glued to it, and handling the frozen wire quickly led to cold fingers. Jenkins, who was carrying the body, got so cold that his fingers lost feeling, and shouted that he couldn't hold the body for much longer. I had to give him my gloves and tie the body to the wire[1]. And yet we had gone only about 200 feet out. The further we went, the more the thinner cables sagged, till soon they became useless as a foot rest. Consequently we had to rely more and more on the main cable, and so the friction increased and it became even more difficult to drag ourselves along.

Over an hour had passed and our progress was at a snail's pace. All this time, we had been completely unaware of the 400-feet chasm below, so difficult was it to move along the wire. But suddenly we heard shouts below, and saw to our consternation that the first workmen had arrived. They were descending the far side, and pointing up at us through veils of fog and frost. Only then did I suddenly become aware of our extraordinary position, dangling in space hundreds of feet above them. But I felt absolutely no trace of exposure whatsoever, and Jenkins later said the same. We could hang there and enjoy it all: here was no "bird's eye view" of the tourist books, but a bird's eye view in reality.

But our composure was shattered as the foreman appeared breathlessly at the top of the quarry near the *Bon Accord* men. He shouted "Call yourselves intellectuals? You stupid b******s"! Realising our insect-like position, as helpless and motionless as whales on dry land, we could only roar with laughter and fully agree with his conclusion. But at this dramatic moment, there was a sudden crunch, and the body of our dummy, sorely tried in our efforts to move it along the wire, came apart from its head. The body sailed gently down through space, the red gown flapping on the way like the wings of a great bird of prey. It came to earth among some small trees near the foot of the cliff, leaving the head with its battered hat, grinning devilishly at us from the wire.

We beat a retreat as fast as we could go. It was much easier now, without the body, and also the frost had slackened and the ice was melting on the cables. Our progress was watched with great interest by the men below, who shouted up a mixture of oaths, laughter and ribald encouragement. Judging from their activity we wondered if they were running a lottery on who would fall first, and how soon. Later, the *Bon Accord* ran the story with photographs in which our blackened faces were unrecognisable and our names kept secret. Later news about the incident came that day from the quarrymen. According to one newspaper report, one of the quarrymen was about to pull the lever that moves the cables so that the men below could get their tools, when at the last minute we were spotted on the wire. The report was written in such a way that people might have thought we were within an inch of death, instead of being safely tied on to the big cable that doesn't move at all.

The finale of these first two incidents was that the students eventually did get interested, Jenkins got his way, and the university and students voted to have the red gown back. So maybe these stunts did have some effect. In the end very few students ever did wear the gown, and student apathy and blocs have been as rife as ever. But that is another story, and I must now tell you about the third incident.

About the autumn of 1951, a rectorial election was held at Aberdeen University, the candidates being Lord Lovat, Captain Farquharson of Invercauld, Paul Robeson, and Jimmy Edwards. Edwards had a vast following right from the start. Most of the Lairig Club members supported Farquharson, led by an enthusiastic Mike Philip, with Bill Brooker as second in command. Almost nobody was interested in Robeson, and it seemed that even in the unlikely event

---

1   We told our plans only to fellow zoology students Ian Forsyth and Sandy Walker. Sandy recalls arriving at the quarry edge with Ian, just as I was giving my gloves to Bill.

Bill Jenkins at Rubislaw Quarry, 12 March 1951

High jinks by Bill Jenkins at Rubislaw Quarry

of his being elected, he would probably be unable to leave the United States, since the McCarthyites were in their heyday at that time. The Robeson faction was led by an extremely clever but rather frail-looking Jew who disliked violence intensely. Eventually came the time for the rectorial fight in the Marischal College quadrangle, a fight which always takes place before the actual election. And it became obvious that the Robeson faction would be unable to put even a five-a-side team into battle. Roy Wilkie, who lived in our digs and was a fervent Robeson supporter, asked us to help. Though the violence of the fight was looked on unfavourably, nevertheless they knew that if Robesonites didn't put up any fight at all, it would be bad for the voting later on. He asked the eight of us Honours Zoology students to help Robeson. None of us had been interested in any of the candidates, but we were all stirred by him enough to help the pitifully outnumbered one or two Robeson warriors. And Jenkins and I began to think of a crafty stratagem.

When all the teams were drawn up, we saw to our horror just how outnumbered we were. There were only about a dozen of us, against masses for every other candidate. The Edwards faction in particular was a minor army. With four teams, two semi-finals had first to be fought, and the first teams drawn were Robeson and Farquharson. Though we had excellent ammunition, including musty fish oil and rat excrement crawling in maggots, the sight of Brooker and Philip laughing derisively at us from the head of their battalion really made us quail. However it was now that we put into action our stratagem for winning the fight even against impossible odds. But first I must explain how the fight is done. Each side in a fight lines up at a door on which the side's flag is nailed very high up to a wooden spar, the opposing side doing likewise at the opposite side of the quadrangle. Each side has attackers and defenders. Whichever side tears down the other side's flag and is first to carry this flag to its home door, wins the fight. Now my idea was to get ready on the roof immediately above one of the doors, and to rope down and throw the flag to Jenkins on the ground, who would be looking out for me and keeping away from other people. The chief trouble was that it was a 50–50 chance that Robeson might draw the door below me, and if so, there would not be time to get across the roof to the other side above the Farquharson door.

The quadrangle was full of men and ammunition, and there were crowds of spectators at the gate, in every window, and scores of them on the roof beside me as I fixed my doubled rope round a suitable projection. Just in case any lunatic Farquharson supporter on the roof tried to cut the rope or yell a warning to his supporters below, I had arranged for Ian Mackay and George Dunnet to be up there with me as stalwarts ready to deal with any kind of trouble. There was a hush as the sacrist tossed a coin, and YES -- Farquharson were to have the door below me! Elated, I got the ropes ready, and prepared to step out, watched anxiously by all the people round about on the roof. A whistle blew, and bedlam broke out below. I swung out in a quick movement, and did a rapid free abseil down the wall below, with the rope simply over my shoulder and between my legs for maximum speed. In what seemed a few seconds after, I tore the Farquharson flag out and started looking for Jenkins. The Farquharson boys were so engrossed in the fight that they hadn't even noticed the loose ends of nylon rope dangling down almost to ground level. Ah! there was Jenkins in an open space, I flung the flag out, and he caught it and ran like a good Welsh-rugger-man, and in a few seconds the whistle blew and the sacrist was shouting that Robeson are the winners. This all happened so fast that I hadn't even time to get to ground level. When the Farquharson men saw what had happened, fury burst out. One of them grabbed the loose ends of rope and swung me about like a yo-yo up and down the wall. Another wildly threw rotten tomatoes. Another threatened "I'll do you in, you b*****"! It was incredible to see how the intelligentsia of Aberdeen could so quickly go berserk. I was in an impossible position, unable to move up or down, now that the ropes were tightly held below. The man holding the ropes was a medical student that I knew but was so crazed meantime that he didn't seem to know me. I announced in the most serious tone I could muster "If you don't let go these ends, I really will give you a hiding next time you set foot in Clifton Road". He complied immediately, and I dropped to earth. All this occupied only a few seconds, and as I reached the ground, the irate Brooker and Co were just arriving at their home door, followed by the victorious zoologists. Bad feelings quickly subsided as the second semi-final was drawn, and all teams combined together in a vain attempt to defeat the vast Edwards contingent.

Some time later, Tom Patey asked me for a loan of a climbing rope, and I told him where he could collect it. After his climb, he asked what gory accident had occurred when I had used that rope, for it was covered in numerous bloody stains. It would have been an opening for a good story, but of course the truth was that the stains of the rotten tomatoes never came out and lasted till the rope was thrown away.

At the next rectorial election, I was on the roof when Kenny Grassick tried to repeat the flag-stealing act. Several of us including Tom Patey and Graeme Nicol acted as guardian angels up above on the roof. Once again, luck held and Grassick's enemy had the door below us. Kenny, instead of doing a free abseil, chose to be let down on a rope from above, so that he could be pulled up if his adversaries used too much violence on him after being defeated. But as soon as he started, we saw the mistake: progress was at a snail's pace compared with a free abseil. Kenny hadn't gone more than a few yards down --- and even this took what seemed an interminable time --- when he was spotted. From then on, tremendous quantities of ammunition fell on him, and the aiming was good. Repeatedly he took a rotten tomato or lump of pig dung full in the face. And anyway the fight was nearly over. We pulled him up and commiserated. He had also suffered from the fact that since the day of my third incident, students at rectorial fights occasionally look upwards as well as forwards.

(1960, *Etchachan Club Journal* 3, 59–70)

The Rubislaw quarry was 466 feet deep, and had been in use for at least 211 years previously. It fell into disuse in 1971 and has since filled with water.

Chapter 13 Thirty miles on ski

Though it was already mid-April, winter still gripped even low ground in the valleys, and the mountains rose in folds of spotless, shiny snow far up into deep blue skies. It was very hard to believe that we were in our own familiar Strath Spey and not in some high valley near the Arctic Circle. But then this was 1951, after the longest cold spell and heaviest snowfalls the central Highlands had seen since 1895. For four days we had been ski-touring back and fore across the Monadh Liath. The severity of the storms up there, and the snow lying right down in the streets of Newtonmore at times, gave us a warning what to expect when we headed up Glen Tromie for the Gaick hills on the 13th April.

AW at start of the Gaick tour (Adam Watson senior)

Loch an t-Seilich of Gaick, 14 April 1951

Upper Glen Feshie with Coire nan Cisteachan on left

It was a very wild morning. Occasional flying showers swept over and enormous snow-plumes hundreds of feet high were billowing into the sky over A' Chailleach of the Monadh Liath. At the top of the glen by Loch an t-Seilich., we had to turn the car, after vainly trying to charge through the drifts. Gaick is notorious for its avalanches, and here several avalanches had recently torn down boulders, mud and snow right to the roadside. That evening, on the long ridge of Sron Bhuirich, I was looking at one of the few double cornices I have yet seen in Scotland; a cornice that had avalanched on both sides. Up at Gaick Lodge, Alick Sutherland had just moved in a week before, after being forced to evacuate as early as December because of the heavy snow and the danger of avalanches. The frost was intense when I turned in at the bothy that night. All around, the immense steep white domes of the hills reared up to a black velvety sky. Not a sound, save at times the faint rushing of some burn far away below the snow, rising and falling as the wind changed.

The next morning was a perfect one: an unclouded blue sky, and a frost of great severity that had even frozen the fast burn down the steep face of Sgor Bhothain. Over the small snow-free patches of ground in the floor of the glen the air was alive with the metallic hum of drumming snipe, the joyous shouting of oyster-catchers and the crying of peewits. It was good to see spring slowly forcing its way up into this snowy wilderness. The unearthly blue of the sky, the heather slopes a rich chocolate colour merging soon with the shimmering snows above, the sun streaming

Looking north to the Cairngorms from Allt a' Chaorainn

through the trees, and the cheery bird songs, all made this one of the finest walks I can remember, in spite of my heavy pack and skis.

I met my father at the dam, and at once we started climbing on ski-skins, away up the great swelling Mullach Coire nan Dearcag. A few hundred feet above the dam, I left behind the last heather and stones I was to see till Geldie Lodge. A wind rose quickly out of the west as we climbed, and dark clouds piled over the Monadh Liath. Twenty minutes later the sun had gone, and menacing clouds of black, orange and white filled the sky. The slope turned icy, so hard that the ski-edges failed to bite; so, for lack of an ice-axe I scraped out edges for our boots with a ski-stick, a slow and tedious job. But then at last here was the plateau, rolling on and on for miles to merge in a grey world of sky and snow. The snow was still hard up here, and we went rattling on at a great pace, the skis slapping on the icy ridges.

As we neared Coire Bhran, there came the quickest weather change we had ever seen. One minute the clouds were overhead and the distant Drumochter peaks still visible, next minute dense cloud all round and a wall of huge snowflakes sweeping down with a loud hiss. It was impossible to see beyond the tips of our skis, so we had to go forward side by side, steering by compass.

Small dips in the snow seemed tremendous gulches and we often fell on flat snow. Afraid of skiing over the cornices of Coire Bhran, we decided to get out. The descent, back the way we had come, seemed endless and desperately tiring, with constant falling on icy snow. We were almost at the dam again, ploughing through three inches of new snow, when out came the sun and there were the snowflakes streaming high above, glistening against blue sky!

We turned again, this time straight into Coire Bhran. In the corrie we parted, my father back to the dam, I to climb to Leathad an Taobhain and beyond. For the last part of the climb, I had to remove skis again and kick steps up an icy slope, while great seas of drift raced past, buffeting my back. Near the top, at almost 3000 feet, I faced back into the gale. Far away to the west, miles away under angry, lowering clouds, a minute black speck stood out sharply in this lonely waste of white. It was my father. I watched the progress of the little speck with interest, as it crawled like some tiny mite or beetle, till the fierce cold forced me to move.

On with the skis. Sailing with the wind behind me, I shot over the top and pointed the skis into the new country that lay ahead. This vast, gently sloping bowl was the Upper Feshie, and today the course of the river was nowhere visible. Now the

Geldie Lodge and An Sgarsoch

snow was powdery on top of a hard-packed surface that had seen no thaw. It was a joy to swing down over waves of snow sparkling in the sun, then to climb again to the tops on the south side. This was the old Mounth plateau, stretching for miles of high ground; there can be few places in Scotland where it would be easier to get lost. Up here it was like being on top of some great ice-cap in the Arctic. There was not a sign of life, no deer, not even a grouse or ptarmigan, nothing, till I spotted a solitary fox crossing the hills. What it was living on and where it was going are a mystery.

Now and again, squalls swept down in a fury of choking drift. At times, I could not even see my skis, but I was always able to press on slowly as I had the wind at my back. But always the squall would pass and the sun would appear again with fierce blinding light. Sometimes I stopped-to watch the drift trails snaking swiftly over the snow, or whirling past like great water spouts. I saw another fox crossing towards lower Feshie, the last sign of life till evening. From the bare top of Carn an Fhidhleir, there was a long run straight downhill for miles towards the Geldie, now over the Spey watershed and into the Dee. Soon I was poling again down in the floor of the glen, and I began to feel tired. It was now five o'clock, and seven hours and 23 miles were behind me since Gaick. Then suddenly round a corner a great black shape loomed: Geldie Lodge!

It was good to sling off heavy pack and skis, collect some blocks of ice to melt for soup, and lie back on a sleeping-bag beside the roaring stove. I soon had a three-course meal, finishing with raspberry jam mixed with powder snow:

Bob Scott and dying stag after a blizzard, morning of 15 April 1951

a magnificent trifle. How strange it was to stand looking out at these broad windows that had seen luxury long ago, away down Glen Geldie and out to Beinn Bhrotain, a terrible arctic wilderness this day. Depressed by the dreariness of the shattered lodge, and feeling in great form again after the meal, at six o'clock I decided to press on for the Linn o Dee.

It was already freezing hard. Outside the lodge I had a bad attack of cramp from sitting too long, but once I was on the move again for half a mile, the last twinges had gone. After climbing the gentle rise to Cairn Geldie, I slid down its far side to the Dee, here hurrying on invisible beneath deep ice and snow. As I was not yet tired, I pushed on up the Fcith nan Sgor hill towards Luibeg, instead of skiing down Glen Dee to the Linn. I had just started the 1000 foot climb when a great storm lashed down in thick black columns.

The slope was very gentle and seemed endless in the midst of heavy falling snow. But at last here was the watershed at Sgor Mor. Just then the snow stopped falling, and the sun peeped out through a hole in the clouds. It glinted on the great waste of Glen Geldie and on the edges of all the hills. Geldie Lodge looked the loneliest place on earth; a tiny black dot in a pool of gold light. I watched the sun sink behind the wild clouds that were to bring an all-day blizzard by the next morning. The Cairngorms turned iron-grey in the afterlight. Away east, down Deeside and far beyond into space, the sky turned from a translucent, duck-egg green to a murky purple. It was time to go.

Northwards I pointed the skis, far away down to the wind-swept corner of the old pine wood on the shoulder of

Ski-run down Luibeg wood as seen on 18 April

Sgor Dubh. Then swoop after swoop on a velvety snow carpet through the trees at high speed, with care thrown to the winds now that I was so near the end of the journey, and at last down the steep bank to Luibeg. It was half-past eight and dusk was falling. I could scarcely believe I had been talking to Alick Sutherland at Gaick only about ten hours before. So many glens and hills and changing scenes had passed on this long trek that it seemed to have taken days. Then I suddenly remembered: it was my 21st birthday! Could any present have been finer than this one that would last a lifetime in the memory?

(1958, *Etchachan Club Journal* 2, 186–190)

Chapter 14 Recollections of the Gaick-Luibeg ski-tour

Here I copy my diary, but the entry for 14 April ended half way through my tour. I add some other recollections that were not in my article.

13 April. Skiing on hills beside Gaick Lodge

A wild morning at Newtonmore, with occasional flying showers and a strong wind blowing huge snow plumes off A' Chailleach. Dad and I drove to Gaick in his car. He would have come to stay there, but isn't quite better yet from a bad cold. The sun came out as we turned up into the glen, though clouds black as night towered over the shimmering white bulk of Meall Chuaich, a fine contrast. The Glen Tromie woods were silent, but we saw a cock sparrow-hawk, and a dipper on the river.

Views were spectacular all the time as we got further into these wild bare hills. There was still a lot of snow on the road. Just beyond the dam, where snowdrifts had collected in the shelter of the birch wood, we had to charge them with the car, and eventually decided it was too risky to go further, especially as the road itself was sticky due to the sun's warmth at noon in this sheltered place. I carried on after seeing the car safely turned with only inches to spare where the slope tumbled to the loch. Avalanches had come down the gullies here and filled the watercourses with snow, mud, and gravel even to the roadside.

Little life stirred among the leafless trees, but at the loch-head and on the marshy flat above, many common snipe drummed, a goosander pair and a mallard pair swam on the loch, and a few oystercatchers called at the loch-side. Peewits swung overhead and the wind hummed in their wings as they tumbled about in display. Many rabbits scampered about on the dry slope east of the road, surprising in view of the severe past winter.

At the lodge a pair of pied wagtails hunted on the short grass. Alick Sutherland was having a meal and in no time I was sitting at table with a mountain hare's leg before me. We had much to tell each other. It's not long since he came back -- he evacuated in December due to the severity of the weather and the risk of avalanches, down to Glentromie Lodge, and since he came back 10–14 days ago his road had been blocked again. The red deer, he said, all went down to Glen Tromie woods, no stags or hinds remained at Gaick, and all went down to the woods, where few have died. Some of them are back on the flats beside the lodge now. The keeper at Sronphadruig has been blocked in since November. He stayed alone and skied to Dalnacardoch once a week for provisions. What an existence. He has been there a quarter of a century. Alick heard that the snow came up nearly to the roof -- Sronphadruig Lodge is in a sheltered hole.

I walked out and across the bridge, then along the flat below Sgor Dearg. The sun was out and only a few cotton-wool clouds raced across the sky. It was good looking across to the wee lodge under the great bulk of Sgor Bhothain, its gullies like great white ribs, packed with snow. Sron Bhuirich was quite immaculate right down to the floor of the glen – here too, on the ridge flung out towards the lodge, a double cornice had formed and avalanched on both sides. You could see it from the lodge. I came to the snowline at once and skied up the glen of Allt Coire an Dubh-chadha. It could have been in the Himalayas -- walled in by great snowy peaks and rocky walls plastered in green ice and snow, below huge cornices from which tufts of drifting snow raced into the blue sky. Avalanches had come down on every face -- some big ones too. Probably they came down yesterday with the softer conditions and big snowfall.

I climbed high on the hill to the south, the skins failed to grip eventually and I had to climb up the ridge cutting small steps by ice-axe. Wind was terrific, yet the sun still shone, only a few clouds. At times though, everything was choking with drift blown from other hills by particularly strong gusts. There were wild views through to Sronphadruig and Beinn Dearg, and the hills of Atholl beyond a Loch Bhrodainn still ice-packed like the floes of an arctic sea. The line of continuous snow ran just above the glen floor, except on sheltered south-facing slopes where the sun was melting it fast. I glissaded to the skis, as it would have been impossible to go higher. There followed a very fast, exciting, and at times almost uncontrollable ski-run down to the bottom of the glen. About 50 stags and hinds were feeding beyond.

I crossed below Sgor Dearg and went up into the corrie of Bogha-cloiche in Coire Madagan Mor. The summit ridge of Sgor Dearg showed a huge edge of snow or ice on its cornice. The cornice on Bogha-cloiche was double (the diary included a sketch showing a cornice at the top skyline and another lower down) -- both had avalanched and big cracks almost like crevasses broke the steep snow slope below and beside the lower cornice. Up in this lonely corrie with the glacier-like cracks and the rock faces on the Sgor Dearg side rimmed with ice and fog crystals, one could have been in the Arctic.

The sun had gone beyond clouds and hills, the frost already hard. I returned to the lodge. We had tea and spent the night till late on, round the fire without a light, chatting away. Late on, I turned in at the bothy. The snow had frozen hard. The frost was severe and though the wind had died, there were slight breezes now and again that penetrated to the bone. There was a magnificent show of stars despite the glorious moonlight flooding the glen. These ghostly looking white hills contrasted with the dark, star-spattered sky, a noise of burns came from far away now and again as wind currents changed, then silence. Gaick? Some folk say, nothing but peat-hags and rotten weather.

14 April. From Gaick to the upper Feshie

My 21st birthday and a perfect morning -- a frost of great severity had frozen even the fast burn running off Sgor Bhothain. The air was alive with the metallic humming sounds of drumming snipe and crying peewits. Breakfast, then I left. Alick was sorry to see me go and tried to get me to stay. I'd intended to go tomorrow, but in view of the uncertainty of the weather decided to go today.

The walk down to the dam was one of the finest I can remember. The crispness of the air, the unearthly blue of the loch and beyond it the heather slopes of rich chocolate colour merging into the sparkling whiteness of the snows, the sunlight streaming through the trees, and the shouting of oystercatchers. Creamy clouds began to drift across the sky, tracing blue shadows on the snow.

I met Dad at the dam and he was feeling in better trim. Last night he went up to Drumochter and saw a remarkable sunset from the Laggan moors, looking towards Creag Meagaidh. We climbed up a couple of hundred feet and put on skis, and then up into the west corrie (Coire nan Dearcag) of Mullach Coire nan Dearcag. The sky was becoming more and more clouded, especially to the west, and a wind getting up, only slight yet. On the upper slopes we found the snow frozen hard, and eventually had to traverse off the face of the corrie and on to the ridge, kicking slight steps. Where the ridge met the plateau, it was almost ice in places.

Then at last we reached the flat plateau, where we slipped on our skis and skimmed along, the skis slapping loudly like shots from small rifles as we crossed icy ridges at speed. The weather to the west was very dirty -- we could see A' Chailleach and Carn Sgulain looking white in very flat light, and then suddenly the clouds dropped several hundred feet. Within a minute or two it was snowing. We continued to ski swiftly, shoving with the sticks at a nice rate. There were extremely wild views over the plateau to Beinn Dearg and through a hole in the cloud to Sgor Dearg rapidly being engulfed in storm, and then the blizzard was on. Within a couple of minutes, visibility was practically nil, we lost the sense of position by visual means and could only guess it by strain or lack of strain on muscles – very tiring. Hardly ever have I seen snow falling so thickly. As the plateau was under a complete covering of unknown depth, and smoothed out, no stones were showing.

In view of cornice danger we decided to get out, and went down to the north, down a steep gully where the new snow had already piled up an inch deep. Skiing was blind with many tiring falls. We stuck together and at last got out of the mist. Snow was sticky as we pushed with sticks down to the moor. Prospects were grim, for the snow was still falling very thickly and becoming wet. We turned back towards the dam and after going some way we saw the sun appearing.

Now we retraced our marks eastwards and after a tour on the flat for some way we skied down better snow to a burn beautifully corniced on both sides. The sun came out and felt like fire on our faces. We were at the foot of Coire Bhran. Up top were huge snow domes, with heavy cornices on the Bhran top and the Mullach Coire, both of which had avalanched. We had lunch – it was 12.30 p.m., fine to sit there in shelter, watching the burn gurgling through snow banks.

We skied on to the next burn -- just then it looked like another storm coming. Dad decided to go back, especially as he had no map. Still I gave him a perfect line for his compass. But to get back he had to face the wind, not very strong but getting stronger, and the skiing in the face of these blizzards had been no fun. He wished he could come on with me all the way (to Geldie) -- I'm sure he could have too, but there it was -- another parting.

Why is it that a parting in the hills is such a sad thing? Had we parted yesterday on the Gaick road, our exchanges *would have been flippant. Soon we'd have forgotten each other. But after a bit of comradeship in the face of trying conditions, it is sad to part. We talked for a while, ate oranges, spoke of everything about today and nothing about the outside world. It seems silly now to think of us then, father and son, one nearly three times as old as the other. It certainly didn't seem so then. Comradeship in the mountains is truly the highest form of comradeship in existence.*

A storm came on and we left, I to plod up to the bulky summit of Leathad an Taobhain, he to return over the lonely moors of Gaick. By now a change had taken place. The falling snow was dry and stinging, the snow beneath my skis crisp and frosty. At the top of Leathad, after a hard climb, for the last part kicking steps in hard frozen snow while seas of drift raced past, buffeting my back, I turned into the wind. Far away over the white space to the west was a black speck. I followed its progression with interest till the fierce cold drove me to action.

On with the skis, and a new country lay on the far side -- the upper Feshie. Beyond lay Carn an Fhidhleir and the Cairngorms, on the right the plateaux stretching out to Beinn Dearg, The sun had come out, shining with powerful light on this white wilderness. I skied to the col lying to the east, where a curious snow whirl had formed a deep gully on a quite open slope. Then with the wind and another squall behind me, I skied into the Feshie basin. Not a black speck was to be seen for miles.

Later recollections

The above ended the diary entry, but here is more that I remember. On 13 April we hoped to drive to Gaick Lodge, but snow blocked the road, so I continued on foot. We agreed to meet next morning at the dam, walk to the lodge, and ski nearby. I had intended to ski to Deeside next day, but the weather was so fine on the 14th that I decided to try that day. Had I delayed till the 15th, gales and snowfalls for days would have precluded a crossing.

After breakfast with Alick Sutherland at Gaick, I walked to the dam. My father, now in better form after a good dinner and a sleep at Main's Hotel in Newtonmore, suggested skiing up the snowy hill above the dam. So we climbed a steep heathery hillside and soon donned our skis.

On the plateau we skied quickly on icy snow, sailing with the wind. It was exciting and we put distance behind in short time. At A' Chioch we turned south and crossed the next plateau when the blizzard struck. In the whiteout I steered by compass, taking bearings with my father as marker. Staying close, we returned to the plateau's west end before I deemed it safe to ski north, eventually beside the snow-covered burn in Coire nan Dearcag. After emerging from the mist, for the rest of the day I did not use compass or map.

The sun appeared, so we turned east and lunched at Allt Coire Bhran. Then we skied east again to the burn of Maschaochan, where we parted. As I climbed to Leathad an Taobhain, dark clouds threatened snow. By now it was too late to turn back and catch up with my father, but I thought that if a blizzard came I could easily ski down into Glen Tromie or round to Glenfeshie Lodge.

On the summit I turned to look west. My father, a small black speck, was conspicuous miles away in a white landscape, moving steadily west. In 10 minutes he would be at his car.

Luck now came with a rapidly enlarging expanse of blue sky. To my right stretched a white plateau to Beinn Dearg and other shining snowy hills above the glens of Atholl. Just left of the broad whaleback towards Carn an Fhidhleir I saw far down the slopes of the upper Feshie. Further left soared the Cairngorms, high above all else. The light reflected by the snow shone with dazzling brilliance.

I put on my skis and shot quickly southeast. Skiing was easy, though the surface streamed with dense ground-drift up to waist height and occasionally above my head. At times I could just see my skis, even though the sun and blue sky shone brightly above. The experience was novel and enjoyable, moving downhill effortlessly so soon after climbing steeply on foot.

As I skied towards the next top, Glas-leathad Feshie, the wind eased, ground-drift stopped, and a quick run ensued in clear light on sparkling fresh powder with some tiny ridges of soft grey old snow. In my diary I noted a gully with a snow-whirl on an open slope. A creature of deep snow and wind, it does not exist in summer. It would be a hazard in whiteout or snowfall if one skied with little care.

At the col west of Glas-leathad Feshie the main climbing was past. It would be easy and swift to continue on packed powder along the broad ridge to Carn an Fhidhleir or An Sgarsoch before dropping to Geldie Lodge. However, just as I was about to start the short climb to the east, without skins, dark clouds appeared above Leathad an Taobhain and the gale renewed, portents of a snow-squall that leaped down furiously within a minute. I decided to move off the exposed plateau and turned north towards the upper Feshie basin.

With the gale at my back, I skied carefully downhill into increasing shelter. When I had descended two hundred yards, snowflakes stopped falling, the gale eased, and brilliant sun appeared. I was standing on a superb surface of packed powder. After a joyous run east of Allt Clais Damh, swinging towards the upper Feshie, I climbed back to Glas-leathad Feshie because the fine weather still held.

Up again on hard-packed powder and icy ridges, the skis slid swiftly, almost effortlessly. A strong wind at my back helped me along, often without using sticks. I crossed the plateau of Glas-leathad Feshie quickly and turned south towards Glen Bruar. I had just reached the next col, looking past An Sligearnach into Atholl, when dark clouds lowered again on Leathad an Taobhain and the wind rose, heralding another snow-squall.

It became very wild up there as the now indistinct horizon edge smoked with heavy drift, and snow plumes raced high into the blue sky. I turned towards Feshie again and came into the Coire Breac, where uniform packed powder extended in every direction. Another snow-squall now darkened the sky, and in the ensuing snowfall and ground-drift I could not see my skis, but I moved slowly on a gentle gradient downhill with the wind at my back.

Shortly the snowflakes stopped and the sun peeped out. However, I decided that the storms were too frequent and thick to continue all the way along the tops to Carn an Fhidhleir, so I turned northeast. Now came a glorious long run down the ridge east of Caochan na Laire Fiadhaiche to the glen floor. Not a stone or plant broke the white blanket.

Then I skied east along the flat moor north of the river Feshie. There were several dense snowstorms with whiteout, but always the blue sky would appear again and the sun shine with brilliant light on newly fallen powder that sparkled with myriads of diamonds. In good light I glided swiftly south of An Eilrig and crossed the invisible Feshie where it turns northeast beside the wee burn of the Cruaidh-alltan.

Now I stopped in mid afternoon to enjoy the views during a sunny spell with less wind. I took a photograph looking back the way I had come, into the light and across miles of snow that shimmered with a silky silvery sheen. The blue sky was dimmed by millions of fine snow particles, blowing as a thin snow-squall passed, and distant ragged clouds in the west threatened a squall to come. However, the wind had eased, snow-squalls had become fewer, and sunshine blazed most of the time. For miles the snow had been so good that skiing was almost effortless, especially with the wind helping me. I decided to go higher for the views and greater variety of ski-running.

An easy climb followed on skins round Meall Tionail to Carn an Fhidhleir. Views were outstanding, with ever more variety of far panoramas, nearby slopes, and snow and rime and hoar frost and ice at or near my skis, an endless parade of sparkling snow and ice and wilderness. Gales had scoured the top of Carn an Fhidhleir, but rime covered the few boulders above the snow, and sheaths of blue-green ice gleamed beside them. To the south, the spotlessly white glens and hills of Tarf and Tilt stretched into distant haze. It seemed an endless snowy world under a vast blue sky.

I turned north for a continuous long run for miles into Glen Geldie. At the end of it I stopped to look back to Carn an Fhidhleir and Meall Tionail, their snowy tops glistening in strong sunlight against a blue sky, and ground-drift smoking as a renewed gale whipped the high ground. Down in the glen though, the wind had fallen to a breeze, enough to drift snow at the surface, but at times mere eddies that could not stir even the finest snow particles.

I came upon a small open section of Allt a' Chaorainn in the shelter of an overhanging snow-bank, the first liquid since Allt Coire Bhran. I drank copiously. During the tour I had sucked rime crystals or snow, a poor substitute. The water refreshed me beyond measure. Just the sight of it running a few yards was a tonic, and the sounds as it hurried round corners before diving under snow were magical restful music after hours of roaring wind and hissing drift.

I felt the sun warm on my skin and clothes. Snow on my boots melted and the leather dried in the warm air. It was good to stop several minutes to relax and appreciate this wonderful spot. That and the drink gave me a great mental and physical boost. I had already had the best day of my life and now was enjoying it more than ever.

Onwards again I skied with renewed energy, east for mile after mile along the wide white glen. I enjoyed some nice long glides down gentle slopes, aided by using the sticks to attain a faster speed. There were occasional short climbs, however, and my arms began to tire with the frequent poling. Then I saw Geldie Lodge suddenly appear, the first large dark snow-free object I had seen since the heathery bank by the dam. Tiredness vanished!

Within a few minutes I reached the front door, took off skis and sticks, and laid them against the stone wall. A small patch of grass shone an unearthly vivid green after miles of snow and ice and cloud and sky. For the first time since the dam I put my feet on horizontal snow-free vegetation and walked on to a flat, solid, stone doorstep. The movements on such easy ground were ungainly and awkward, a strange feeling after hours of the different rhythms of skiing and stepping on snow of varying texture and softness. Suddenly also, the need for concentration, determination and willpower had passed. It was almost an anticlimax. My enthusiasm and passion for being on the tour were also no longer relevant or important.

I walked into the big downstairs room, my boots banging on the wooden floorboards, a harsh, noisy contrast from the soft crunching and whispering and tinkling of skis and sticks on snow. Next I heaved my rucksack on to the floor with another thump. The room with its plaster walls and ceiling and its wide glass windows was silent and dry, out of the wind and the snow. The sudden change after many miles of snow and storm felt very strange. Inside, the air was cold and frosty, colder than in the sun outside. I could see my breath. The air felt humid and damp. At first the room seemed almost half dark after the brilliant sun and glistening snow outside, until my eyes became used to the dim light.

That moment's contemplation while I stood was long enough -- now for action. I pulled out the contents of my rucksack in readiness for a comfortable warm dry night, fetched snow to melt for soup and tea, started my primus stove, and made and ate a large meal while lying on my sleeping bag against the rucksack. I finished with a trifle of raspberry jam mixed with powder snow, a recipe I had often used on tours, followed by cups of hot tea.

Afterwards I stood at the broad front window to look at the view. The meal along with the physical and mental rest for an hour had done wonders, psychological and physical. In the article I described how I decided to ski to the Linn of Dee that evening instead of next morning. I packed my rucksack, closed the front door, and put my skis on again for a fast run on partly icy snow down to the Geldie Burn and across it on a continuous safe snow-bridge. I was delighted to be on the move again; gliding downhill and covering the ground more quickly than in summer.

As I began to climb the far side, cramp seized my legs, but with a good skiing rhythm I recovered, and climbed easily without skins up the gentle slope to Cairn Geldie. From there it would be short work to ski to the White Bridge and along the road to the Linn of Dee, downhill with the wind behind me. I reckoned I would be seeing my friend Willie Grant, deerstalker at the Linn of Dee Cottage, well within the hour.

But tiredness had gone, I had developed a fast easy rhythm, the sun shone from a blue sky peppered with only a few white puffs of cloud, and the wind had died to a cooling breeze. I decided it would make a better tour to climb the Feith nan Sgor hill and end the day with a long run to Luibeg, instead of down the Glen Dee road to the Linn. So I skied quickly down the slope northeast of Cairn Geldie and skimmed across the river Dee on a deep firm blanket.

I had just started the long climb with skins up Sgor Mor, when dark clouds quickly obscured the sun. Snowflakes began to fall in windless humid air, and within a minute a storm descended with heavy snow falling in thick black columns, accompanied by a rising west wind that lashed the snow. I pressed on, full of energy and confidence on ground that was increasingly familiar to me. Heavy snow fell throughout the climb, which seemed very long because at most I could see only a few yards in any direction. Just as I reached the rime-sheathed granite tors at the summit, the snow ceased and out came the sun through a big hole in the clouds. What a bonus!

After a few minutes to look at the view, certainly the most striking of the whole tour, there followed a long run down to Luibeg. The last glide through the old pinewood was superb, the best I had ever seen it, undoubtedly the best downhill run of the day. The snow was superlative, a deep carpet of velvety packed powder, so uniform in texture and firmness that I could make my own slalom time and again as I whirled around old pines or swooped between them. A final rush down the steep bank beside the fenced field led to flat ground past the barn. The bothy was empty but a light shone in the cottage window.

I took my skis off, laid them against the porch, and knocked on the door. Wearing slippers, deerstalker Bob Scott opened it. "Faar (Where) have ye been wi that muckle pack, Adam?" "Gaick", I said. Astonished, he exclaimed "Gaick? God almichty, fit a lad ye are! Come in oot o that caal nicht". He ushered me to the kitchen, where his wife Helen beamed happily. For years they had treated me like a son and had been used to my appearing, often without their knowing, day or night, over the Cairngorms from Speyside or up from Braemar. But Gaick was something different! Bob said snowdrifts had blocked his road to the Linn of Dee and he had never seen so much snow.

Other comments on the tour

I saw no birds or deer, and no tracks. They had deserted the whole area. Even in lower Glen Geldie, where some heather was snow-free, I saw none. Single foxes were the only animals seen on the ski-tour. Each was a loner like me, crossing miles of snow. I enjoyed the distant company.

My wooden ex-army skis with steel edges weighed 20 lb the pair. The Kandahar bindings had three positions, the loosest for heel-lifting. On the tour I used the loose one, but changed to intermediate for steeper downhill runs. I used brown wax, and white for sticky snow. Ski-sticks were of heavy bamboo, painted white, with leather handles and wide wooden baskets held by leather thongs. For tying each boot to its ski, so that skis could not come off in a fall and be lost, potentially fatal on long remote tours, I used thick bootlaces of whale-hide from the eastern Canadian Arctic, as traditionally worn on boots in northeast Scotland.

Ski-skins with white canvas backing were heavy, with leather thongs and metal clips. I wore ordinary hill-walking boots with curved profile, because we could not buy ski-boots with edges of straight profile. Vibram soles gripped well when I took skis off to cross hard snow or ice. Army-type ankle gaiters kept most snow out of my boots, but less effectively than the later snow-gaiters. Ex-army goggles reduced the bright light very well.

My rucksack was heavy, with a metal frame. I carried spare pairs of trousers, socks and gloves, sleeping bag and groundsheet, primus stove and pans, kettle, spare paraffin, meta fuel, matches, food for three days, mug, plate, fork, knife and spoon, hunting knife, camera, binoculars, notebook and diary, sun-cream, one-inch to the mile map, and a heavy ex-army prismatic compass. Clothes were woollen: vest, pants, shirt, trousers, jersey, socks, gloves and balaclava, plus leather mitts attached to a strap for going round my neck, and a canvas hooded anorak.

I had used my ice-axe at Gaick on the 13th, but next morning left it in my father's car, thinking I would not need it on the gentler slopes to Geldie. In fact, it would have saved much time and effort on icy snow at Mullach Coire nan Dearcag.

Retrospective thoughts by my father

My father recalled the Gaick trip after skiing from Coire Cas to Ben Macdui on 22 April 1956 and writing in his diary *It's grand to be away from Coire Cas and the mass of humans, but in a longer tour like this, the shared enjoyment is missing when alone. One is 'keyed' up to the need for judging how far one can get with the snow conditions and the weather. There's a tremendous feeling of comradeship too when accompanied on the biggish outing. What is finer in all this weary world's possessions than true companionship, and undoubtedly the acid test is on a mountain trip. I still have lingering memories – sad to think they are so far back-– of saying goodbye to Adam when he did the Gaick to Luibeg trip in the one day. He, off to the tops and a wonderful day, I, back to the Gaick road, and returning alone. I felt he was off on a great adventure, and gladly, I would have joined him and gone through, than retrace my steps while often looking back to see how he progressed. What a companionship there is to be found in the lonely spaces.*

Hallucination after I left Geldie Lodge

As I wrote in the article, outside the lodge I had a bad attack of cramp from sitting too long, but once I was on the move again for half a mile, the last twinges had gone. These were cramps in my legs. Half a mile to the northeast, I stopped on a hillock to remove goggles and take a photograph into a gleaming pool of silvery light up the glen. I scanned with binoculars, but saw no deer or grouse or human, any of which would have been obvious miles away.

Then to the west I noticed a person 500 yards away, conspicuously black against the snow. The figure walked slowly towards me and then vanished behind a dip. I waited a minute, but nothing moved. Skiing to a higher ridge where I could view the dip, I saw no dark object even through binoculars. So I stopped being concerned, donned the goggles again and continued on ski, though still curious and turning a few times to look back.

Two years later, after a more strenuous journey alone in arctic Canada, I became used to hallucinations. Several times I saw a tall man waving beside a tent beside a frozen lake. I waved and shouted, but as I came nearer, the apparent man and tent became real boulders. After no sleep for three nights and no meal for three days, and laborious wading uphill in deep snow, I began to suffer cramp in my legs. Also I was expecting to see Pat Baird the expedition leader, because he had said he would come to meet me on that day. Earlier in that forenoon I had come across his fresh footprints in the deep snow, recognised his boots from the footprints, and then used the footprints to ease my walking. It struck me then in Baffin Island that I must have had a hallucination at Geldie, owing to cramp and perhaps looking into intense light too long without goggles.

Chapter 15 Through the Lairig Ghru in four hours using skis

It was 23 April 1951 and another frosty sunny morning dawned at Cannich village. Cock chaffinches sang loudly and incessantly in the gardens. On a treetop a mistle thrush piped boldly, that wonderful song of the stormcock. It rose defiantly above the rush of the river, high with snow-melt after three warm days.

My parents, elder brother and I left by car. What a perfect morning this was in the heart of the Highlands. Every bend of the road down Strath Glass and winding among the tall dark trees high above the river Beauly revealed a fresh picture of bursting spring. On the low ground towards Inverness, two vast snowy bens dominated the land, the real Ben Wyvis to the northwest, the other its reflection on the calm waters and shining mudflats of the Beauly Firth.

At Inverness I could have continued the leisurely journey by car to Turriff, followed by bus to Aberdeen next afternoon, before resuming university classes the following morning. My choice, already made at Cannich, was to go to catch a train from Inverness to Aviemore, walk and ski through the Lairig Ghru, and then next day walk to Braemar and bus to Aberdeen. With the hills so deep under snow and the weather so bright and settled, I had not the slightest doubt. Leaving most of my equipment in the car, I took the very minimum into Inverness station: skis and sticks, and a small rucksack with ski-skins, laces for tying ski-bindings to boots, leather mitts, ski-wax, suncream, goggles, sunhat, camera and binoculars.

As the train climbs the long bend above Culloden, it gives one of the best views of the Highlands. Today was superlative, with ever more snowy peaks appearing as the engine puffed and pulled higher and higher above the Moray Firth. I stood at the corridor window, gazing at range after range of hills. It seemed a pity to leave this fantastic snow wonderland. All too soon, the wonderland fell behind as the train headed south. But then a new exciting prospect opened as the train thundered from the Slochd moors down into the great pinewoods of Strath Spey. Ahead, the high long rampart of the Cairngorms gleamed, still spotless. In the middle of the rampart beckoned the Lairig Ghru, a great snowy V. It was coming ever and ever closer by the minute.

As I dismounted at Aviemore to cross the station footbridge and walk south down the street, the sun was warm, the sky cloudless, and only a slight eddy stirred the leafless twigs of the silver birches. Ahead, the snow seemed no less continuous than when I had skied off Braeriach four days before. In the Pot Luck tearoom in the south end of the village I ate a good lunch, followed by cups of tea. At the next table sat a few English hill-walkers about to return south by rail. Laborious wading in deep snow had confined them to the woods. Pointing to my skis, they asked "Where are you going tomorrow"? I replied "I'm about to leave this afternoon to ski through the Lairig Ghru to Luibeg". They were astonished that I would leave so late in the day, until I told them of my recent ski-tours. I said "I expect to reach Luibeg at the latest by nine in the evening, before dark". They came to the door to wave and wish me good luck.

At 2 o' clock I left. Shouldering skis and sticks, I strode down the road towards the Spey and Coylumbridge. Then I took the path to the Cairngorm Club footbridge and beyond, one of my favourite walks in Scotland. I hardly felt the weight of my skis and small pack, for I was now very fit. Obviously the anticyclone still held sway, but the sun was the warmest this year, so I knew that the snow would have softened.

Much snow still lay in the upper parts of the wood and in open glades with heather. The snow was loose and wet. Among the outer trees, however, the air became markedly cooler. Suddenly I came to continuous snow and put on my skis, just before half past three. At once I saw that the surface was exceptional. The sun had softened it enough to give the skis a grip for ascent without skins, and yet I sank no more than an inch. I had never seen so much snow in the pass, burying every boulder, peat-hag and burn under a deep smooth packed blanket. I could point the skis in a straight line uphill and travel at more than four miles per hour. An invigorating cool breeze blew down from the south, and a few puffy thin clouds formed on the skyline edge south of the March Burn. I found the going almost effortless and developed a nice rhythm. It was much quicker and easier than walking the rough wet path of the Lairig in snow-free conditions.

My film had one exposure left. I saved it for a view of the Lairig summit from the Pools of Dee, pools that now

Looking north from the Pools of Dee, afternoon of 23 April 1951

lay invisible under deep snow. On the south side I pointed my skis straight downhill for a run at about 20 mph. The snow was so uniform that while skiing down I could turn my head to look back at my tracks down from the summit, or sideways at the striking views up to the Garbh Choire Mor. The heavy wide ex-army skis gave good stability, splendid on spring snow.

As I reached a gentler gradient my speed slowed, but I still kept up an easy six miles per hour by using the sticks for extra push, and continued almost as quickly on the flat stretch by Clach nan Taillear. Then I began the climb up easy gradients to Sron Carn a' Mhaim, keeping the route as near a straight line as possible. Because of alternate slight thawing and freezing, the snow had become far more uniform than on my tour past here on 19 April. I flashed on at a great pace on the long traverse round Carn a' Mhaim. Soon I was looking down a steeper slope to the Luibeg Burn and the ancient pinewoods of Glen Luibeg. Today it gave a fast exciting ski-run on uniform firm spring snow, in brilliant sunlight.

Taking off my skis for the first time since Rothiemurchus, I clambered down the boulders at the footbridge to the first water I had seen since near the Cairngorm Club footbridge, and took a long drink, always marvellous to a thirsty skier! It was good to be back in this glen that I knew so well. Behind, snowy Carn a' Mhaim peeped through gaps in the bottle-green foliage of the old pines. After miles of snow, the rough reddish bark made a fine contrast, and felt warm to the touch. I could smell the resinous scent. Ahead, Lochnagar's snows were suffused in the evening sunlight with a creamy glow. In windless air, the only sounds came from the restful rush of the Luibeg Burn. The glen was peaceful, perfect.

Four days before, I had skied from the gate of Luibeg cottage all the way along the path to the footbridge. Since then, sunshine had melted much snow on the path, but the north-facing slope south of the burn still held continuous wide cover. I slipped on the skis again to slide on perfect snow under the dappled shade of the old pines of Preas nam Meirleach, and then swiftly down the moor. A short climb ensued to the hillock with many fallen trees at the corner of the main wood on Sgor Dubh. From there a grand new prospect opened, downhill across the pines to the green grassy flats of the Derry, speckled with many grazing stags. Blue smoke curled upwards from a chimney of Luibeg Cottage. What a delight!

Below me now stretched the best run of the day, an exciting swoop on deep snow through the wood. I whizzed down around the old trees, on spring snow that had started to firm with the coming of evening frost. Whenever I turned, my skis swished through tiny plates of loose ice that flew out with tinkling sounds. I decided I must return at the weekend to ski on this superb run. (I did, with my father and Norman Tennent).

Continuous snow ended at the foot of the wood. There followed a short walk on foot, traversing the steep bank above the burn. I saw small dark trout in midstream, swaying their tails in the clear water above spreads of pale coarse sand. Past the barn and bothy I strode, and soon was speaking to Bob and Helen Scott in their kitchen. The time was 6 o' clock, an easy four hours since Pot Luck. It had been my shortest crossing of the Cairngorms, yet leisurely.

Had the morning frost been less hard or the afternoon air warmer, the snow might have been sticky and the skiing laborious. As it was, the tour excelled. I had been fortunate indeed. It was by far the most carefree tour I had ever done across the Cairngorms. On the Gaick trip nine days before, the weather was so stormy and cold that a serious mistake could easily have resulted in death, and I knew it. The Lairig was the opposite, with such settled weather and superlative snow that I felt less tired on reaching Luibeg after 18 miles than when I strode down the tarmac road out of Aviemore.

Next forenoon I left my equipment at Luibeg, apart from binoculars, sunhat and an exposed film, for I would return to ski at the weekend. Then I walked down to Braemar. It was yet another glorious day. Chaffinches chirped in the old pines around the cottage, and a robin and a wren voiced their ownership of the henhouse and barn. From far up the steep wood of Sgor Dubh came the strong sweet notes of a stormcock, like the one at Cannich yesterday morning. On the grass field a pair of oystercatchers called excitedly in a crescendo of loud notes, proclaiming their solitary domain of Luibeg and the Derry.

I strolled across the flats to the Derry, and then down the long dusty road of Glen Lui, where much snow still lay deeply. For the first time in two days I saw red grouse, in small packs on the snow-free ridges. At times they bickered noisily, a sign that soon they would disperse to take territories and pair for the nesting season. Many mountain hares sat on snow-free heather, beginning to show some of their dark new summer coat. In the Lairig Ghru, Glen Dee and Glen Luibeg, the snow cover had been too deep and complete to afford worthwhile feeding for grouse or hares, so they had left, for months. They had moved quarters, for miles.

Golden plovers piped mournfully in song-flights over the peat-bogs. Nearby, curlews sang their magical music of wailing followed by tremulous bubbling as they glided above grassy patches, their long curved bills pointing down at the chosen domains where they would soon nest. Hundreds of thin stags grazed quietly there, while others lay chewing the cud on dry heather banks, enjoying glorious warm sunshine after a desperate winter. They were the fortunate survivors, for hundreds of their fellows had fallen in the blizzards of early and mid April, not to rise again.

From the Black Brig I climbed up the track towards Mar Lodge through the finest stand of ancient pines in Scotland, with superb views of the Cairngorms and the hills of Ey and Geldie. I could see much of the route of my tour from Gaick on 14 April. The upper glens out to Leathad an Taobhain still lay under unbroken snow. But mistle thrushes now sang from the pines, and blackcocks bubbled at their display-ground lek on a grassy clearing in the old birkwood of the Garbh-allt above Claybokie. Spring was pushing strongly into an exceptionally wintry landscape for 24 April.

In Braemar I mounted the red Strachan's bus to Aberdeen and sank into a comfortable red-cushioned seat. As usual there was a feast of colour from Braemar to Ballater as the bus whirled downhill among sunlit trees. I sat at a south window to see the Ballochbuie pines, the sparkling Dee, the splendid high snows of the White Mounth and Lochnagar, the silver birches of Coilacriech. They are all hard to beat.

Later the bus threaded the busy streets of Aberdeen to Strachan's depot at Bon Accord. I walked down Union Street and took a clanking noisy tram up George Street to the foot of Clifton Road. Then a short walk followed past the Northern Hotel and up the pavement of Clifton Road to Lilybank Place and my lodgings. The sun shone warmly and the stonework of Aberdeen granite sparkled in the sun, but I felt deprived without the snow. My kind landlady made tea and sandwiches. Cannich was far away and long ago. It seemed ridiculous and incredble to think I was there only yesterday!

Next morning I would start the summer term of science studies and examinations at Marischal College. I wanted to be back at the Derry on my skis!

Chapter 16 With Tom Patey

Tom Patey, born in 1932 at Ellon in Aberdeenshire, became a mountaineer of world renown because of pioneering ascents of Muztagh Tower and Rakaposhi, and remarkable climbs in the Alps and Scotland. In Scotland he took part in the first ascent of the Old Man of Hoy with some of Britain's best-known climbers. He featured much in books by Joe Brown, John Cleare, Chris Bonington and others. Before this I knew him very well at an early stage of his development as a mountaineer, when he had a big influence on me. Here I tell something of those days.

On 8 September 1949 I first met him at Luibeg. After attending Braemar Games, Willie Campbell Dyer and I cycled up and had a meal in the bothy. In my diary I wrote *Afterwards two young bodies, one Patey of Ellon and another of Aberdeen, wandered in and created a hell of a mess of spilt oatmeal, porridge and paraffin.* Willie and I were glad to leave the now smelly bothy at midnight for a walk up Sgor Dubh in moonlight.

On Tom's first trip to Luibeg, his father had asked Bob Scott to keep a friendly eye on his son. So much for allowing the young Thomas to flower independently! In those early days, Tom and his friends 'bagged' Munros. He stopped this after a few years and moved to climbing. In 1962 he criticised his own early Munro-bagging, in his perceptive article *Cairngorm Commentary*.

On an early trip to Luibeg Bothy with pals from the school of Robert Gordon's College in Aberdeen, he tried to dry his wet boots by heating them over a primus stove. One boot hardened and twisted so much that Tom could not get his foot inside.

I next met him at Aberdeen University in 1950 when he came to study medicine. Now he associated with the university Lairig Club and climbers in the Etchachan Club and Cairngorm Club. Having ditched Munros, he had taken enthusiastically to rock-climbing. I recall having coffee with him in the Students' Union as he showed me tiny photographs of new routes he had climbed on the sea-cliffs of Longhaven with fellow student Mike Taylor of Peterhead. Knowing that my first impression in 1949 was too brief to be reliable, I changed my opinion radically.

We both appreciated coming from Buchan in Aberdeenshire. Our regard for the Cairngorms and Lochnagar went beyond climbing routes to involve a rapport with the area, including the glens leading to the corries. He liked the long walk to or from a climb, as evident in his article *Cairngorm Commentary*. Aberdeen climbers appreciated this too, and Malcolm (Mac) Smith praised it in his Introduction to the first *Climbers' Guide to the Cairngorms*. We contrasted the Cairngorms unfavourably with Glen Coe, where the climbs start near roads. This emphasis on the long walk to the cliffs later became widely known as 'the long walk-in'.

Tom and I shared a deep interest in knowing terrain from even brief acquaintance. We developed this even on fine days with no chance of fog. Neither of us took a map or compass on hills we knew, except in snow for some high hills and plateaux. We liked doing without a map when fog rolled in, for it helped us to know terrain and take the best route unaided.

Shy and self-effacing, he was not gregarious, and had an aversion to dancing and competitive team-games. He looked out at the human world, and his enthusiasm for the popular parties that arose from his music-playing signified him as a leader to the crowd rather than a part of it. Highly articulate in spoken and written English, he possessed a wide vocabulary and a good knowledge of phrases used by past writers. Also he had a great sense of humour, well manifested by the calypsos and other songs that he composed. Some involved praise with humour, such as *Freddie and Sticker*, while others deflated the pompous side of mountaineering.

Brought up by an English mother and Irish father at Ellon's episcopal Rectory, he lacked fluent northeast Scots as a first language, unlike many climbers in Aberdeen and around. Despite this, as an Ellon pupil he knew enough to understand it well, and used many words himself. He had an educated northeast voice, with the addition of a slight rolled *r*, a frequent northeast feature. In his last school year he attended Robert Gordon's College in Aberdeen. There he met Gordon (Goggs) B. Leslie, whom I had known as a lone visitor to Luibeg bothy.

With Goggs, Tom burst out of previous constraints with the first winter ascent of the feared Douglas-Gibson Gully on Lochnagar in December 1950. It had a reputation of being highly dangerous and almost unclimbable in summer, so the first winter ascent was remarkable, technically and psychologically. His elder peers in the Etchachan

Club suddenly took notice. He continued to make first ascents in the early 1950s, though not yet the dominant figure that he later became at the centre of northeast climbing.

On return from Canada in October 1953, I registered at Aberdeen University for a PhD study on ptarmigan and became an assistant lecturer in the Natural History Department. I joined the Etchachan Club, who appreciated my slides of arctic peaks in Baffin Island. Dr Lil de Kock in the Department offered me a two-bedroom flat in her house at 10 The Chanonry, and Mac Smith was seeking a flat, so we joined forces. Mac had many books and journals on mountaineering, and no one knew more about possible climbs in the Cairngorms, which he had long explored for this purpose. He contemplated the first guide to the climbs, and our flat became a powerhouse of information. Tom, Mac and the other main mountaineering pioneers lacked a car, but my jeep could hold six passengers, with plenty of room in the back for rucksacks. We shared petrol costs.

Mac was a central figure in the Etchachan Club. He and Bertie Duguid, Roy Greig, Gordon (not Goggs) Leslie and Ken Winram met each Friday evening at the Victoria Restaurant, where climbers sat at the same table. Tom and I attended regularly. Although some of them voiced suspicion of other Aberdeen groups and strangers, Tom had access to all, because of his experience, honesty, classless attitude, and above all enthusiasm for the Cairngorms. With his continual mutual exploration of climbs he increased their cooperation, and by 1955 the Aberdeen climbers had become a closer group, largely due to him.

Tom Patey behind Luibeg Bothy, 5 June 1954

Another reason brought Tom and me close together in 1953. A keen player of piano and accordion, he liked singing. Unlike him I was no musician, but I had brought back rousing songs from my Swiss team-mates in arctic Canada. To Tom, songs and music were almost as good as climbing, and the two together formed a whole that exceeded the parts. He soon learned the Swiss tunes, and excelled at playing them while singing the songs.

Tom often invited me to his home, where his parents welcomed me like one of the family, and occasionally I stayed overnight. His father enjoyed talking with me, including discussions on new books that I had bought, some of which he borrowed and enjoyed. Soon Tom encouraged his parents to host gatherings of climbers younger than them, which had a rejuvenating effect on father and mother.

In the winter of 1953–54, Tom Weir was due to lecture in Aberdeen on his recent Himalayan expedition. Shortly before the date, he phoned me to say he had flu and his doctor in Glasgow had advised him to cancel the trip. I was sympathetic and considered a possible replacement speaker. When I told Patey, he phoned Weir. He dismissed the Glasgow doctor by asserting "Most GPs are fools. The best medicine will be good company in Aberdeen". This persuaded Weir to come, and I met him at the rail-station. After the lecture I asked him to stay the night with me, using a sleeping bag on a camp-bed, but Patey kindly asked Weir and me to the rectory, where we would have a bedroom each. Weir was still suffering the after-effects of flu, so next morning he contemplated an easy day, walking and birdwatching by the estuary. Patey now overwhelmed Weir with enthusiasm for the Longhaven cliffs. The easy day vanished!

Before or since, I have never met anyone as persuasive as Patey, part of his extraordinary force of personality. The cliffs on that winter morning were at their most spectacular. Pale blue waves from a North Sea gale crashed over the lower rocks. Patey chose Stepped Ridge, but to reach the foot of it we had to cross the lower rocks. A scramble normally sufficed, but today we had to wait until the rocks were clear of a wave, even though covered with foam and water flowing out from an earlier wave. Roped, Patey made a run for it to the foot of the first pitch. Then Weir and I followed, one by one, each watching the waves. The climb was short, steep and exhilarating, with a tearing gale sweeping up the exposed chimney at the top. It was so violent that I felt it helped me climb upwards.

Len Lovat, a Glasgow climber in the vanguard of new routes in Glen Coe and Ben Nevis, and a good friend and climbing companion of Weir, followed with a lecture at Aberdeen. Tom Patey invited Len and me to stay the night at the rectory after the lecture, and we had excellent discussion on Scottish climbs and mountaineering. Next morning we climbed a dozen good routes at Longhaven, which greatly impressed Len, before I drove him to his train at Aberdeen, accompanied by Tom.

On 31 December 1953 the jeep had a full load of six climbers including Patey and Johnny Morgan, heading for Aviemore to meet Weir and other SMC members from Glasgow. On the way to Huntly, the party reached the climax to a Swiss song with a hoarse shout, at the very moment when a tyre exploded with a loud shot. A year later, the jeep took Tom, two lady friends of his, John Hall, Jenny and me to Aviemore, to meet Glasgow climbers. In my diary I wrote: *the best New Year party I've attended. Tom's band was great. He was on the accordion, John Hall on the fiddle, and Tom Weir on the drums. Dan McKellar excelled as master of the ceilidh, which ended at 4 am.*

In early 1954, plans for Mac's guide became formalised. The SMC would publish it, and Tom Patey would assess routes done so far. He would lead most routes himself, with close colleague Mike Taylor leading some. I was the main second, but others also seconded him, including Aberdeen climbers and a few from Glasgow such as Douglas Scott. We checked hundreds of routes and I measured the heights of the main cliffs with a big surveyor's aneroid barometer. With this foundation, Tom went on to climb many new routes, often following lines noticed during the checking. By 1954 he had become such a confident climber that he did not need anyone seconding, or indeed a rope. However, he found it useful to discuss the route in detail with his second throughout the climb and indeed with anyone else on his rope.

At the start of June 1954 I took the jeep to Longhaven one evening with Mac, picking up Tom at Ellon and finding five girls there, four of them his former Ellon school-mates and a new friend Dorothy (Dot) Mitchell from Cove. On the moderate climbs opposite Scimitar Ridge, I led Mac, and Tom led the girls. Though inexperienced, Dot had natural ability as a rock climber and was unafraid of exposed places. Then Tom led me, Mac and Dot up Diagonal Crack, a magnificent route high above the sea. When we returned to the jeep, *the Ellon girls were in a very merry state because they had taken about a nip and a half of whisky each while we climbed. Tom had difficulty restraining them.* To sober them before Tom's parents saw them I ordered a walk along the track. A salty breeze off the sea along the exposed cliff-top quickly cooled them off!

An early day of checking I recall in 1954, when I drove to Braemar on 4 June with Tom and Dot. Also I took Graeme Nicol and Kincorth Club stalwarts Freddie Malcolm and Alec (Sticker) Thom, who dismounted at Invercauld on their way to Beinn a' Bhuird. Tom, Dot and I stopped at the Fife Arms public bar in Braemar. The Swiss songs by Tom and me, with him at the piano or his accordion, and with me using a kazoo or harmonica, brought the house down. The crowd cheered and clapped, and the barman offered us free drinks if we returned on another evening. Tom's face glowed with enthusiasm, occasionally contorted as he concentrated on his playing.

Tom and Dot Mitchell look at the cliffs of Coire Sputan Dearg, 5 June 1954, about to ascend all known rock-routes there for a climbers' guide

I was astonished at his excitement. Dot and I enjoyed the evening, but Tom seemed supernatural. Far from being tired, he was elated. Far from being mentally duller with each whisky that he downed, he seemed to burn it like fuel and become mentally sharper. I was to see many more evenings like this at the Fife over the next few years, and at other hotels and bothies. He carried a bag of music in the jeep when we went on trips, so that he could play good music on piano or accordion, irrespective of whether it was a bothy, campsite, public bar, or private house.

When the Fife bar closed on that evening of 4 June, we crossed to Bruachdryne cafe for tea. The owner's son had a French accordion and music. Tom and he joined to play with gusto, and then discussed accordions and music. We also had more singing. Tom enjoyed all this and said it was the best evening of his life. When he finally came into my jeep on that evening and many others, he behaved quietly and normally as if he had not been at the bar. We went to Luibeg on a gorgeous evening with soft velvety light on the Cairngorms. I drove the jeep through the Luibeg Burn to the bothy. Tom had a notebook containing Bill Brooker's accounts of his pioneering climbs, including Coire Sputan Dearg, and we now read it. Bill's enthusiasm and graphic descriptions of the rock impressed us greatly.

Next day, Tom enjoyed the walk into the heart of the Cairngorms where the magnificent granite cliffs of Coire Sputan Dearg soared ahead. We climbed Crystal

Tom glissades at Coire Sputan Dearg, 5 June 1954

Ridge and then Hanging Dyke, a steep route on sun-warmed granite, full marks to Bill for finding such a fine unusual route. Tom shook my hand at the top, a nice ceremony that he repeated on many days at the top of a new route or a route that neither of us had climbed before. While Dot sat in the sun, Tom and I then climbed more routes.

After each one, we descended from the plateau by a fast standing glissade on steep snow down one of the gullies. We both liked glissading, and came down close together, near enough to talk about the thrill and the snow's quality. On this occasion and others in summer, we had no ice-axes. As a skier I did not need one on spring snow, and non-skier Tom did not need one because he had good balance and experience of different kinds of snow. Later I wrote in my diary: *I had a lovely dook* (bathe) *in icy cold water in a pool* and climbed Derry Cairngorm to study ptarmigan, while Tom continued until he had checked every route previously climbed in Coire Sputan Dearg. The value lay in the same person leading and comparing different routes in the same conditions. His phenomenal energy and enthusiasm that day were immense and impressive.

Next morning was even hotter. Dot had an easy day, while I went to my study area on Derry Cairngorm and Tom alone to check routes in Coire Etchachan. In the afternoon I strode to look over the corrie edge down to the cliffs and noticed Tom on the steep grey southern buttress, the Talisman. He was a tiny pale spot, dwarfed by the immense wide corrie and boulder slopes sweeping up to Beinn Mheadhoin. The spot moved slowly, forever upwards. It was the most remarkable sight I have witnessed of climbing in the Cairngorms or anywhere else.

In the evening we called at the Fife, where Tom surpassed his earlier performance, *Tom in great form at the Fife piano, plied with drinks from every side.* Then at Invercauld I picked up Freddie, Sticker and Graeme. We stopped at Inver Inn, where Tom again played the piano with gusto. Despite the noisy engine, on the way to Aberdeen we had enthusiastic discussions about the

At Coire Etchachan, Tom climbs Talisman solo, on the cliff edge half way up, 6 June 1954

Tom Patey at his party for Housi Weber at Ellon Rectory, 30 June 1954, from left Mac Smith, Rev Patey, Dot Mitchell, Tom, AW, Housi, his fiancee Marianne Lienhard wearing AW's Inuit summer anorak, Graeme Nicol, Mrs Patey, Goggs Leslie, Betty Davidson

routes, and Tom planned future weekends to climb and check all the known routes. On the whole, poor weather marred that summer, with much rain and little sun. This did not deter Tom, and did not deter me in seconding him on what Mac Smith in his guide called *a host of routes often in atrocious weather*.

J. R. (Housi) Weber, Swiss geophysicist and mountaineer who had been in Baffin Island with me, came to Aberdeen in mid June to stay with me. His fiancee Marianne Lienhard arrived before the belated Housi. Tom invited Marianne and me to Ellon for an evening, and asked if I could pick up a new friend Betty Davidson, who lived in Aberdeen near me. An associate member of the Cairngorm Club, she had impressed Tom with her singing.

When Housi eventually arrived, he was delighted to hear how popular the Swiss songs were with Tom and others. Tom now planned showpiece climbs for Housi on the first weekend. In high hopes I drove on a Friday evening with Housi, Marianne, Tom, Dot and Johnny Morgan to Luibeg bothy. Alas, it *turned out a hellish weekend. It rained all day on Saturday. Fortunately we had Tom's accordion in the jeep, which I took right to the bothy door last night. In the afternoon I drove up a distant glen to check an eyrie, where we found a big strong eaglet. We also did some climbing, but the rock is very smooth and loose. Tom feared that my laden jeep would fall through the ricketty plank bridges, but they held. We then went to the Fife and had a good night with the accordion. Sunday was again a foul wet day, so in the afternoon we went to Longhaven, expecting better weather at the coast, but it was worse, cold and wet with a gale blowing heavy showers. In these conditions the traverse of the normally easy Scimitar Ridge was a serious undertaking. Betty Davidson joined us at Tom's home and sang Gaelic melodies while Tom played the piano, and then Housi led the singing of some Swiss songs.*

While Housi and Marianne stayed two weeks with me, Tom arranged evening parties at the rectory for them and as many of his climbing friends as could come. The company, singing and music were memorable. I took photographs of the group outside on a June evening. Now, 56 years later, I discern a striking happiness in the party. Tom in particular looks radiant and relaxed.

When he was scared about the jeep falling through bridges, he had dismounted at each bridge and ran quickly to join us at the far side. He also feared being in a car where one sees and hears a river underneath and the car rumbles loudly while crossing. The water surface lay only five feet under the bridge and the stony bottom just another foot, so his fear was irrational, but no less real. Yet he did not fear waves battering the low parts of coastal climbs, which terrified most people. Tom feared adders and had an obsessive dislike of fleas and ticks. During December 2001, Mac Smith in a letter to me recalled *those glorious moments of hilarity at the Chanonry when, climbing the stairs, I heard gales of laughter coming from you. Mystified, I entered your room to find you sitting on a chair, convulsed in non-stop laughter at Tom kneeling in the buff, frantically searching through his vest, pants, shirt and trousers stretched out on the floor for the flea he had picked up on the bus.*

On 9 July, Tom and I returned to Luibeg bothy and Coire Etchachan with W.W. (Hutch) Hutchison. In the middle of the face, a line of overhangs runs along the upper steep section, above an easy lower section where slabs lead to grassy scoops. Tom had looked at the face in June and seen a feasible route threading the overhangs. It proved so when we climbed it. Tom suggested calling it the Bodkin. In wet greasy conditions, he led the crux pitch (severe) in his stocking soles.

I drove on 30 July to Luibeg with Tom, Betty, John Hay, and Bill Potts of the Natural History Department at Marischal College. Next morning dawned cold with slight rain. We walked to Coire Etchachan and all climbed Quartzvein Edge, with John and me on one rope, taking alternate leads behind Tom and the others. Next day was rainy and misty, but Tom and I climbed a new route on Stacan Dubha above Loch Avon, after a rebuff on the northern section. Later we climbed Beinn Mheadhoin with Betty and descended in mist and heavy rain by the Dubh Lochan and Glen Derry.

On the following Sunday, he, Betty and I climbed Red Tower at Longhaven. *The tower and opposite face were very fine, the face of beautiful pink granite being quite vertical, and yet no harder than mild severe, on sound rough rock. The evening light on the North Sea, the steep cliffs, the sea pinks and the sea birds were magnificent. We are fortunate to have this wonderful coast on our doorstep.* Other good days we had at Longhaven in fine weather, when Freddie Malcolm and my father joined Tom and me in good climbs, especially Diagonal Crack. Tom had a great respect for my father, who did his first rock scrambling with me at Aonach Eagach when 51 and his first rock-climbing in his mid and late 1950s. He got on well with Tom's parents, and later they and Tom appointed him as their solicitor.

By now I knew Tom better than any other hill friend up till then. I spent some days exploring the Buchan coast and castles with him. I knew the Moray Firth coast better than him, but he knew the coast from Peterhead to Collieston very well. Sometimes it would be just an afternoon when he had no medical classes, or an evening, but often a whole day, usually the two of us, but occasionally with Betty also. Tom liked Tolquhon Castle and other old sites, and criticised the folk who valued them less than pseudo-castles with aristocratic inhabitants.

I recall a day when, unroped, he and I climbed very steep grass up to rocks on a coastal face. We climbed side by side, and when he stopped for a fag he said "You've a very fine technique on steep grass. I don't mean that as sarcasm, but praise. Climbing steep grass safely is a difficult art, yet it seems easy and natural to you". I said I had often climbed it on the Moray Firth coast when a schoolboy, later at eagle eyries, and very often in the Lofoten Islands.

Besides the SMC Climbers' Guide to the Cairngorms, Tom in the mid 1950s began to promote the idea of a climbers' guide to coastal cliffs, produced by the Etchachan Club. All known routes would be checked and graded, and obvious new routes climbed. As usual, his enthusiasm resulted in volunteers helping, but Tom covered the main climbing ground at Longhaven. John Hay, helped by Tom and Alan Will, covered the cliffs south of Aberdeen down to the sections at Cove, and I did a cursory exploration from Macduff to Rosehearty. The Club produced the first edition in 1960.

In August, Tom planned to check routes in the Garbh Choire of Beinn a' Bhuird. I drove on the 29th with him, Mac, Gordon, Ken Winram and Bertie. I switched off the engine to coast silently to a gate in sight of the headkeeper's house, but it was a wet gloomy evening and he did not come out. Tom was greatly amused by this. Then we walked to Freddie's howff on the moor. Freddie and Sticker, who had pioneered routes on the cliffs of Coire na Ciche, joined us on a night of mist and rain. Until very late we had eager talk on religion, supernatural phenomena and metaphysics. After this, Freddie said he would not fancy going far outside in the dark that night.

Next day we woke to *a dirty morning with a strong west wind, mist at times, and cold, but later it cleared partly*. Tom had planned a full day, and we all rose too late. Eager to be off, he did without a cooked breakfast. Used to this from long days in Baffin and elsewhere, I did not demur, but Gordon made forcible comment. He and the others would join us later, after a proper cooked breakfast.

Tom started up the path at a cracking pace, and I with my long stride could easily follow. On any path you can take alternative routes for a few yards to avoid boulders, wet patches, and so on. If you walk fast, you choose the alternative rapidly, usually in a split second. On this day and many others I noticed how Tom invariably picked the best alternative when he was in the lead.

Fog draped the hills and rain fell. As we descended into the corrie, its outstanding feature the Mitre Ridge soared into mist, an impressive dark wall of steep granite. A breakthrough in Cairngorms climbing came here in summer 1933, when two parties climbed new routes on one day. Previously, most climbing had been in gullies, eschewing open faces. Wedderburn, Baird and Leslie climbed the Direct Route, hard severe in nails, and Cumming and Crofton a severe route to the west. Both routes, especially the Cumming-Crofton route, had become big challenges to Aberdeen climbers.

Tom and I climbed a new route on the buttress east of South-East Gully, with fine views across to the East Wall of the Mitre Ridge. Then we climbed down North-West Gully alongside the impressive vertical West Wall. Tom now went up Commando Route and descended the gully. We then climbed the Cumming-Crofton route. In his *Climbers' Guide*, Mac described it as: *The finest route on the Ridge and one of the best in the Cairngorms. The climbing is continuously difficult and exposed*. To us it seemed one of the steepest climbs in the Cairngorms. On the crux, a granite slab, Tom climbed in stocking soles, for the wet rock offered little friction in boots. Past a vertical wall leaped an impressive view down Slochd Mor. We finished by Bell's Variation to the Direct Route. Just then, Ken and Mac appeared at the top of our first route on the eastern buttress. We strolled to join them and ate some mandarin oranges, whereupon Tom named the new route Mandarin Buttress.

Mac and Ken returned down the glen, because the rain was heavy and the mist low. Then Tom and I climbed North-West Gully. While I measured the cliff's height by aneroid, he raced across to Stob an t-Sluichd to explore routes on long ribs of rock, and on the way back, remarkable man, he climbed a new mild severe route alone on the East Wall Direct of Mitre Ridge. I walked back via Mac's howff in Coire nan Clach to pick up food for later use. Later we all met at Freddie's howff to walk to the jeep and then I drove to Inver Inn for tea. Here we re-organised the party. Mac, Ken and the others would go by bus to Aberdeen, while I drove with Tom to Speyside for climbs on Sgoran Dubh.

For weeks he had planned to check all known climbs there, where the SMC did some climbing in 1902 and 1904, followed by further routes by SMC members and a few others in later decades up to the 1940s. However, very little had been done since, and Aberdeen climbers had not gone to these big cliffs to repeat any route. Tom organised a strong party, with Aberdeen University students Mike Taylor and Leslie (Fally) Fallowfield coming in Mike's car to join us. I had asked Douglas Scott, who would come from Glasgow and meet us on the first day. In the jeep, a long tiring drive followed till 11 pm at Coylumbridge. There, Tom and I met Mike and Fally at the campsite, where they had a tent. Tom and I slept in the back of the jeep.

On Monday 30 August we awoke late. *The first job was to get permission to drive up the glen, so I drove with Tom to Inverdruie to see Lt. Col. J.P. (Ian) Grant. Tom explained that a key would enable us to check all routes in two days. Ian Grant couldn't have been more helpful and gave us the key, though warning us about a landslide on the road. The four of us now set off, without sign of Douglas, on a grey day with clouds but no rain. The landslide had no great terrors for the jeep, which we nicknamed The Roaring Fart, but I forced it too far at a rough section further on, and tore a small bit off the back. We were far up the glen and it wasn't a long walk to Sgoran Dubh.*

Tom and I climbed the steep Robert's Ridge on great rock, probably the best route on the Sgoran, with a spectacular finish, and then up Cram's routes on No. 1 Buttress, while Mike and Fally tried to find Bell's route alongside. Tom and I went beyond Sput Seilich to climb the original route to the Northern Rampart. After that we began to waste time on the Rampart trying to find routes, and saw Douglas at the top of Robert's Ridge too! Tom forced a way up one groove on the Rampart and landed in serious trouble because of lack of holds and poor friction. I had a good belay on a wide ledge close below and could have held him easily if he had fallen, but he made the more difficult descent carefully without mishap. We thought this must be where H.I. Ogilvy and Miss S. Robson had been killed. Then we climbed to the top of the Rampart by its southern edge. The Rampart was a rather horrible-looking face and we were pleased to leave this spot. We met Douglas, who joined Tom to climb Diamond Buttress, while I walked to Sgoran Dubh Mor to measure the cliff's height. I felt tired towards the summit, due to the different action from rock-climbing. On the descent my strength returned and I strode quickly back to extricate the jeep before darkness fell. We all camped at Coylum.

Tuesday 31 August was another similar day, with rain at night. Douglas climbed with Tom, as Fally decided not to climb. With Mike I climbed Bachelor's Buttress, which is really a chimney, then Central Route on No. 1 after much wasted time, and over to climb No. 5 gully, filthy and wet. The pinnacle of A' Chailleach was great, especially with a wild wind raging through the gap. Later, we had a wild view from the beach of Loch Einich up storm-tossed waters to hills dark in the gloom of clouds and rain. All recorded climbs on these cliffs have now been checked.

Next day was tantalising, a lovely day, warm, sunny and cloudless except for a few puffs of white cumulus, but we had accomplished our task on Sgoran Dubh. We drove up Glen Feshie, to be faced by a locked gate, and next to Loch an Eilein for tea at the tearoom and a delightful stroll through the wood by the lochside. Then we visited the old Rothiemurchus kirk at the Doune, a place of great atmosphere and peace on this beautiful day. We were all especially held by the story and sight of the grave of Shaw Mor Fiaclach with its fine ancient black stepping stones.

After arriving late at Aberdeen and dropping Tom off, I had to drive to Luibeg, for I had arranged with Bob Scott that I would accompany the stalking party for a day as an unpaid gillie to take photographs. After striving against sleep and having to walk outside the jeep near Coilacriech to be fully awake, I arrived at Derry Lodge in the wee smaa oors, and stretched my sleeping bag on a bed in the gillies' room without wakening them. I spent two days on the Derry beat, but the shooter failed to shoot a stag, thus limiting the photography.

Tom made another foray on Cairn Gorm while holidaying with his parents at Aviemore. When I arrived on 10 September, he enthused about the clean rough granite on new solo routes on Creag an Leth-choin. My parents came from Turriff with our hill-walking friend Willie Campbell Dyer of Kent. *Next morning, Tom, Willie, my father and I set off in the jeep, a dry day and the hills clear. First of all, Tom and I went to Coire an t-Sneachda and climbed Aladdin's Buttress. Safeguarded by me from the side, Tom climbed the Lamp Direct route, and later I finished by Aladdin's. We all went up the Lamp and the rocks at the top. Campbell Dyer enjoyed the fine situations. Tom and I climbed a route up Fiacaill Buttress, with a fine wee chimney at the top.*

We then crossed the Fiacaill Ridge into Coire an Lochain and round to its west side for Savage Slit, a remarkable feature cutting far into West Buttress, a sensational vertical route on clean rough rock. Tom and I next climbed Ewen's Buttress. Then Tom, my father and I ascended the Western Route on No 4 Buttress, an interesting climb. The crux is hard, and I gave a shoulder for Tom and my father to get up, and I found it very hard getting up last. (Tom wrote of it as: *The last man needs wings* and Mac in his *Climbers' Guide* stated: *Still technically severe -- a nice problem confronts the unfortunate last man.*) *Back at Aviemore, I showed slides, Tom played his accordion and we sang till 1.30 am. My father said it was a wonderful ceilidh.*

Sunday was cool but sunny and clear. With the same party we walked to Coire an Lochain where Tom climbed Vent, very dirty, and then we all went up Vent Rib alongside. Tom tried the VS finish to Central Crack, with a top rope dropped by me from the plateau above, but ice on some of the crucial holds rebuffed him. He and I walked over the plateau and down to the foot of Hell's Lum crag at Loch Avon. After we climbed the bottom easy-angled slabs unroped, Deep-Cut Chimney gave a fine route, spectacular at the top. Tom continued to Coire an t-Sneachda to climb a variation on Aladdin's, while I measured cliff heights in Coire an Lochain.

Tom now proposed that we check all routes in Glen Geusachan and Braeriach's Garbh Choire. He could not come on the first day, but Mike and I started. *On Saturday 25 September I drove after breakfast from Aberdeen up to Luibeg. Mike and I walked up to Corrour Bothy on a bad day with low clouds, sleet and a cold northwest wind. Suffering from some flu, I was not in the best form. In the afternoon we went to Glen Geusachan, climbed Tiered Cracks in Coire Cath nam Fionn, and explored the rest of the corrie. Snow fell during the climb and lay high up.*

On Sunday, Mike and I left Corrour early. At Garbh Choire Dhaidh in mist we found Mac Smith and Gordon Leslie at their howff, and Mac pointed out climbs in a brief spell when mist cleared. The first was an unclimbed discovery of Mac's, the Great Rift. Mike and I climbed it, 500 feet of exciting variable open gully. Snow fell heavily for most of the day, so the climbs were wet and cold. At one of Bill Hendry's routes, Chimney Pot, cascades ran over us as we clambered up dirty chokestones. Mike and I took turns leading alternate pitches on it, and on Pisa and Helicon Rib.

Then we went to the howff, and found Mac and Gordon crouched over a stove. They had gone to Garbh Choire Mor but bad weather repelled them. Mac reported two old snow-patches, one now very small. Mike and I went there to investigate Sphinx Ridge. When first climbed on 25 May 1952 by a party, Mac rated it very difficult, but noted that as snow receded below the cliff, *so a smooth nose is brought to light which has so far prevented ascent of the Ridge in the later months of the year (Climbers' Guide to the Cairngorms Area).* My diary records: *The nose rebuffed Mike and me due to poor friction with wet snow falling and water streaming down smooth rock. Gordon joined Mike to climb the last two routes that remained unchecked, while I walked to Corrour. Heavy snow fell, and by night lay down to the bothy. Several folk had arrived, including Tom and Freddie, and the bothy was full. Freddie had carried up Tom's accordion so we had a good singsong. On the way to Corrour, Tom had explored routes on the cliffs of Carn a' Mhaim. He and Freddie planned to climb on Lochnagar next day, confident that Mike and I would have checked all the Garbh Choire climbs, so they decided to go to Corrour for good company, singing and music. This sent my flu packing.*

On Monday we rose early to a wonderful morning with rosy sun on the snowy tops and a dusting of sparkling frost and snow on the heather. After making tea we walked to Luibeg, where we met Tom Weir and Ian McNicol, up for the weekend. I dropped Patey, Mac, Gordon, Mike, Freddie and Sticker at Ballochbuie gate for a climb on Lochnagar, and waited for Weir and Ian there. By the time they came, it was too late to catch up with the others, so we had a wonderful afternoon in Ballochbuie wood, rich and mellow in the sunlight, with snow on the hills.

Now Ian and Tom Weir left for Glasgow, and I drove to the road-end beside the Falls of Garbh Allt to await Patey and the others. Two shiny land-rovers were parked there, and several men and women standing outside in the sunshine introduced themselves as the queen's equerry and others. I explained that we had come to check routes for the SMC Climbers' Guide. They could not have been more pleasant, said the royal party had gone to shoot stags up Feindallacher Burn, a long way from our route to the cliffs of Lochnagar, and so we would not have disturbed the royal sport. They awaited gillies with ponies carrying stags. I awaited Patey and the rest. It turned out that they had climbed a new route, a remarkable chimney which Patey had aptly named The Clam.

An extraordinary contrast now arose, between the well-dressed smiling shooting party having a picnic and a dishevelled serious Tom Patey appearing fast down the path, wearing a white jersey dirtied by the wet grimy rocks of The Clam and carrying a dirty climbing rope. Mike, Gordon, Freddie and Mac followed. I introduced them to the shooting party, who nodded pleasantly. Then we mounted the jeep and roared down the road to cheery waves from the party.

Mac Smith told me another interesting royal story about that time. He, Kenny Winram and a third climber from the Etchachan Club had been up climbing on the cliffs at Creag an Dubh Loch on a hot sunny day. In mid afternoon they returned to their bicycles in the wood at Glas- allt-Shiel. By now they were so hot that they decided to put all clothes in their rucksacks and cycle down to the Spittal of Glenmuick in the buff, wearing only their boots on the pedals. As they skimmed down past the lodge at Glas-allt-Shiel, too late to stop they saw a few persons picnicking on the lawn between the road and the loch. It was the Queen, the Duke of Edinburgh, and their children, entirely on their own. The climbers passed them just yards away. The Duke waved, and the trio waved back briefly to whizz out of sight down the road!

On 6 October 1954, Bruce Forman in the Zoology Department asked me to take him to Ben Macdui to search for spiders, and booked a university shooting brake. Tom met us on the previous day in the Students' Union when Bruce and I were planning our trip, and asked if he could get a lift with us to Braemar. Bruce agreed. Freddie Malcolm and Alec Thom had done good climbs in Coire na Ciche and Tom had not yet checked them. After an early start in Aberdeen, Bruce drove quickly to Braemar on a dry steely grey day, overcast with high cloud. West of Braemar, we

Beside AW's jeep at Luibeg Bothy on 26 June 1954, from left Housi Weber, Marianne Lienhard, Patey, Dot Mitchell, AW, Bob Scott

dropped off Tom to wade across Dee and walk far to the corrie. He would meet us at Invercauld at dusk.

Bruce and I had a long day, and during it I descended Castle Gates Gully to measure cliff heights by aneroid. Small snowdrifts lay on the highest ground, and in exposed spots a slight wind blew. Tom had a grand day's climbing on dry warm rock in the shelter. Alone, he climbed all known routes in Coire na Ciche. At Hourglass Buttress, climbed on the first ascent with the aid of a piton that Alec and Freddie had left, Tom used it, next decided he could do without it, climbed back down the crux, and removed the piton on the way up! He rated the climb as very severe without the piton.

In those years I became so used to climbing unroped with Tom on easy rocks that I began to climb some routes solo, as an interesting way of travelling from one place to another during ptarmigan studies. Also, cock ptarmigan had territorial lookouts on crags, from which they took off on song flights. I climbed Crystal Ridge, Flake Buttress and Pinnacle Buttress in Coire Sputan Dearg, and other such climbs in other corries. Although only moderate in standard, Pinnacle Buttress offered an exposed steep route on good rough rock with magnificent views. On Lochnagar I climbed Black Spout Buttress, particularly interesting because ptarmigan often lived at high density in the northeast corrie and used the buttress for lookouts.

In November 1953 after a climb with us on Eagle Ridge of Lochnagar, Tom Weir told Tom Patey, Mac, Mike and me that he wished to propose us as SMC members in 1954 and hoped we would agree. We did, and the SMC accepted us. In December, all four went in Mike's car to the meeting, which put SMC recognition behind a Cairngorms Climbers' Guide.

Tom's enthusiasm extended to hill-walking meets of the University's Lairig Club in winter. I remember a small but happy busload in November 1954 to Glen Isla and Glas Maol, returning for tea to Kirriemuir, where the hotel gave us a hall for the evening. On the next meet, Tom persuaded so many to come that it required three buses to carry the 100 or so who signed for the Sunday trip. In the evenings after these meets he excelled with accordion, piano, and singing.

For my wedding in March 1955, my father said he would like to pay for a party at the Udny Arms Hotel in Newburgh, close to Ellon. He generously accepted a small list of relatives named by Jenny and me, and hoped I would suggest climbers and others. So it turned out, with Aberdeen climbers such as Mac, Gordon and Bertie, Prof Vero Wynne-Edwards and his wife, arctic explorer Pat Baird and his wife Jill, Pierre and Lil de Kock, and Bob and Helen Scott from Luibeg. After a memorable speech by my aunt Elsie, there came singing and music. Tom and I sang the Swiss songs from Baffin Island, and even the normally reticent Wynne-Edwards joined with gusto in a Swiss duet along with me, and in other Swiss songs with Tom and me. Tom and I sang some songs that Tom had written about climbers and climbing. He was in his element, enjoying playing his accordion and piano as well as singing. Once again, his enthusiasm bubbled over to stimulate others. Had he not been there, the party would have been good, but not such an extraordinary memorable event.

Tom graduated in medicine in 1955, having passed his examinations fairly readily without much fuss and without any obvious detriment to his climbing. In his pre-registration year he worked at Stracathro Hospital and then Inverurie Hospital. Stracathro in the Mearns lay too far from his usual haunts and friends. Undeterred and still car-less, he cycled 20 miles up Glen Clova, carrying his accordion and rucksack on the five miles of the Capel Mounth track, and met us at Lochend Bothy beside Loch Muick for a splendid evening of song, music and conversation till midnight. *Next day he did the return trip to Lochnagar (fifteen miles) climbing three routes and returning to Clova, his bicycle and Stracathro, ready to commence night duty at the hospital* (Brooker and others, obituary notice).

In the heat-wave of August 1955, Tom joined Bertie, Jenny and me for a weekend to Luibeg. We spent an evening at the Fife Arms public bar, where Tom excelled at the piano as ever, and then we had tea at Bruachdryne. Late on a beautiful night we left, and enjoyed driving up Glen Lui. The Cairngorm Club had a lease of Derry Lodge, and Tom suggested we enter and make tea, but the door was locked. Although a parked car stood outside, we saw nobody about, so we thought the inhabitants must have gone to Luibeg. However, I noticed that a big sash window was unlocked and had a tiny crack which allowed access to finger tips. With several sets of finger tips in concerted effort we lifted the window, walked in, and switched on an electric light.

Tom walked straight to a piano at one end of the big room. Before anyone had time to cough, he played the Death March. At first taken aback, Bertie, Jenny and I smiled broadly, and then suddenly we heard a crash upstairs, as someone flung a door open, and an imperious voice let fly.

Bertie said quickly "Christ, it's Ada Adams"! A strong walker who had gone to the hills for many years, she had taken charge of the Cairngorm Club's cleaning, tidying, and other domestic maintenance at the lodge. She even had committee members and club presidents doing minor errands in the lodge instead of going to the hill. Jenny remembers seeing Pat Baird, expert arctic explorer, mountaineer and CC president, walking with boxes of nails on some ploy of Ada's. As Bertie, Jenny and I walked towards the door and the hallway, we looked round to see our room empty, with the window still wide open. Tom had crept quietly into the darkness. Having wakened the formidable Ada, he had deserted us. We faced a different kind of music.

Ada had switched on an electric bulb over the stair, and in its strong light we now saw a ghastly apparition as she emerged at the landing. Large and rotund in body, she stood swathed in what seemed like blankets, with thick brown muscular legs protruding. Thick oil on her face reflected the light in small pools of silver. Metal hair curlers stuck out from her head, resembling tiny electric insulators. She viewed us for a few seconds, her height on the upper floor adding dominance. Then her mouth opened in a curl and she delivered a withering comment.

"Bertie Duguid. You've nae business comin here at this time o nicht and makkin sik a din. You're nae even a Cairngorm Club member. As an Etchachan Club member ye're nae supposed to come in unless your club secretary applied in writing and got a booking in advance". I said he could come as my guest, for I was a CC member and the CC rules said a member could use the lodge without prior booking, provided this did not prevent use by other members who had booked. The latter point clearly did not apply, because only her very small party was in the lodge. I

Tom climbs Alligator Crawl solo on Longhaven sea cliffs, 8 August 1954

said none of us had played the piano. I insisted we use facilities to make tea. She kept on railing at Bertie, but I asked her to calm down and go to bed. I offered to close the window and let ourselves out of the front door, ensuring that we locked it on the inside before we left. She relented, but gave a parting shot that Bertie would be hearing from his club secretary.

After the apparition vanished, we had tea in the kitchen and then drove away. As soon as we had gone safely out of earshot, an explosion of laughter rang inside the jeep for several minutes, and tears of mirth ran down our three faces. When we came into the cool dark night nearer Luibeg, we could hardly stand up, due to infectious laughter. Tom came out of the bothy and gales of laughter broke out again. We could hardly stop.

A few days later, Bertie received a note from the Etchachan Club secretary, delivering Ada's complaint. Bertie rightly said he had been a guest of Cairngorm Club member Adam Watson. I received a letter from Jim Bothwell, CC Secretary, asking me for a written apology to Miss Adams. I got on well with Jim, and went to see him at his office in Bridge Street. I told him that according to Club rules I had done nothing wrong, and likewise my guests Bertie and Jenny. He did not deny what I said about the rules. It boiled down to the club being grateful to Ada for her work at the lodge, and so being unwilling to accept its own rules by going against her wish for a written apology. She ruled the roost at the lodge, or, as Bob Scott put it aptly, "She wis the sergeant major". Clearly she also ruled the roost in the committee, and the committee was prepared to ignore its rules because of her domineering influence.

So, I resigned from the Cairngorm Club, after being a member since the late 1940s. Though pleased to be in the Etchachan Club and SMC, in 1955 I thought that some CC committee members in those years had snobbish attitudes. Someone in our ranks coined the phrase 'Just a Cairngorm mannie' for them, and Patey enjoyed using this innuendo with sarcasm. Later the CC changed for the better. After the Lurcher's Gully inquiry in 1981, when I gave the main scientific evidence, the president asked if I would accept honorary life membership, and I agreed.

For some months in the short days of winter, Tom worked at Inverurie hospital, quite near Bridge of Don where I lived. On several days he suggested we climb on Bennachie. After coffee in his room, we would dash in the jeep up a woodland track to snatch a few climbs on the Mither Tap and other tors. He knew every such place like the back of his hand, including every track and path in the Forestry Commission plantations, in darkness as well as daylight. With him at my side I needed no map of the complex network of vehicle tracks in the FC plantations. After we returned in the dark, he played records while we drank coffee, and occasionally he used his accordion and sang with me. Always I remember his extraordinary enthusiasm, whether we had time to go on the hill or not.

In summer 1956 he joined an expedition that put all four members on top of the Muztagh Tower in the Karakorum, previously often regarded as impossible. This was a major breakthrough in Himalayan climbing, a forerunner of many alpine-style small expeditions with high technical standards.

When he returned he spoke of other impressive peaks. The Trango Tower above Baltoro Glacier fascinated him, and he longed to organise an expedition to climb it. He said I would make a good support member for the summit climbers, because of my energy, determination and team spirit, but the Arctic attracted me, not the Himalaya. He never organised that expedition because other commitments prevented it.

In 1957–60 as a naval medical doctor attached to the Royal Marine Commando he climbed hard new routes on the granite sea-cliffs of Devon. During 1958 he joined a services expedition to Rakaposhi, where leader Mike Banks and he reached the summit. While in the Navy he returned to Ellon on leave, and my diary for 2 March 1957 gives a brief note *Up to Derry gate in van with Jenny, Edith* (a friend of Jenny's) *and Tom Patey, after a great night in the Fife, Tom with accordion and bag of music. After a big thaw the road was too soft for vehicles, so we slept in the van at the gate, after a display of aurora.*

Betty Davidson and Tom had become close. When visiting Tom, his parents, and half brother Morris at Ellon rectory, Jenny and I would give Betty a lift from Aberdeen. Afterwards we took her to her home at Seaton near the Bridge of Don, close to Pat Baird's house at Inverdon where Jenny and I lived. Betty often spoke at length with Jenny and me in my jeep and later in the butcher's van that replaced it, and her mother and father gave us tea. She was keen to marry Tom. They did marry in 1958 at King's College chapel. Jenny recalls how we drove from Glen Esk to attend the ceremony, and sat at a table for an enjoyable lunch with Bill and Margaret Brooker, Jerry Smith, Kenny Grassick, Graeme Nicol, and Mike and Dorothy Taylor.

Tom and Betty moved to a house in King Street, where Jenny and I visited them often. Jenny was still nursing baby Jenny, who slept in a pram in the separate cab at the back of my long land-rover, with the pram secured firmly by climbing rope. While Betty gave us tea, baby Jenny slept soundly in the rover. Tom had to meet a climber at Aberdeen rail-station, and I offered to drive Tom to meet him and take him to the Station Hotel on our way back to King Street. Tom and I set off, met the climber, and dropped him at the hotel. He asked us in for coffee, and, forgetting baby Jenny in the back, I joined Tom and him. Half an hour later I drove Tom home. As we bumped over the rough granite setts that covered Aberdeen's streets then, Tom said he thought he heard squeaking at the back and asked about the suspension. Used to hearing squeaks from the rover, I dismissed this.

Meanwhile, Jenny was concerned because it was time for baby Jenny's breast-feed and the rover had not returned.

Tom and Mike Taylor at AW's jeep in Coylumbridge campsite, 1 September 1954

When Tom and I came into the house, she immediately went to get baby Jenny. Only then did it strike me like a bolt out of the blue that I had been oblivious about the baby. Hungry, she had made the squeaking that Tom had heard! Once she had been given her feed and lay satisfied, we all laughed. Tom said "Adam, you're the archetype absent-minded scientist".

On a later visit to King Street, Jenny and I saw the first Patey baby, not long into the world. Betty was out when we called, but Tom took us to see the baby. He asked Jenny what she thought of it, adding with a smile, "Go on, it's an ugly little bugger. Feel free." Jenny said, "Yes, I agree. It is an ugly little bugger." Tom said "Fine, but can you not be more specific? Let's have a good descriptive adjective and noun." At once Jenny said "An irate beetroot". Tom burst out laughing. He said, "When you show your new-born babe and ask folk what they think of it and they say 'It's an ugly little bugger', or 'An irate beetroot', you really know they're your friends and not hypocrites. They aren't bonny, are they, the new babies?" The whole episode was classic Patey.

During another visit by us to see Tom at King Street, Betty came in after seeing her GP. She announced: "He says I have got external rhinitis". Tom dismissed this with a wave of his arm and a chuckle. "That just means a running nose", he said.

When I went to live in Glen Esk in 1957 I saw him less, but I returned often to Aberdeen to Etchachan Club meetings and to some Friday evenings at the Victoria Restaurant. Tom usually came to the Victoria. Keen incoming climbers went there, to sit on the fringes of the climbers' table, where they would be regarded suspiciously by some native veterans. Tom and I would approach the incomers, and good climbers such as Englishman Jerry Smith felt less awkward and could join the main table while sitting beside Tom or me. Jerry soon showed his mettle by climbing very hard new routes in the Cairngorms, and then was treated like a native veteran of old! His English accent was immediately forgotten and considered of no consequence! A critical soil scientist, Jerry and Sandy Walker stayed with Jenny and me in Glen Esk while they surveyed soils in Angus, and we had grand discussions. It was a tragic loss to mountaineering and soil science when Jerry died from a fall in the Alps.

After moving from Glen Esk to Strachan in 1961 and Crathes in 1962, we saw more of Tom. Always a loyal friend, he would call unannounced of an evening, even though we had not been in touch for weeks. Sometimes he invited us to parties when he did locum work at Braemar or when he worked at the Aberdeen hospital. A brilliant storyteller, he held us in fits of laughter with his tales of doughty matrons, inebriate doctors and demanding patients.

In one winter, Hermann Buhl lectured to the Royal Scottish Geographical Society at the Music Hall in Aberdeen about his first ascent of Nanga Parbat in 1963. Hundreds packed the hall, including many northeast climbers. Tom, Graeme Nicol and I sat together. Graeme was very excited, for he had long modelled himself on the famous Austrian. He liked mentioning Buhl's habit of carrying a snowball while walking in the streets of Innsbruck, as a method for acclimatising one's hands to the cold. Buhl gave a good lecture and spoke eloquently of his solo ascent, bivouac, and exhausting descent next day.

Afterwards he came into the audience for a few minutes. We could not wait and went straight to him. Thanking him for an impressive lecture, we introduced ourselves as local mountaineers and I said I had climbed in arctic Canada and Lofoten, and he shook hands with us warmly. He asked about local peaks, and we explained that most cliffs were in corries. He asked their height in metres. Thinking usually in hundreds of feet, Tom and Graeme did not know immediately. Considering the highest ones at Creag an Dubh Loch and Shelter Stone Crag, which I had measured for the climbers' guide, I said up to 300 metres. Graeme and Tom nodded impressively. Buhl commented "Small cleeffs, small cleeffs"! For all that, he enjoyed being among mountaineers, and nobody else from the audience really engaged him. We asked if he would like to see the cliffs and climb with us, and offered to take him next morning, or to climb sea-cliffs if he lacked the whole day needed for a visit to Lochnagar or Creag an Dubh Loch. With a tight lecturing tour, however, he had to go south next morning. He said he would have liked to come with us, and hoped to do so if he returned to Scotland. The last I remember was his happy grin as he waved to us above the crowd, shouting "The best of luck to you". All three of us left in a buzz of excitement, especially Graeme, to whom this meeting face to face had been a dream for years.

Tom became general practitioner at Ullapool, where he climbed scores of new routes, mostly solo. Once when he came to my Crathes house he told me of a crag that lay miles up a wild glen at Alladale and of the unusual rock on his pioneering climb there. The description was so vivid that I would not forget it, even though I had never been there. It was part of his magic with words, sharing an unusual experience with others.

He asked if I knew Orkney, because he considered climbing the Old Man of Hoy. I told him of Hoy in July 1947 and read my diary when I *walked across short heath at the top of St John's Head, and finally the last few yards towards the edge of a huge abyss. As I crawled to peep over the edge, I looked down a vertical 1200 feet of sandstone to the Atlantic far below. Fulmars, puffins and other sea birds fluttered, adding to a feeling of immense space. To the south, the striking pinnacle of the Old Man jutted darkly against a shimmering silvery sea that caught strong sunlight.*

He listened keenly as I described the most impressive sea-cliff I had ever seen, apart from Faroe and also Kaxodluin at Cape Searle in Baffin Island. I loaned him maps and my copy of the book *Orkney the Magnetic North*. Years later he ascended the Old Man and repeated it on TV, as usual after thorough care in preparation. Now he was climbing with a wider set of people, including some famed names of mountaineering.

Like many of his Aberdeen friends I saw little of him at Ullapool, but he continued to visit me on the way to see relatives. My father often drove to Oykell or Ullapool for hill-walking, and Tom would always join him for an evening at Oykell pub or at an Ullapool hotel, and entertained him at Tom's home. My father filmed hard new routes being climbed solo by Tom. He said Tom was a devoted family doctor in a practice with big distances between the more remote houses.

On the evening of 20 May 1970, Betty phoned Jenny to say "There's been an accident today when Tom abseiled solo from a sea-stack near Whiten Head in north Sutherland. Tom fell to his death. Could you ask Adam to come at once with his father as family solicitor? I've already phoned Mike and Hamish MacInnes. Mike has said he'll come from Peterhead in his car and pick up Mr Watson and then Adam".

My father had just spent his 70th birthday ski-touring on Carn an Tuirc. He learned about the tragedy only when he called at our house for tea on his way to Newburgh, and went there at once to prepare for the task. Mike drove from Peterhead to pick up him and then me.

It was a beautiful night, barely dark in the northern sky. Betty plied us with tea and sandwiches, and told as much as she knew. Mike and I shared a room in the house while my father booked into a local hotel. Because of the shock, I remember little else that night, save that Hamish MacInnes called, looking grave and saying little, like all of us.

We returned to Aberdeenshire next day. At the funeral in the east episcopal church in King Street, I had never seen such an unusual group of mountaineers. As well as many northeast climbers, SMC members had come from Glasgow and elsewhere, including Malcolm Slesser and Hamish MacInnes, and from further south Chris Bonington, Chris Brasher, Joe Brown, John Cleare, Ian McNaught Davis, and others. I remember the heavy sorry of the big crowd as Mike and I with Tom's half-brother Morris and others, I think maybe Hamish MacInnes, carried Tom's coffin. I was close to tears, and am in tears now as I type this sentence 40 years later. Burial took place at the church beside Ellon rectory. After a reception at an Ellon hotel we drove to Aberdeen, where Margaret Brooker's parents welcomed us at their large house to join in camaraderie and happy remembrance of many good days with Tom.

It was fitting that he ended his *Cairngorm Commentary* article in 1962 (p. 81) with two striking sentences. *Good climbing and good company often go together: each is essential to the enjoyment of the other. In the Cairngorms they are inseparable.*

Chapter 17 Eagle Ridge and a night tour of Balmoral Castle

On Saturday 28 November 1953, Tom Weir gave an illustrated lecture at the annual dinner of the Cairngorm Club in the Caledonian Hotel at Aberdeen. In those days, virtually all at the dinner sported resplendent evening dress. The men in their black and white dress bowed stiffly when greeting one another, like displaying penguins. Tom Patey and I, who had met Weir off the train from Glasgow, wore suit and tie, as did Weir. We three had agreed beforehand our flouting of the convention on evening dress. The lecturer could hardly be prevented from attending because he wore a suit, so Patey and I reckoned we were in strong company!

Tom Weir had brought boots and clothes for climbing next day. After the lecture, he stayed overnight in Aberdeen with a Club Committee member, but it had been agreed that four of us would call for him after breakfast, for a climb on Lochnagar. Next morning I set off from The Chanonry of Old Aberdeen in my jeep, and in Aberdeen city I collected Tom Patey, Mike Taylor, Bill Brooker, and Tom Weir last but not least.

To afford Weir the best views, I asked him to join Patey on the wide front seat beside me. Then I drove to the Spittal of Glenmuick. On the way up Deeside, Patey said to Weir "We'd like to show you Eagle Ridge. It's the finest rock climb on Lochnagar. It will be in great condition today". This was Patey optimism and enthusiasm *par excellence*. In fact it was a raw cold cloudy day, typical of the end of November, with fog clipping the tops of Lochnagar and the eastern Cairngorms, soaking wet ground after rain, portents of sleet and snowfall to come, and the beginnings of a wind that would be very strong on high ground and next day a hurricane on Cairn Gorm summit! (My father wrote of next day, after descending from Cairn Gorm with a Sheffield student: *We struck NW into Coire Cas, battling against the gale, it was a very stiff climb down and we were buffeted very badly and fell time and again*).

The view of Lochnagar from the Spittal of Glenmuick is uninspiring, almost disappointing, revealing just a small upper part of the cliff, with Eagle Ridge out of sight. Only on reaching the col at the Meikle Pap could Tom Weir appreciate the height of these precipices of Creagan Lochnagar, rearing upwards steeply for 700 feet. Dark, almost black, they rose into curling scarves of grey mist. It was far more impressive than in summer sun.

I spotted a pack of 20 ptarmigan at the col, and we stopped a minute to watch them resting as they crouched among boulders. Tom Weir and I saw 12 cocks and eight hens, each cock with a distinctive winter stripe of black feathers along the side of the head. Already the birds showed many white feathers of the oncoming winter dress. The whitest, a hen, had upper parts over 90% white, the darkest, a cock, only 20% white. On average the white covered about two-thirds of the upper parts. Each bird had feathers puffed out to form a ball, for insulation. With heads tucked in, they sat unmoving like sphinxes, cleverly out of the wind, conserving heat and energy by not moving. These small arctic ghosts of the Meikle Pap watched us pass.

Patey stopped to explain to Weir the detailed layout of the cliffs and the main climbing routes. From here we looked straight across to Eagle Ridge and saw its pale sharp edge and towers, conspicuous against the darker cleft of Parallel Gully A to the right. Patey pointed this out to Weir and excitedly described the main sections of the route.

Descending into the corrie and traversing above the dark loch, we found the boulders wet and slippery, and put hands on them for balance. The clumps of dark green moss on the boulders felt like cold wet sponges. A wind stirred the loch below, sending white-tipped wavelets flying along the surface. It was going to be very windy up on top!

All five of us gathered on the scree at the foot of the gloomy Douglas-Gibson Gully, where no old snow remained from the previous winter. It was very sheltered, and windless apart from an occasional slight eddy from the corrie below us. Spots of light cold rain fell, and water from earlier heavier rain streamed down the lowest rocks of the cliffs. Eagle Ridge soared steeply into the mist on our right.

Near the foot of the ridge, a conspicuous wide inset corner formed the start of the route, heading steeply to the right for 60 feet. Patey led, with Mike second and Weir last. Bill and I climbed on a separate rope behind them, coming close to them throughout, and at times standing beside them while Patey forged ahead. Knowing the climb intimately, Bill swarmed rapidly up the first pitch. Though steep, it had many rounded holds, cold and wet today, but no more than Very Difficult. It reminded Tom Weir and me of our climbs on similar rounded holds during rain on the peaks of Lofoten in north Norway during 1951.

There followed easier climbing at a lower angle to about mid-height on the cliff. The climbing now led up to a 50-foot tower of Mild Severe grade, and then up to an apex edge ending on a vertical 12-foot wall. That wall was the crux, Severe in standard, an exposed spot with cliffs plunging precipitously on either side into gloomy gullies. Wet and slippery, the rocks were cold, but throughout the climb we moved fast, which warmed us. The steep granite greatly impressed Tom Weir, who pronounced Eagle Ridge a fine natural line.

As we scrambled unroped up the last easy broken rocks, wet snowflakes came streaming past. A strong wind blasted us when we reached the top of the ridge and walked on to the edge of the exposed flat plateau. There we met John Hinde and members of the RAF Mountain Rescue Team from Kinloss, who had just climbed Eagle Ridge ahead of our two parties. We stopped briefly to chat, Tom Patey the most animated and taking quick puffs on a cigarette.

Climbers half way up Eagle Ridge, which ends at the pink boulders, October 1964

All three parties sped to Lochnagar summit as mist and snowflakes swept down in dark veils. Hurrying clouds and snow showers hid the Cairngorms. Then we all raced back across the plateau with the wind at our backs, pushing us along like sails, and later reached the Spittal of Glenmuick as darkness fell. Cold light rain filtered down through the sheltering thick spruces and pines. At the jeep we put our wet equipment in the back, and then piled inside to drink hot tea from flasks and talk about our day on the hill. The windows steamed with condensation, but we were warm and happy. John Hinde's party left in a land-rover down the public road to Ballater.

For variety on the return journey to Aberdeen, I offered to show Tom Weir the moorland glens to the north, instead of just driving down to Ballater on the same public road that we had come up in the morning. He and the others agreed enthusiastically.

In those days the rough vehicle track from the Spittal to Allt-na-giubhsaich and the gravel road beyond it were unlocked, though private. I lacked permission to drive there, but I cruised past the Spittal, down the track to the wooden bridge that spans the river Muick, and over the moor to Allt-na-giubhsaich. Next there came a glide down the private road on the west side of Glen Muick beside the pine plantations, and then a fork left along the edge of the wood above Inchnabobart. Lastly we crossed the boulder-strewn moors of upper Glen Girnock. The rain turned to sleet, streaming in grey blobs past the innumerable granite boulders and heather banks.

Many white hares bolted headlong across the road, sometimes just a few feet away. I slowed carefully to avoid them and afford right of way to the real native inhabitants of the hills. Reflecting our headlights, their eyes shone brilliant red. The eyes of the scores of hinds, calves and stags gleamed green. As I drove miles over the moor, time and time again we saw the red and the green, watching us.

Eventually we came down the long straight brae to the deer-fence at the Buailteach fields, where many stags trotted across the road above the fence, the last shining green eyes we were to see that evening. Since at least back to 1944, Balmoral estate had no locked gates, but in 2010 for several decades past there has been a locked gate near the Spittal and one at the Buailteach, as well as many others elsewhere on the estate. On that evening in 1953, however, I drove the jeep where I chose. No one was out in the sleet to say yea or nay!

From the Buailteach I drove along the public road past the Lochnagar Distillery and down the steep brae through the woods to Balmoral. The sleet turned to cold rain as we dropped lower towards the river Dee.

Passing the shop at Easter Balmoral, I drove on the private road to tour the complex network of private roads and buildings further west. This included a spin round Balmoral Castle and its many nearby houses and buildings, then out to the public road again and over the metal bridge to Crathie. We saw lights in a few houses, but nobody outside on this cold wet night and no vehicles on the roads. The Castle was a massive tall stone pile, brooding silently in total darkness, impressive but ugly. My passengers enjoyed the tour, shouting encouragement, and laughing and joking. There was wonderful merriment and hilarity in the party. A stranger entering the jeep might have decided we had been drinking whisky, not tea!

At Ballater we stopped for hot fish and chips. Then we roared down a largely deserted main Deeside road to Aberdeen. Tom Weir sat beside me as I drove the left-hand-drive jeep, with Tom Patey on the far end of the big front seat, while Mike and Bill leaned forward eagerly from the back seat. Above the loud din of the tired old World War Two engine and its noisy wheels, Patey shouted his ideas for the climbers' guide.

"We've agreed that I'll climb most of the known routes and Mike the rest. While we're doing that we'll also explore any obvious unclimbed routes. Adam will second most of the routes to provide continuity, and he'll measure the cliff heights with his big aneroid barometer. Mac Smith will be the editor and main author. Mac already has many notes and descriptions of the cliffs and corries. He knows them far better than anybody else. For years he has been exploring every cliff and corrie with a sharp eye for possible lines. We're well ahead already". And we were, for this was fact, not just Patey's optimism.

As usual, Tom Weir was a great catalyst, and said the Scottish Mountaineering Club should publish the guide. He would propose us and Mac as SMC members in time for the 1954 AGM. The club would then be more likely to back the idea. He would strongly recommend their backing and promote publication by the SMC.

The atmosphere in the jeep was electric. Already stimulating all the way from the Spittal, it now reached a crescendo. The jeep seemed almost ready for take-off into mid air! I had not experienced such a tangible buzz of electric team dynamism before, or since. It was a fitting end to a remarkable day on the hill.

Chapter 18   February 1955, severe frost and first try for the six tops

After the long winter of 1951 and my ski-tours in April that year, I began to think I would like a tour crossing the four highest Cairngorms tops, or better still the six main hills including Ben Avon and Beinn a' Bhuird. The next winter was too mild, except in January but it had too few hours of daylight. During early 1953 I lived in Montreal, and 1954 was mild.

In 1954–55 there came another severe winter, not as prolonged as 1951, but a January and February with deeper, more continuous snow and harder frost than in 1951. The winter day was too short in January and early February for such a long tour, but by late February had lengthened greatly. The light from continuous snow added extra daylength. By now in any case, I had become used to skiing at night in moonlight and in the dark without it.

19 February. Severe frost at Luibeg

Dad came from Turriff to Aberdeen, meeting Jenny and me at Marischal College at 5 p.m. and leaving his car in the quadrangle. We went into my jeep and I drove up Deeside in deep snow on a starry night with a very low temperature. The engine stopped twice because the cylinder-head gasket had begun to fail as water leaked into the oil. After ¼ hour in hard frost the engine started again, but often faltered as if about to stop, and required much coaxing and use of lower gears. Eventually we reached the locked gate more than two hours later than planned, at 9.15.

Leaving on skis up the snow-blocked road, we enjoyed a wonderfully bright night and ghostly snow everywhere. In deep soft snow we arrived on ski at Luibeg footbridge at 11.15, just as the scullery light went out. Bob must have still been up, so Dad knocked and Bob opened the door.

He welcomed us to a warm fire in the kitchen and lit a stove. I suggested he go back to the box bed in the kitchen, where Helen sat up to instruct me where to find food. I cooked bacon and potatoes on the stove and made tea for all five of us. My father described this in his diary. *We went to bed. It was bitterly cold -- the coldest this winter at Luibeg. I lit a night light and had on three pairs of socks, trousers, pyjama jacket and balaclava.*

Next morning dawned with severe frost and brilliant sun. Dad wrote, *Up at 9 a.m. and after breakfast we set off on skis to Carn Crom, low temperature. Brilliant sun and colours were on the snow, opal blue, wonderful to see Carn a' Mhaim and Monadh Mor. I climbed above the rocks on Carn Crom and had great running, finishing with a spectacular run-out through the wood.* Everywhere the snow sparkled. Skiing from Carn Crom was excellent. Ominous clouds had gathered, however, threatening heavy snow. In the afternoon we skied to the locked gate, arriving just before dusk as the first flakes fell from a leaden sky.

The jeep engine would not start in the severe frost, but eventually I managed to fire it after many turns of the starting handle, a hard job with such a big machine. My father wrote that *Adam had jeep trouble again at the locked gate, but ultimately started. He must be very tough to turn the handle of such a machine.* In heavy falling snow we roared down the road, with the engine showing no faltering. The reason for this was that the water which had previously gone into the oil had frozen. As the engine warmed and melted the ice in the oil, however, it began to falter again, worse than last night. At Crathie it stopped completely and I could not re-start it. In the hard frost, my fingers stuck like glue to the metal starting handle.

My father wrote that *opposite Balmoral the engine petered out in the middle of the worst snowstorm we had experienced in the low country, 5½ inches in 2 hours. Ultimately I joined a bus at 9.30 p.m. for Ballater, and got a taxi to return to Crathie and tow us to Ballater, stayed overnight at the Towers hotel.*

There we spent a comfortable warm night after a late supper. My father wrote: *Adam deserved a good rest as he stuck it out during the snowstorm trying to start the engine -- all during a temperature of 10 below zero Fahrenheit, the coldest place this night in the country.* Not for the first time that evening I said to Jenny "We should have taken my father's car!"

After heavy snow overnight, next morning we had a hot early breakfast at The Towers. My father wrote that we *left Ballater at 7.15 by train to Aberdeen. Wonderful snow effects in Ballater town, but a snowstorm began and we were late*

AW senior skis up Sron Riach with Lochnagar far beyond, 27 February 1955

AW senior skis towards Stob Coire Sputan Dearg, 27 February 1955

in reaching Aberdeen. My car was almost invisible in the quadrangle and I decided to return home by bus. The jeep I had left at a Ballater garage for gasket renewal.

26 February. A try for the six main tops

On the next weekend, the last in February, I decided to try for the six tops. My father picked me up at Inverdon near the Bridge of Don in the early evening, after driving on snowy roads from Turriff. My jeep still lay at a Ballater garage for repairs. In Aberdeen, my father and I picked up Etchachan Club member and keen ski-mountaineer Bertie Duguid, before motoring to Braemar.

On that frosty evening of 1955, we stopped for tea at Bruachdryne cafe in Braemar, where we met another Etchachan Club member and ski-mountaineer George Davidson. George later joined us in the car. My father wrote in his diary, *Adam was all set for the 6 Tops Tour, but Bertie Duguid reported a radio forecast of bad weather coming next day.* The Derry road had been blocked for months, so the four of us left the car at the Linn of Dee and skied up Glen Lui to reach Luibeg at 11 p.m. My father wrote that it was not unusually cold while skiing.

His diary next day runs, *A beautiful morning, in fact the most wonderful morning I've seen in the hills, everywhere plastered white, the sun shining, perfect snow and wonderful tints.* Despite this, I gave up the idea of the six tops, for I noticed ominous alto-cirrus cloud in the west, a sure sign of impending change, confirming Bertie's forecast. I skied with my father up Glen Luibeg to Ben Macdui. *We left at 10.30 a.m., great skiing snow, wonderful snow on the Sron Riach, all the near hills standing out in the sun.* On the plateau and summit the sun had gone and a biting cold wind blew, moving the powder snow in whirls and little clouds.

My father wrote on this. *Very cold on top, I thought I'd be frostbitten before I got skins off and into my pack, then a wonderful run down to Loch Etchachan, and down Coire Etchachan, crusty in some parts and softer in others, but I stuck to the north side of the corrie. Adam was a small figure in the bowl when I was still on the side of it. At Loch Etchachan we had thought of going home via Derry Cairngorm, but the weather was changing quickly and very cold, so we skied down the corrie to the hut, a poor substitute for a hut, and after a quick snack, on to the Derry flats, reaching Luibeg at 5.15 p.m.*

A grand dinner there and off at 6 p.m. with Bertie and George to ski in the dark down to the Linn of Dee. *Reached car but couldn't get it started on account of intense cold, so Adam skied to the phone box at Inverey to phone Mrs Grant in Braemar and ask if Alistair could come in a taxi and give us a pull.* He later came in a big Austin, by coincidence the car that my father had sold to Mrs Grant! *Alistair with AV7656 gave us a pull and off we went. I reached Turriff at 2.30 a.m. on Monday morning, many drifts between Aberdeen and Fyvie.*

Notes

The dated accounts above rest partly on my diary and quotations from my father's diary. I skied round the six tops in April 1962 (Chapter 21), but thought of doing this in February 1955 and April 1958, when I was fitter, after skiing more than in 1962. Despite short daylength in February 1955, the tour would have been easier if weather had been good, because the snow was the best of all three occasions, and hard frost reduces one's overheating while skiing. In 1958 (Chapter 20) it would have been easier than in 1962, had I risen earlier, because snow was better, with more powder and less ice.

Chapter 19 Four winters on the Glen Esk hills

In 1957 I became a senior research fellow at Aberdeen University, studying red grouse, and my wife Jenny and I moved to Fernybank Lodge in Glen Esk. My colleague David Jenkins started work there in late 1956, concentrating on the moor near Tarfside but occasionally visiting higher moorland. In view of my mountaineering experience, it was agreed that I would extend the high areas up to the Braid Cairn at 2900 feet. I would have a land-rover for the work. I would also get a middle-aged big white English setter dog called Harra, gifted by Sir John Brooks at Midgay on the Dornoch Firth, from a line that included setters from Altnaharra, hence his name.

David drove the land-rover with me on 17 October 1957 to see the high area that he had studied, and the Invermark beat gamekeeper Jimmy Robertson and a Millden gamekeeper Eck Stewart accompanied us. We drove up a rough track past the Hill of Kirny and left the rover on a ridge beyond, called Aikenstock by the gamekeepers. Beyond lay a shallow peaty valley drained by the Easter Burn, rising to the Hill of Saughs. All around us for at least a mile stretched an undulating plateau, mostly covered by thick peat and peat hags. The keepers called it the Leg o Moss, an apt name, for it forms a long leg of peat-moss. Away to the northwest rose the Braid Cairn, called by the keepers the Braid Cairns.

When we reached 2000 feet, a vast panorama opened out. We stood at the edge of a gently rolling plateau of peat-hags, bogs and heathery hilltops, east to Mount Battock, north to Braid Cairn, west to Glen Clova and Loch Muick with Lochnagar and Broad Cairn rising prominently beyond, and south towards Glen Esk. Further south on the far side of Glen Esk stood a narrower plateau stretching to the Hill of Wirren and upper Lethnot.

The great space struck me as unusual. In my diary I wrote, *what it would be like here during a blizzard? It is difficult to think that this area is at the same altitude as the floors of the upper glens of the Cairngorms such as Glen Dee, Dubh Ghleann etc.* After an hour's walk we drove down the Hill of Kirny. Later, I went there so often at all seasons, leaving the rover on the top ridge or skiing up from the low ground, that some local folk nicknamed me The Laird o Kirny.

On 21 December 1957 a force 8 gale blew despite a mostly sunny sky, breaking many branches off trees down in the glen. On the Leg o Moss at 2000 feet, nearly all red grouse were in shelter along peat-hags and burnsides as I walked along the plateau with Harra. *Grouse were extremely wild, rising mostly at 200 yards. Even single birds rose at 150 yards, and many of the packs at 300 or even 400 yards, but in spite of the gale, the light was excellent and grouse easily seen with the sun glinting on their wings. Gale all day and I saw a hare bowled clean over by the wind as it ran along the top of a ridge among hags.* The gale could easily have knocked down a man or dog, and I had to take care while walking. Harra stayed close to me, sometimes buffeted by strong gusts. On this and other wild days, however, I never saw a red grouse or ptarmigan bowled over, even though they ducked low during violent gusts.

Heavy snow fell in January to March 1958 and I had magnificent ski-touring. Mostly I skied to the Hill of Kirny and beyond to observe grouse on the study areas, but on other days to Mount Battock, Hill of Wirren, Craig Maskeldie, Glen Lee, Water of Unich, the Green Hill of Clova, Glen Mark, Mount Keen, Braid Cairn and Hill of Gairney.

Hard frost continued on many cloudless days, often with hoar-frost crystals festooned on birches and snow surfaces. When the crystals melted in the sun, water drops glittered in brilliant spots of light showing all colours of the spectrum, each drop changing colour as it moved. Even in January sunshine, the snow sparkled with diamond brilliance. It gave perfect conditions for skiing on ascent and descent, and I recall many long runs, swishing for a mile straight downhill to the fields.

On 16 February a temporary thaw came with a gale, sleet and blinks of warm sun. My father and I climbed on skis to Allrey below Mount Battock. I wrote *wind force about 8, spring snow drifting, skiing slowly uphill at one stage, without using sticks, so strong was the gale at my back, one good run of ¼ mile straight downhill on uniform snow.*

We had a memorable short tour on 23 March, starting at 650 feet at a road near my house. On skins we climbed to Craigangower where a strong sou-easter blew, and skied down the corrie, a continuous descent of 1300 feet before I stopped. My father wrote: *What a run, excellent snow and the wind behind me. It was steep so I veered over and came on Adam's tracks going down. It was most exhilarating with rough and smooth parts, and I decided it was one of the best*

Jenny and Harra below Braid Cairn, 13 January 1958. Neil Baird and friend Swanney skiing far right

Spiggie near Braid Cairn, 13 January 1958

skiing days I have had. I saw Adam's figure far below. One could have gone back if it was not so stormy. I got home to Turriff at 6 pm after a most enjoyable weekend and perfect skiing.

I had never seen so much snow covering everything in the landscape as in December 1958. On the 12th my notes for the glen bottom record *torrential rain and sleet, falling as snow on the hills* and on 14th *torrential wet snow began at 0900, by afternoon turning to sleet and finally cold rain in late evening,* and on 15th *Heavy rain and sleet much of the day.* On the 15th I noted that our rain gauge at Milton Cottage showed four inches since the 12th, equivalent to four feet of snow.

When I skied that day, I found *four inches of snow at 1000 feet, a foot at 1500 feet, 18–24 inches at 1700 feet, and 2–3 feet with many deeper drifts at 2000 feet. Above 1700 feet, snow covered everything deeply, and even the Kirny Burn flowed silently below. Snow filled the six-foot deep peat-hags beyond the top of the Kirny Burn, level to the ridges on either side, and drifts at least 15 feet deep lay on the lee side of the Hill of Kirny. Now well consolidated, the snow had fallen moist and then froze. Today, fresh snow drifted along the hard surface and lay in many fresh drifts. The dogs and skis sank in no more than an inch in the fresh snow and just left small marks in the harder surface.* Not a black speck broke the white expanse, and over many years in the Cairngorms I had never seen such unbroken snow.

During days when deep drifted snow covered most ground, the red grouse formed big restless packs, which I could see two miles away with the naked eye. As I appeared on skis at a hilltop and saw packs afar, often they flushed a mile away, and at greater range when a flying eagle appeared .The packs favoured ridges where wind had blown snow off the heather shoots that the birds ate. Over big tracts I could count them easily against the white snow. Often I counted all grouse on our high areas totalling 1750 acres, by skiing to the Hill of Kirny and the ridge beyond the source of the Easter Burn. On 8 January 1961 I noted *Deep snow, on skis, 549 grouse seen on high areas.*

On 15 January 1959 I saw a huge pack land at Badalair on deep snow while I stood ½ mile away. In the bright sunlight they appeared black against brilliant white snow. I had just finished counting 950 when they took off with a roar of wings and swept out of sight.

Down on the low moor near Tarfside, sometimes a heavy fall of moist snow came in calm air, with no drifting or very little. When this happened, almost all grouse vanished on the first day. I could scan a moor where hundreds had fed on the previous dusk as snow began to fall, and now see none. They could not have flown away, because I had seen them preparing to roost on the previous dusk, and now not a wing-mark or footprint broke the surface.

Harra at Inverarnan of Loch Lomond, 1 January 1958 (Tom Weir)

Sunset on the Hill of Gairney from the Hill of Kirny, January 1958

When I investigated on skis, I found the grouse underneath the snow in the places where they had roosted overnight. Well insulated by a thick snow blanket above, they stood in pockets of air. Often they stood on snow-free ground, because thick heather above their heads had stopped much of the snow from falling through the foliage to the ground. Some did a little feeding underneath, as shown by freshly-bitten shoots, but many fasted. Such conditions never lasted more than a day, because the weather would change with drifting or thaw, and next day the birds would fly in packs to feed on the surface.

I observed many snow roosts. Usually the grouse scraped a small hollow, but on fairly cold nights a deeper one with their heads level to the rim and looking out, just above the surface. In hard frost they made holes with the entrance open, but in severe frost burrowed wholly underneath, after filling the entrance with snow kicked back with their feet.

After deep snowfalls followed by thaws and hard frost, the snow on 3 February 1959 was so hard that I could drive the land-rover in a straight line uphill or across country over burns and hags that had vanished out of sight. My notes described it as *Very hard snow with a heavy deposit of ¼ inch of hoar-frost crystals like soap flakes on top. The rover wheels went in less than an inch on drifts 3–4 feet deep.* The surface had a gritty feel, with enough friction for tyres and walking. It reminded me of the gritty surface on sea ice, lakes and rivers at Baffin Island in June.

On one day of drifted deep powder I left the land-rover on the Hill of Kirny and went with Harra to the Braid Cairn to count grouse. In mid afternoon I had finished and began walking back, with Harra close behind. Suddenly I became aware of no noise behind, and looked round, seeing no sign of him. A white snowy expanse, shining in the sun, extended everywhere. However one can see a white setter on fresh snow, because the dog looks creamy-white. Through binoculars I scanned my recent route in vain. I knew he could not have chased a hare, because I would see his tracks, so I assumed he had fallen into a hole.

With mounting anxiety I walked back 400 yards, following my earlier tracks, and then with great relief heard him

Harra and Solitaire in exceptional snow cover on the Hill of Kirny, 15 December 1958, at sunset

Sheep await farmer for a sunset meal below Burnside, February 1958

Down Glen Esk to the North Sea from the Hill of Kirny, February 1958

barking, a strange distorted sound from under the snow. I ran to the spot, came to a dark opening two feet from my homeward tracks, and saw him at the bottom, barking loudly. He stood on snow above firm peat about nine feet down, in a circular peat-hole about 3–4 feet wide, whose entrance had been covered by drifted snow. As soon as he saw me, he stopped barking and wagged his tail. He looked at me, longingly.

I decided that I must try to get Harra out quickly. A glance into the hole was enough for me to see a safe way to get him out and me afterwards. The way was to clamber down the hole and stand on the floor, lifting him up with both arms until he could scramble out. I could then extricate myself by backing up, as in a rock chimney. I could see that the hole was of the right width. So it proved. I clambered to the foot, and in a fast movement lifted him above my head and threw him sideways. After his body landed on the edge of the hole, he tore into the snow with his fore-claws and swarmed out, to shake himself and await my arrival.

Vertical black peat formed the walls of the hole, with little snow. Water in the peat had frozen into small bands and patches of glossy ice, but most of the frozen surface of the walls was rough because of frost, offering much more friction than in a thaw or in summer. Only at the very bottom was the peat partly unfrozen, slightly wet and greasy. Putting a foot against the far wall, I leaned until my back rested against the near wall. Next I put the other foot vertically against the far wall, and proceeded to move towards the circle of blue sky above. Because of friction from the frozen peat, this took more time and energy than in most rock chimneys, but I could more easily stop and take a rest at any point.

Eventually my head came above the snow surface and I saw Harra wagging his tail, pleased that I had appeared. I moved slightly sideways, with my bottom and both feet resting against the snow at the top edge of the hole and my back above the surface. Then I rolled sideways on to firm snow, stood up, and shook snow off. What a relief!

The morning after very deep windless snowfall at the Milton with Hill of Wirren beyond, 25 February 1958

AW about to ring a grouse chick that Solitaire pointed on the Hill of Kirny, June 1958 (Tom Weir)

Harra and I walked to the rover without further ado. He stayed close at heel, with no sideways wandering!

Another Harra event featured the Braid Cairn in winter again. On this day, no snow lay on the lower slopes. After finishing a grouse count at the foot of Braid Cairn, I called Harra to heel and walked towards the rover on Hill of Kirny. He came at heel for a few hundred yards, but again, as above, I became aware of no sound and looked round. He was lying down in tall heather half a mile back, pointing at something. I whistled and shouted, but when on point he was the steadiest dog I ever had. He continued to point. I then thought that if I sat down, he would tire of waiting, would break his point, and come to me.

After five minutes with him still motionless, I decided it would be interesting to see how long he stayed on point. I thought I would have to sit a few minutes. After 40 minutes he made his first slight move, merely raising a foreleg and taking a single step forward. Then he lay on point again, but the movement had unnerved his quarry, and now I saw through binoculars a cock grouse lift its head. It gave escape calls and a moment later flew. Harra then ran straight to me.

The grouse had raised its head about three yards from where he first pointed, and doubtless thought it best to sit tight, hoping the dog had not noticed and would depart. The grouse and I made the same error. There is an apocryphal story in some books of a staunch setter pointing at a partridge, out of sight of its master and not returning to him, and of how months later someone found the bones of dog and partridge together, neither having wished to move.

On one cloudy November day I went with Harra and my English pointer bitch Solitaire to the Hill of Kirny to count grouse, but the weather deteriorated rapidly as we walked the first transect along a ridge south of the Easter Burn. The already strong wind became a gale so strong that I could hardly face it when I turned. Torrential wet snow and hail swept down in sheets, and wisps of mist tore past. Knowing the unreliability of a count in such conditions, I gave up this one. As I turned to walk half a mile uphill to the rover in the teeth of the gale, I had to crouch as I faced the wind and the dogs ran low to the ground, close at my heels. Our slow progress concerned me, and I considered turning with the wind at our backs. We would then have come quickly to sheltered low ground, but that would have entailed abandoning the rover temporarily, maybe longer if a blizzard came.

Using every peat-hag, hillock or burn-side to reduce the force of the gale, I moved in zigzags and curves, closely followed by the dogs. Eventually after a slow journey the rover loomed dark on the horizon. Yard by yard we came nearer, and eventually it stood beside us. Immediately it broke the strength of gale and wet snow. As soon as I opened the back door, the soaked dogs jumped in, shook themselves and lay close, while I battened down openings in the canvas back-door. Aware that the gale might wrench the driver's door off its hinges if I opened it, I used the passenger's door at the lee side. I entered a different world of dry air and calm.

Outside, the gale battered and shook the vehicle violently, and wet snow plastered the windward side. Would the engine start in this wet air? After a single turn it sprang into action, I pushed my foot on the accelerator to make it roar, and drove off in a little cloud of whirling snow. Soon the heater made the cab a warm haven as I descended to the sodden rain-swept moor, and I opened the window at the back of the cab to let heat into the back for the dogs. They were sound asleep. I called at the Milton to see farmer Vic Strachan and his wife George (Georgina), who gave me tea and a scone while I stood steaming at a blazing fire.

By late 1960, botanist Gordon Miller and assistant Dudley Pinnock had joined us. Gordon had often been on the hill but Dudley not, for he hailed from southern England. However, he assured us he had much experience of yachting and navigation off the south coast. On 8 November, a winter day of fresh snow, I drove the rover to beyond Hill of Kirny with Gordon and Dudley. Each of us had a separate job, I with dogs to count grouse on Hill of Gairney. The sun shone brilliantly from a cloudless blue sky upon sparkling fresh snow and hoar frost. After walking together for a mile to a ridge west of the Hill of Saughs, we took three routes, I to go furthest.

Shortly after we split up, fog formed at ground level for a few minutes, on an area about 600 yards across. Through the thin fog I could still see the sun and blue sky. In a few minutes I emerged into bright sunshine for the rest of the day. In late afternoon I returned to the rover and Gordon came soon after. Seeing no sign of Dudley, we walked to the ridge beyond the Kirny Burn. From there, any person would have been conspicuous against the white snow, for miles. We agreed to retrace our outward route until the point where Dudley had left us.

After fast walking in snow, we came in 20 minutes to the spot where the morning's tracks diverged, and then followed Dudley's track. For about 200 yards he had gone in a straight line, and then suddenly his track went at a right angle when it should have continued straight. At once I realised what had happened. At the end of his first 200 yards he had come into thin fog that disorientated him so that he went in the wrong direction. We followed his new track for some way, and with binoculars I saw it continuing towards the lower moor. Obviously he had been in bright sun soon after starting his altered new track, and later saw the low ground.

Now Gordon and I returned to the rover at dusk. I drove to the Milton, where Vic opened the door to say Dudley was inside. While George gave us tea, a shame-faced Dudley told his story. When fog came down, he became disorientated, and recognised nothing when the fog vanished. He saw unfamiliar snowy hills everywhere and it felt like being on the moon. However, he saw low ground, and the burn near him flowed in that direction, so he went there. Eventually he reached Baillies farm, which he recognised, and walked the road to the Milton. On arrival there in early afternoon, he suggested walking to meet us, for he knew we would be anxious. Wisely, Vic had forbidden this, and told him to await our return.

Aware that this had badly shaken Dudley's confidence, next day I drove with him again to Hill of Kirny, to teach him a lesson in recognising terrain and sun direction. I showed him how no two ridges or hilltops are the same, and how every bit of ground is unique when you know how to look at it. He showed much interest. Never again did Dudley become lost or disorientated on the hill. It had been a good lesson.

Chapter 20 The four highest Cairngorms on ski

On Friday 11 April 1958, I drove from Glen Esk to Corndavon moor, and spent most of the day counting red grouse with my English setter dog Harra. The two sections of moor north of Crathie held consolidated deep snow after a long winter, and I estimated snow cover on them as 70% and 80%. Not a cloud dimmed the sky. I noted the wind as Beaufort force 0–1, and at 1400 feet the snow was thawing in the sun but freezing in the shade. In late afternoon I drove to Luibeg, hoping for a long tour next day.

After a cup of tea with Bob and Helen Scott, I skied with Harra to Carn Crom to look for ptarmigan. The view northwest to Braeriach was striking as the snow turned golden in the evening sun, the shadows dark blue, the rocks almost black. The south side of Derry Cairngorm lay deep under continuous snow in great folds that shone creamy in the sun, gradually turning golden and then pink. I watched the sun set and then descended quickly to Luibeg, with Harra running straight downhill behind me as I zigzagged in one swooping ski turn after another.

There had been a temperature inversion, with warm sun on Carn Crom, but down in the glen a sharp frost had set in. I laid my sleeping bag in the barn and slept with Harra in the straw beside me. Before turning in, I arranged with Bob to look after him next day. At first I considered taking him, but then decided to leave him. He had put in a hard day's work on the hill, and the tour would be long and perhaps too icy for him.

I intended to rise at 4 am in anticipation of skiing round the six main tops of the Cairngorms, but slept soundly till 6. Now I regretted not having taken an alarm clock, for the lack of two hours might scupper my plan. By the time I left at 7 after a good breakfast, Bob had risen and took charge of Harra. I told him I intended to ski round the four highest tops and go to the two eastern ones if daylight allowed. He said I should have asked for an alarm. As usual he gave a great send-off with a shout, and said he would see me in the evening after I had crossed much of his beat.

On a beautiful morning of hard frost and cloudless sky I walked up Glen Luibeg. I carried a heavy pack with a pair of wooden Canadian downhill skis which had steel edges and a binding for climbing, aluminium ski-sticks, straps for attaching ski-bindings to boots, ski-skins, a pair of heavy Canadian ski-mountaineering boots, an ice-axe, crampons, goggles, camera, binoculars, food, a cup, suncream, sunhat, leather ski-mitts, and spare clothes. After a snowy winter when I had daily walked or skied in Glen Esk, I hardly noticed the heavy pack and skis.

At the last pines by the Lairig path I donned the skis and climbed on hard-packed powder to the shoulder of Carn a' Mhaim, and then to the footbridge over Dee near Corrour Bothy. The snow had melted on some parts, with many boulders projecting, and had turned icy in other places. Nonetheless, when I reached the bothy I had taken only 1½ hours from Luibeg. Now there followed a long climb on skins up Coire Odhar on hard-packed powder. Towards the top I had to remove skis and climb on foot, kicking and cutting steps because of a steep bulge of hard snow and then soft cornices. The sun felt very warm and I treated each step on soft snow carefully because of avalanche risk, but past the top a cool light breeze blew.

On skins I climbed fast up the Buidheanach on hard-packed snow with smooth powder on top, and made steady progress to the top above Coire an t-Saighdeir. A few puffy clouds had formed about 500 feet above the plateau, but evaporated as they moved slowly towards Glen Geusachan. Some boulders projected through the snow on the final rise to Cairn Toul, but I managed to keep the skis on by climbing narrow drifts. I had to remove them for only a short section where boulders with soft powder blocked the way to the summit. Only 3½ hours had passed since I left Luibeg and the settled weather tempted me to consider the six tops again.

After skiing down a partly bouldery slope towards Sgor an Lochain Uaine, I travelled fast on good snow round the south side of the Sgor to the col at Garbh Choire Mor. There I slipped on skins and climbed beside immense cornices to the plateau. Much of the cliff lay under snow, rime and ice, but steep buttresses had become partly free of snow and ice. A haze enveloped the distant landscape, and Beinn Bhrotain and Cairn Toul rose in a strange silky sheen of sunshine glistening on snow. Patterns of light on the snow differed visibly on different kinds of snow, even two miles away. The most spectacular view of the day opened from near the top of Garbh Choire Mor, past huge cornices to the snowy depths of Glen Geusachan.

Skiing almost effortlessly on the plateau past the unseen Wells of Dee, I reached the top of Braeriach at noon, five

Looking south from above the Garbh Choire Mor on 12 April 1958

Rime-encrusted cliffs of Coire Bhrochain from Braeriach summit on 12 April 1958

hours from Luibeg. Regarding this as quite fast, I again considered a tour round the six tops feasible, despite losing the two early hours. At the rim of Coire Bhrochain near the summit cairn, the buttresses showed not a speck of rock, buried under thick rime and ice below overhanging cornices, and shining with a strange pale purplish light. Now I left to ski down to the col with Sron na Lairige on rough bumpy sastrugi and patches of ice. I slowed to a stop as I neared the steep edge of Coire na Lairige.

Carrying skis, I began to plunge on foot in deep drifted powder down the top of the steep slope, but it carried a large convex bulge due to drifted soft snow, and soon I had to take care, step by step. I noticed small snowballs rolling from under my feet and picking up snow as they descended. The snow had become unstable due to sunshine and warm still air, with a risk of avalanche. Slowly and carefully I climbed back, watching every step and walking on firmer snow where possible, and then skied south on a horizontal traverse along the top of the wreath at a gradient too low for an avalanche.

Having reached the boulder ridge at the east side of Coire Bhrochain, I climbed down it, a slow, tiring descent. The exposed ridge had caught the wind, so most snow had blown off. Soft snow partly hid the boulders, slippery and harder to see than in summer. Care had to be taken with every step. Eventually, however, after a time-consuming descent of 600 feet, I reached a snow slope at a lower angle, put skis on, and moved swiftly down to the glen south of the Pools of Dee. The Pools lay invisible below a deep mantle of drifted snow.

Four sets of tracks in the snow along the bottom of the Lairig Ghru showed where walkers had passed, and a man walked south past the Pools as I skied up the slope towards Ben Macdui. The boulder field in the Lairig lay under deep snow, but a few ridges leading into the foot of the Lairig from either side held little or no snow because of severe drifting.

Now I faced east, and climbed over 1000 feet to the edge of Ben Macdui plateau north of Allt a' Choire Mhoir. At first I followed a snow-free ridge for 200 feet, and then had to climb hard snow. The skyline edge above seemed far away, but I ascended steadily and carefully, and it was good to reach the half-way point.

Just then I suddenly thought it would be less tiring to keep the skis on by moving south and then up continuous snow on the broad ridge east of Coire Clach nan Taillear. Despite the detour and longer distance, I thought it would be faster, but it was now much too late to change tack.

Every step on the upper steep half of the slope had to be taken carefully, because of a mixture of icy rocks, hard snow, and patches of soft snow that hid boulders. Now a big sweep of hard snow ran steeply below me, shining in the sun and falling into the depths of the Lairig Ghru. As well as the crampons, I had to use my ice-axe often for steps and occasionally handholds, and found the warm still air oppressive and tiring. However, I knew that the snow could not avalanche, and the skyline edge approached, slowly but surely. At last there came relief and satisfaction, the plateau edge. As I breasted it, I appreciated a sudden rush of cold air flowing from the snowy flat expanse beyond. I had taken two hours from Braeriach, far longer than expected when I began descending Coire na Lairige.

After a snack, I donned my skis and faced Cairn Gorm, whose snowy dome rose white against the blue sky to the northeast. From the plateau edge, good skiing conditions on hard-packed powder stretched all the way to Cairn Gorm. As I passed the top of the March Burn, I noticed that a big party had come up earlier today or yesterday, leaving huge bucket steps in the steep slope. It would have been almost effortless compared with my ascent route. However, the deep soft steep snow faced the sun, and the air in the Lairig had been warm, so the avalanche risk would have been high. My route had been by far the safer of the two, though more consuming in time and effort.

A few downhill skiers sat at Cairn Gorm summit, which I reached in quick time. Then I skied south to Ben Macdui, finding the going excellent and achieving such a good rhythm that I did not notice my heavy pack. At Ben Macdui cairn I stood some minutes to appreciate the views of snowy hills in all directions. There followed a magnificent long run to Loch Etchachan and then another all the way down Coire Etchachan to the Lairig an Laoigh path at the top of Glen Derry.

Should I continue to Beinn a' Bhuird and Ben Avon, or descend Glen Derry to Luibeg? I felt fitter than in the morning, and had I risen two hours earlier would have continued without hesitation. I was tempted to continue, for skiing conditions were now excellent, with a slight frost making the snow surface less soft. All the steep difficult slopes lay behind me. Earlier in the day I had noticed unbroken snow from the Lairig an Laoigh path to Moine

Bhealaidh and the North Top of Beinn a' Bhuird. At Corndavon and towards Braemar the day before, I had seen unbroken snow on Cnap a' Chleirich and Ben Avon.

However, I reasoned I would come off Ben Avon to Glen Quoich at dusk. A long walk on foot would follow through trackless tall heather in the glen, with enough snow to make walking difficult but not enough for skiing. As an alternative, I reckoned that there would be enough snow for skiing along the steep woods on the north side of Carn Elrig Mor, but the light would have been failing and the risks increasing accordingly. After either of these alternatives, I would have to come into tall heather in the trackless wooded Glen Quoich. Skiing along the south side of Meall an Lundain would follow in the dark, and then a walk down the moor to Derry Lodge. Although I had a small hand-torch, it gave very poor light compared with today's head-torches. I reasoned that a long walk floundering in the dark with a heavy pack, especially in Glen Quoich, would take the edge off a wonderful day.

So, south down Glen Derry I pointed the skis and removed them below Glas Allt Mor. There I had a good drink from the burn and lay five minutes in warm sunshine, drying my boots and appreciating the fine light on the outpost pines. Slipping on skis again, I followed ribbons of snow down to the footbridge and then walked down the path to Derry Lodge and Luibeg, which I reached at 7, as low evening sunlight shone creamy and silvery on the far snows of Beinn Bhrotain and Monadh Mor. Twelve hours had passed since I left.

At Luibeg, Helen Scott gave me hot tea, the finest drink I could wish. Bob had enjoyed Harra's company. After feeding Harra his meal of the day, hot oatmeal brose laced with milk and boiled mountain hare, I chatted with Bob while Helen gave me soup. It felt like old times at Luibeg, except that I could not stay, for I had far to go.

Bob and I drove separately to the Invercauld Arms bar in Braemar, where I stood him a big dram and a pint while I had a thirst-quenching lemonade shandy. He had come for a good sitting with local men, but I had to leave all too soon. There followed a long drive down Deeside and over the Cairn o' Mount to Glen Esk in the noisy land-rover. I had to charge through deep drifts on the snow-blocked Cairn road and creep over ice on the south side, with one wheel on gravel and heather at the side to prevent the vehicle careering on slippery ice right off the road. After midnight I reached home at Fernybank. Jenny said eagle expert Leslie Brown had arrived from Kenya on Friday evening, spent Saturday searching for eyries, and had gone to bed in one of the lodge's many bedrooms.

As I put Harra to bed amongst deep straw in an outhouse, the stars shone brightly and frost gripped the ground under the tall trees. I thought of the day just gone. The main impressions were of innumerable shining slopes and ridges in an unending series in all directions, the swish and tinkle of skis on the snows of the high plateaux and corries, the muffled sound of burns below the snow, and the sight of unearthly bright green grass and dark green pines after many miles of snow and ice. I returned to the house and listened to the radio while having a last cup of tea to quench my thirst. The weather forecast reported a marked change, with cloud on the hills and snowfalls for several days, and that proved to be the case.

In the next two days, winds were cold, snowflakes and hail biting, and clouds low as Leslie Brown in his kilt and I in winter clothes did grouse counts with Harra at 2000 feet on the Leg o Moss. It would not have been suitable for a long solo ski-mountaineering tour across the high Cairngorms. I was glad I had snatched the opportunity for an outstanding fine day on the hill.

Later I reckoned the distance as about 22 miles and the total height 6900 feet. Continuing to the eastern tops would have added another 12 miles and 3500 feet. Had I risen at 4 in the morning as intended, I think I would have been on the top of Beinn a' Bhuird by 5 in the afternoon, Ben Avon before 6, the south slope above the first Quoich pines by 7, and Luibeg easily by 9.

Chapter 21 Cairngorm langlauf

It was a Saturday in April 1962, and I'd been burning heather all day on a Deeside moor just below the snow line. We had marched off the hill hot, tired, and thirsty, but a sudden frost soon had us shivering at the contrast from the blazing inferno of a few minutes before. I was looking forward to a long lie in bed next morning. But later that evening I began to wonder. This was the first April since 1958 with so much snow. If I got up early, and the weather held, what a fine langlauf tour could be done on the Cairngorms! I nipped over to the little shop up the road at 11 o'clock, and bought six tins of fruit, knowing I'd crave sweet liquid rather than food the next day.

I rose very sleepily at three, and after breakfast drove swiftly up Deeside. The sky was cloudless and moonlit, and the ground iron-hard, as I set off at 5 o'clock from Invercauld through the pine woods towards Gleann an t-Slugain. A frosty mist hung over the Dee, magnifying the craggy low hills and the tall spruces into a landscape more like the Rockies. I was carrying a pair of long narrow skis, weighing only 7 lb., which I'd bought at the hamlet of Kaaresuvanto in Lapland for 50 shillings, and a fairly full rucksack with ice-axe, sleeping bag, camera, binoculars and food. I was determined not to continue with the ski tour any longer than I was enjoying it, and to sleep at Corrour or some other place if the day became too much of a penance.

From the upper Slugain onwards, the snow lay deep and continuous, so hard that it bore my weight with scarcely a mark. On with the skis, and I rattled away at great speed over the icy surface towards Ben Avon. It was already dawn and cock grouse were cackling all around, standing up on every big snow-free patch and shouting defiance to their next-door neighbours -- a cheery Deeside morning sound seldom heard in the barren far west. The sun was flooding in a rosy glow over the great bulk of Beinn a' Bhuird and down into the old green mushroom pines of the Quoich. It was good to be climbing at last, up towards Carn Eas. Skins were needed for a grip and soon afterwards a problem appeared. The steep south side of Carn Eas was ringed from end to end by a massive cornice which had been avalanching in yesterday's strong sun. There was only one narrow line of weakness without a cornice -- a 45-degree slope which had thawed partly the day before and was now very hard. It was a case of kicking steps in a long traverse below the cornice, then cutting steps straight up over the line of weakness. Having done no climbing whatsoever for four months, I was glad to inch gradually over the bulge and off this icy slope that swept far down into the murky shadows of the Gairn valley.

At Carn Eas I was now on the Ben Avon plateau and looking down over the vast Aberdeenshire grouse moors, mostly covered by an early-morning cloud sea. Up here some of the snow had evaporated in the dry sunny air, exposing bits of green moss and grass, and the golden plovers were back, flying like butterflies in their courtship and piping mournfully--always a welcome sign of spring on the hills of Deeside. I tore on at a great, but jolting, pace over hard ridged snow, and soon the black rocks at the summit loomed up above. An icy east wind blew there, showering the fog crystals from the rocks. There was a view of utter desolation towards Tomintoul, where the bleak flat Banffshire moors were an unrelieved expanse of white almost all the way to the Moray Firth. Through binoculars I watched cars crawling like ants on the road towards Glen Livet. It was 8.30 a.m., and I was 3½ hours from Invercauld. Already very thirsty, I sucked fog crystals at the cairn till the cold sent me off. I turned west towards the finer prospect of the Mitre Ridge and Beinn a' Bhuird.

A few minutes and half a mile later, the plateau was behind after a fine run on smooth powder snow. But afterwards the fairly steep descent to the Sneck was slow and tiring on very icy ridged snow, where the long narrow skis were difficult to control. I went down painfully, with a few tumbles and undignified scrapes. Then up the other side, with a spectacular airy view on the right along the great ice-plastered wall of Mitre Ridge.

From Cnap a' Chleirich to the North Top of Beinn a' Bhuird, it might have been an Arctic ice-cap--not a black speck in sight, and psychologically very tiring with the intense glare, flat snowscape and no view. But at last at 10.30 a.m. the tip of the North Top cairn peeped through, and a fine view opened out to the west. The 2-mile descent to Moine Bhealaidh was the best ski run of the day, with glistening hard-packed powder in every direction. I swooped leisurely from side to side all the way down Coire Ruaraidh, and finally far out on to the Moss in a last straight run. But out on the flat glaring expanse of the Moss I again felt tired, in spite of the perfect snow surface, and started

Ben Macdui from Beinn a' Bhuird on 16 April 1962

getting cramps up and down my legs. No doubt about it, I wasn't in form, what with no skiing at all for over six weeks, and that -- of a day yesterday tasting the preliminaries of hellfire hadn't helped. It was tempting to think what a good finish it would make to ski quickly all the way down to Derry Lodge and have a brew of tea over a fire. This was a signal that it was time for a good rest, and I opened a tin of fruit.

Refreshed, I pushed on swiftly and was soon edging down the steep slopes into Glen Derry. Here the snow was very icy, and the endless fast traverses and kick turns brought the floor of the glen up slower than if I'd been on foot. The Derry Burn was showing at one place, the last water I was to see till Glen Dee, and I drank a good quart. Coire Etchachan was suffocating -- no wind, blazing sun, a dark blue sky and utter calm. Every step was an effort, relieved only by watching the infinitely more painful progress of two heavily laden parties on foot. As I climbed, a cornice cracked and tumbled down the 500-foot red wall of Creagan a' Choire Etchachan, and the whole corrie had an air of menace. It was so calm that I could hear my heart thumping as if it was outside my body, and the 'silence you most could hear' swishing in my ears. Some ptarmigan were quietly dozing on top of boulders in the hot sun, their eyes closing lethargically from time to time. I rested for a while on a boulder near them, feeling quite spent.

There was a refreshing change at last up at Loch Etchachan where a cold wind blew over the flat white invisible loch. I was tempted to go down by Derry Cairngorm, but now felt slightly better, so I plugged on uphill mechanically and took heart when I caught up with two skiers from Yorkshire. The snow was smooth but our pace slow to the Ben Macdui cairn, where about six people had gathered. For the third time I felt like ending the tour by heading off south, but some food and a rest for an hour in good company changed my mind. Ken Armstrong and a friend appeared from Glen More and shortly after headed back, flashing down at a great speed off the North Top. How I envied their fine downhill technique and the stability of their heavy skis. By the time I had wobbled down unsteadily on my birch boards from Lapland, they were distant specks. Still, the plateau was a continuous sheet of silky smooth snow, and now on the flat, my skis had the advantage, I felt stronger, and soon I'd passed ahead of them. After leaving my pack at Lochan Buidhe I felt like jumping in the air with relief and I now flashed quickly on to Cairn Gorm, through scores of skiers and walkers thronging the summit and the Coire Cas ridge.

Not long afterwards I was ski-ing gingerly down the top of the March Burn. The slope was now 45 degrees and had softened dangerously in the strong afternoon sun, so I fixed the skis to my pack and trod carefully downwards, shoving my ice-axe well into the snow and sending off minute avalanches all the way down. I skied down the last 200 feet in a glorious steep swoop to the invisible Pools of Dee and suddenly out of warm sun into freezing hard shade.

I ate two more tins of fruit and took stock. It was 5 o'clock and the cramps and weariness of the forenoon had all gone. However, I was now finding climbing very tiresome with the pack but easy without. So -- why not leave the pack in the Lairig Ghru below Coire Bhrochain, ski round, back a short distance for the pack and on to Corrour Bothy? This meant some extra distance and loss of height, but I couldn't enjoy any more climbing with the pack.

The steep climb up Braeriach on skins was easy, on snow so hard in the shade that the skis scarcely left a mark, and yet not so icy and steep that the skins didn't grip. An hour later I was at the top, looking down a Coire Bhrochain precipice heavily sheathed in ice and frost. A bitterly cold breeze was blowing but the few clouds in the sky were all vanishing rapidly. It was good to look away from the glaring snow and ice for a moment, down past the cone of Carn Eilrig to the warm reddish-brown moors of Strath Spey, the green fields of Tullochgrue and the houses at Coylumbridge among the pines.

I moved off in a long run downhill to the plateau, and an easy 50 minutes later I was on Cairn Toul, looking west over the Moine Mhor towards Glen Feshie. This was obviously the grand finish to my tour -- a long 2-mile run down to the Moss, then another steeper 2-mile run to Achlean. But with a pack in the Lairig Ghru and a car at Invercauld, I had to turn east. I clambered down the bouldery ridge of the corrie below the summit and soon came on a drift stretching 2000 feet to the Dee. No place for a solitary fast glissade, but the surface was safe enough for a fast trot downhill, and I was at the bottom within 20 minutes.

I had a good rest at my pack and ate the last two tins of fruit. Dark blue shadows were spreading rapidly in the glen and already tiny daggers of ice were visibly thrusting out over the pools of melt water.

It was good to warm up again, gliding quickly down the moraines to Corrour Bothy, where I took my skis off to go inside. The last sun rays were burning red on Ben Macdui. By contrast the bothy was dark and gloomy, and I was

Sunset at Corrour Bothy, where John Pottie gave AW tea on 16 April 1962

feeling not at all tired, so I moved on across the snow-covered Dee and up round Carn a' Mhaim. The snow was no longer continuous and many stones appeared, but it was still much quicker to scratch and push forwards with the skis. Finally a last run down to the pines of Glen Luibeg; there was no snow down there, so I had to walk the remaining mile and a half to Luibeg. I was now so used to the ski-ing motion that I felt I could have kept that going all night, but I found the new movement of walking very tiring.

It was getting dark at 9 o'clock as I reached Derry Lodge, where I met Bob Scott and my father. My father had been ski-ing at the Moine Mhor and Glen Geusachan, and wasn't long off the hill himself. Back to Bob's for cups of tea, and then down the road in my father's car to Braemar where we swung into the welcoming lights of the hotel for a dram and pints of beer with some of the residents. We left after midnight and collected my car in the Invercauld wood at 1 a.m. The greatest mental effort of the day was now required to drive down Deeside without falling asleep.

I'd had a good 24 hours' worth, seeing the whole Cairngorms range and other parts of the North-East from innumerable viewpoints. Time had passed so slowly that it seemed more like a week -- a good indication of a day lived to the full.

I worked it out later at about 38 miles, with 34 on skis and 8700 feet of climbing. It is certainly no more than a hard but enjoyable day in good weather to a lightly laden man, and I would carry a lot less if I did it again. Without a push I think I could have done the tour in 14 hours instead of 16, and still enjoyed it. But I don't think the time could be cut much more without making the day a matter of physical effort rather than of enjoyment. It is a grand way of re-exploring familiar hills, and the Cairngorms, noted originally as a paradise for hill-walking and shown by the recent Guide to be equally enjoyable for rock-climbing, should become famed for a third aspect of the sport -- ski-mountaineering. Langlauf provides the opportunity, and I'll be back as soon as I can -- and this year looks like giving another opportunity.

(1963 *Scottish Mountaineering Club Journal* 27, 348–362 and photo opposite p. 347). On the evening before, my father at Turriff phoned to say "I'll come for you tomorrow for a ski trip together". When I told him my idea for the six tops, he decided to drive straight to Luibeg, ski at Glen Geusachan hoping to meet me there or at Luibeg later, and take me at night to my car at Invercauld. However, when I left my heavy pack in the Lairig Ghru to ski lightweight to Braeriach and Cairn Toul, I knew I could not meet him at Geusachan. Apart from ski equipment, I took only an iceaxe, and binoculars to see the best snow for the route ahead. On return to my pack to ski down Glen Dee, at sunset I halted briefly at Corrour Bothy. Climbers John Pottie and Hugh Spencer were staying there and had found the deep snow restricting and tiring on foot. They recall giving me a cup of tea when I looked into the bothy.

Bibliography

Baird, P.D. (1957). Weather and snow on Ben MacDhui. Cairngorm Club Journal 91, 147–149.

Brooker, W.D. and others, and H. MacInnes (1971). Thomas Walton Patey. Scottish Mountaineering Club Journal 29, 433–438.

Duff, J. (2003). The ruining of a good day's sport at Mar. Leopard 296, 23–24.

Duncan, I. (1972). Bob Scott o' the Derry. Scots Magazine 97, 434–441.

Eagle, R. (1991). Seton Gordon. Lochar Publishing, Moffat.

Elseley, E.M. (1951), Alberta forest-fire smoke – 24 September 1950, Weather 6, 22–24.

English, C. (2008). The snow tourist. Portobello Books, London.

Etchachan Club (1960). Rock climbing guide to the cliffs of the north-east coast of Scotland. (Compiled by T. Patey, J. Hay, A. Will, A. Watson). EC, Aberdeen.

Gordon, S. (1912). The charm of the hills. Cassell, London.

Gordon, S. (1925). The Cairngorm hills of Scotland. Cassell, London.

Gordon, S. (1927). Days with the golden eagle. Williams & Norgate, London.

Gordon, S. (1944). A Highland year. Eyre & Spottiswoode, London.

Gordon, S. (1948). Highways and byways in the Central Highlands. Macmillan, London.

Gordon, S. (1951). Highlands of Scotland. Hale, London.

Gordon, S. (1963). Highland days. Cassell, London.

Gordon, S.P. (1980). The golden eagle. Re-publication by Melven Press, Perth.

Gray, D. (2007). The last of the grand old masters. (Tom Patey, a personal memoir). Scottish Mountaineering Club Journal 40, 463–470.

Patey, T. (1962). Cairngorm commentary. Scottish Mountaineering Club Journal 27, 207–220.

Patey, T. (1971). One man's mountains. Gollancz, London.

Pruitt, W.O. (1970). Some ecological aspects of snow. Ecology of the subarctic regions. Proceedings of the Helsinki Conference, 83–99. UNESCO, Paris.

Robb, R. (2007). Thomas Weir. Scottish Mountaineering Club Journal 40, 645–646.

Scott, D. (2007). Thomas Weir. Scottish Mountaineering Club Journal 40, 645.

Smart, I.H.M. (2007). Thomas Weir. Scottish Mountaineering Club Journal 40, 643–644.

Smith, M. (1961, 1962). Climbers' guide to the Cairngorms Area, Vols 1 & 2. Scottish Mountaineering Club, Edinburgh.

Tewnion, A. (1999). Ferla Mor. Cairngorm Club Journal 39, 342–347.

Watson, A. (1959). Through the Lairig Ghru on horseback. Letter in: The Scotsman, 29 July.

Watson, A. (1975). The Cairngorms. Scottish Mountaineering Club District Guide.

Watson, A. (1979). Foreword. The immortal isles, pp. vi–xx. Melven Press, Perth.

Watson, A. (1977). Seton Gordon. Scottish Birds 9, 307–309.

Watson, A. (1982). Bob Scott o the Derry. Scottish Mountaineering Club Journal 32, 292–293.

Watson, A. (2007). Tom Weir. Appreciations. Scottish Mountaineer, November, p.72.

Watson, A. & Allan, E. (1984). The place names of upper Deeside. Aberdeen University Press, Aberdeen.

Watson, A. & Clement, R.D. (1983). Aberdeenshire Gaelic. Transactions of the Gaelic Society of Inverness 52, 373–404.

Author

Adam Watson, BSc, PhD, DSc, DUniv, was born in 1930 at Turriff in lowland Aberdeenshire and went to school there. Lifelong interests in winter snow began in 1937, snow patches in 1938, the Cairngorms in 1939. While a student, he used the first part of the summer vacations to climb in the far north and the second part to work as a deer-stalking gillie in the Cairngorms. As a mountaineer and ski-mountaineer since boyhood, he experienced Scotland, Iceland, mainland Canada and Baffin Island on foot and ski, and climbed in Norway, Swedish Lapland, Newfoundland, Finland, Switzerland, Italy, Vancouver Island and Alaska. In 1954 he seconded Tom Patey when they climbed most of the rock routes in the Cairngorms during checks for the Scottish Mountaineering Club's first climbers' guide there. Later in 1954 he became a member of the SMC and since 1968 author of the Club's District Guide to the Cairngorms. In 1971 he was Chief Expert Witness to the Crown in the Cairngorm Disaster Fatal Accident Inquiry. For many years independent scientific monitor at the three downhill ski areas in the Cairngorms, he has also given technical advice at Scotland's other two ski areas. His main professional research was on the population biology, behaviour, habitats and environment of northern birds and mammals, and he contributed hundreds of scientific publications on these and other topics. In recognition of this, during 1971 he was promoted to Senior Principal Scientific Officer with Special Merit in Research. Since 1990 he has been a retired research ecologist, continuing to do fieldwork and write scientific papers, for instance publishing 16 on snow patches since 1994. During 2008 his book *Grouse* was published by HarperCollins as New Naturalist No 107. In 1986 the Royal Society of Edinburgh awarded him their Neill Prize for 'your outstanding contribution to Natural History and in particular to your study of Red Grouse and the environmental impacts of developments in mountainous countryside'. He is a Fellow of the Arctic Institute of North America, Centre for Ecology and Hydrology, Royal Meteorological Society, Royal Society of Edinburgh, and Society of Biology, and is an Emeritus Member of the Ecological Society of America.

Some other books by the author

1963. Mountain hares. Sunday Times Publications, London (with R. Hewson)

1970. Animal populations in relation to their food resources (Editor). Blackwell Scientific Publications, Oxford and Edinburgh

1976. Grouse management. The Game Conservancy, Fordingbridge, and the Institute of Terrestrial Ecology, Huntingdon (with G.R. Miller)

1982. Animal population dynamics. Chapman and Hall, London and New York (with J. Ollason and R. Moss)

1974. The Cairngorms, their natural history and scenery. Collins, London, and 1981 Melven Press, Perth (with D. Nethersole-Thompson)

1975. The Cairngorms. Scottish Mountaineering Club District Guide, published by Scottish Mountaineering Trust. Second edition published 1992

1982. The future of the Cairngorms. The North East Mountain Trust, Aberdeen (with K. Curry-Lindahl and D. Watson)

1984. The place names of upper Deeside. Aberdeen University Press, Aberdeen (with E. Allan)

1998. The Cairngorms of Scotland. Eagle Crag, Aberdeen (with S. Rae)

2008. Grouse, the grouse species of Britain and Ireland. HarperCollins, London, Collins New Naturalist Library No 107 (with R. Moss)

2010. Cool Britannia, snowier times in 1580–1930 than since. Paragon Publishing, Rothersthorpe (with I. Cameron)

Milton Keynes UK
~ram Content Group UK Ltd.
IW022148160424